KNOWLEDGE ENGINEERING TOOLKITS

ELLIS HORWOOD BOOKS IN INFORMATION TECHNOLOGY

General Editor: V. A. J. MALLER, VM Associates; Visiting Professor in Computer Studies, Loughborough University of Technology; formerly of Thorn EMI Information Technology Ltd.

Consulting Editors: Dr JOHN M. M. PINKERTON, Information Technology Consultant, J & H Pinkerton Associates, Esher, Surrey, and formerly Manager Strategic Requirements, International Computers Limited; and PATRICK HOLLIGAN, Department of Computer Studies, Loughborough University of Technology

M. Barrett & A. C. Beerel	EXPERT SYSTEMS IN BUSINESS: A Practical Approach
M. Becker, R. Haberfellner & G. Liebetrau	ELECTRONIC DATA PROCESSING IN PRACTICE: A Handbook for Users
A. C. Beerel	EXPERT SYSTEMS: Strategic Implications and Applications
A. C. Beerel	EXPERT SYSTEMS: Real World Applications
K. Bennett	SOFTWARE ENGINEERING ENVIRONMENTS: Research and Practice
A. C. Bradley	OPTICAL STORAGE FOR COMPUTERS: Technology and Applications
P. Brereton	SOFTWARE ENGINEERING ENVIRONMENTS
R. Bright	SMART CARDS: Principles, Practice and Applications
D. Clarke & U. Magnusson-Murray	PRACTICAL MACHINE TRANSLATION
V. Claus & A. Schwill	DICTIONARY OF INFORMATION TECHNOLOGY
D. Cleal & N. O. Heaton	KNOWLEDGE-BASED SYSTEMS: Implications for Human–Computer Interfaces
I. Craig	THE CASSANDRA ARCHITECTURE: Distributed Control in a Blackboard System
T. Daler, *et al.*	SECURITY OF INFORMATION AND DATA
D. Diaper	KNOWLEDGE ELICITATION: Principles, Techniques and Applications
D. Diaper	TASK ANALYSIS FOR HUMAN–COMPUTER INTERACTION
G. I. Doukidis, F. Land & G. Miller	KNOWLEDGE-BASED MANAGEMENT SUPPORT SYSTEMS
P. Duffin	KNOWLEDGE-BASED SYSTEMS: Applications in Administrative Government
C. Ellis	EXPERT KNOWLEDGE AND EXPLANATION: The Knowledge–Language Interface
J. Einbu	A PROGRAM ARCHITECTURE FOR IMPROVED MAINTAINABILITY IN SOFTWARE ENGINEERING
A. Fourcin, G. Harland, W. Barry & V. Hazan	SPEECH INPUT AND OUTPUT ASSESSMENT: Multilingual Methods and Standards
M. Greenwell	KNOWLEDGE ENGINEERING FOR EXPERT SYSTEMS
F. R. Hickman *et al.*	ANALYSIS FOR KNOWLEDGE-BASED SYSTEMS: A Practical Guide to the KADS Methodology
P. Hills	INFORMATION MANAGEMENT SYSTEMS: Implications for the Human–Computer Interface
E. Hollnagel	THE RELIABILITY OF EXPERT SYSTEMS
R. Kerry	INTEGRATING KNOWLEDGE-BASED AND DATABASE MANAGEMENT SYSTEMS
K. Koskimies & J. Paakki	AUTOMATING LANGUAGE IMPLEMENTATION
J. Kriz	KNOWLEDGE-BASED EXPERT SYSTEMS IN INDUSTRY
M. McTear & T. Anderson	UNDERSTANDING KNOWLEDGE ENGINEERING
W. Meyer	EXPERT SYSTEMS IN FACTORY MANAGEMENT: KNOWLEDGE-BASED CIM
U. Pankoke-Babatz	COMPUTER-BASED GROUP COMMUNICATION: The AMIGO Activity Model
J. M. M. Pinkerton	UNDERSTANDING INFORMATION TECHNOLOGY: Basic Terminology and Practice
S. Pollitt	INFORMATION STORAGE AND RETRIEVAL SYSTEMS: Origin, Development and Applications
C.J. Price	KNOWLEDGE ENGINEERING TOOLKITS
S. Ravden & G. Johnson	EVALUATING USABILITY OF HUMAN–COMPUTER INTERFACES: A Practical Method
S. Savory	EXPERT SYSTEMS FOR THE PROFESSIONAL
P. E. Slatter	BUILDING EXPERT SYSTEMS: Cognitive Emulation
H. T. Smith, J. Onions & S. Benford	DISTRIBUTED GROUP COMMUNICATION: The AMIGO Information Model
H. M. Sneed	SOFTWARE ENGINEERING MANAGEMENT
M. Stein	BUILDING EXPERT SYSTEMS MODEMS FOR DATA TRANSMISSION
R. Stutely	ADVANCED DESKTOP PUBLISHING: A Practical Guide to Ventura Version 2 and the Professional Extension
J. A. Waterworth	MULTI-MEDIA INTERACTION WITH COMPUTERS
J. A. Waterworth & M. Talbot	SPEECH AND LANGUAGE-BASED COMMUNICATION WITH MACHINES:Towards the Conversational Computer
R. J. Whiddett	THE IMPLEMENTATION OF SMALL COMPUTER SYSTEMS

KNOWLEDGE ENGINEERING TOOLKITS

C. J. PRICE B.Sc.
Department of Computer Sciences
University College Wales

ELLIS HORWOOD
NEW YORK LONDON TORONTO SYDNEY TOKYO SINGAPORE

First published in 1990 by
ELLIS HORWOOD LIMITED
Market Cross House, Cooper Street,
Chichester, West Sussex, PO19 1EB, England
A division of
Simon & Schuster International Group

Printed and bound in Great Britain
by Hartnolls, Bodmin, Cornwall

British Library Cataloguing in Publication Data

Knowledge engineering toolkits. —
(Ellis Horwood books in information technology).
1. Expert systems
I. Price, C. J. II. Series
006.33

ISBN 0–13–517178–4

Library of Congress Cataloging-in-Publication Data available

Contents

Introduction

This book concerns one of the main problem areas for people aiming to use knowledge-based systems (KBS) technology — *what applications are suitable for implementation with KBS technology, and what tool is the right one to use for each application?*

Over several years working for an expert systems shell vendor, I observed many potential users pass from excitement over the technology through a phase of implementing simple applications to either serious use of expert systems or serious disillusionment with the very idea. Examination of the failures revealed several possible reasons for the disillusionment:

- wrong selection of application area for the simple test system;
- over-ambitious selection of application area for delivery system;
- wrong selection of tools for delivery system;
- bad software engineering practices.

This book attempts to help the knowledge engineer with each of these areas. It should be noted that there is a further cause of failure which occurs frequently, and which is beyond the scope of this book — choosing to build a system that no-one would ever want to use.

The type of tool used to build a simple investigatory system is very often an expert system shell (and a fairly cheap one too), and the test application is limited in size and scope in order to be tractable in a short time, while giving some idea of the usefulness of the technology.

The main trouble with expert system shells is that they often have a very limited set of representation and reasoning tools, and do not even provide the ability to construct more tools when they are needed. By contrast, there is now a wide range of software that could be referred to as *knowledge engineering toolkits*. These toolkits claim to provide all the tools that a knowledge engineer will need in order to build knowledge-based systems, and yet even they are not suitable for building all sorts of systems.

Between the knowledge engineering toolkits and the simplest expert systems shells, there is a wide range of available tools, varying in price from £100 to £100,000. They also vary widely in performance, and in usefulness for different types of problem. It is hard to understand what are the benefits of the more expensive systems without buying each of them and trying them out. Such an exercise can prove very costly both in cash and in manpower, and yet without experience of a particular type of toolkit, *how do you decide whether it is capable of solving a particular problem which is beyond the abilities of your present shell?*

The goal of the book

The aim of this book is to help knowledge-based systems developers overcome the learning curve associated with discovering the abilities and limitations of different kinds of KBS tools. The book is intended to enable people with a particular knowledge-based application in mind to judge whether different types of knowledge engineering tool or toolkit can sensibly be used to implement that application. Alternatively, it will help people who already have a particular toolkit to understand whether it is powerful enough for a new application that they want to build.

The ability to match toolkit and application comes from understanding what the different possible components of knowledge engineering toolkits are, what can be built with each of those components, and how the components fit together in different types of toolkit.

The approach of the book

Unlike many multi-authored books, this is not intended to be just a collection of vaguely relevant papers (where that does seem to be the case, the fault lies with the editor). The reason for so many authors is that the range of experience needed to write about all of the different toolkits mentioned was too great for any one person. In some cases, (for example, the lists of toolkit questions in chapters 2 and 12), some overlap between chapters has been left because the difference in outlook between authors shines extra light on the problems involved.

The contents of the book can be split into the following general sections:

Building Blocks: *Chapters 1 to 3* of the book provide the necessary understanding of the most important types of component which make up a knowledge engineering toolkit, with emphasis on what is available in toolkits commercially available today.

These first three chapters could be considered building blocks for comprehension of part two of the book. They explain the representation and reasoning issues that are a basis for the descriptions of different toolkits.

Because this book is about using toolkits to build knowledge-based systems for real applications, this part of the book also explores the idea of applying a standard software building lifecycle to knowledge-based systems in *Chapter 4*. In doing this, it stresses the additional problems that arise when attempting to engineer robust knowledge-based systems (instead of just building prototypes that are never seriously used). *Chapter 5* examines useful types of knowledge engineering tools that are absent from most commercial toolkits at present, but which become more important as attempts are made to build more complex knowledge-based systems.

Tools and Applications: The second part of the book looks in detail at sample systems and the applications for which they can be used.

Chapter 6 considers example commercial offerings from the whole range of commercial knowledge engineering tools and toolkits, from an expert system shell costing a few hundred pounds to a workstation-based knowledge engineering toolkit costing tens of thousands. It should be stressed that for each of the systems reviewed there are examples of successful applications. None of the tools is without a range of usefulness.

In *Chapter 7*, we explore what sorts of applications have been built using KBS technology, and the types of toolkit needed for each type of application.

Case Studies: For each type of knowledge-based toolkit, a specific case study is given showing how that toolkit was used. These case studies (in *Chapters 8 to 11*) try to give an appreciation of how it feels to build a system using that particular toolkit. Each of these detailed case studies is different, reflecting to some extent the capability of the toolkit being used.

Each of the knowledge-based system building toolkits outlined in the case studies is intended to be representative of one kind of toolkit rather than necessarily the best of its type. Further information was given in chapter 6 about other toolkits which are similar to the ones explored in detail.

Summary and Future View: *Chapter 12* sums up what has been learned through the detail in the second and third parts of the book, providing sets of questions for use when trying to select a toolkit. This theoretical methodology for selecting a tool to use on an application is backed up by four examples of using the methodology.

Appendix A looks at research trends in knowledge engineering and in artificial intelligence, highlighting research areas which will lead to improved toolkits in the future. This information will enable knowledge engineers to plan ahead, and to identify applications which are too difficult to attack today, but which might become amenable to artificial intelligence techniques over the next 5 to 10 years. When new versions of existing toolkits are released with extra features, this information should also help the knowledge engineer decide whether those features will be of use in real applications.

Chapter 1

Knowledge representation and reasoning

Michael Z. Bell

...He that increaseth knowledge increaseth sorrow.
Ecclesiastes 1:18

1.1 Introduction

A Shareware expert system shell can be bought for as little as US$25, while a full-scale Knowledge Engineering toolkit can exceed $50,000. Why might someone pay $50,000 instead of $25? How does a top of the range toolkit differ from a simple toolkit? And when might the $25 shell perform equally well or better than the $50,000 toolkit?

A major difference between the two systems will undoubtedly be the facilities provided for knowledge representation and reasoning. The expensive toolkit will offer a range of alternative facilities, the cheaper shell just one or two. This is important because, (put simply) if knowledge cannot be represented or reasoned with, it cannot be exploited. The range of facilities provided to represent the knowledge required to solve the problem, and to reason with it, will quite often determine whether or not you can solve that problem.

A basic understanding of knowledge representation, reasoning, and related issues is therefore essential when evaluating knowledge engineering products: it should determine your choice of product; it will affect the feasibility of your project; and it might also save you $49,975! The basic elements of representation and reasoning are therefore what this chapter is (mainly) about.

1.2 The four elements of problem solving

The problem-solving process can be split into four key elements: data, knowledge, reasoning, and control.

Data is that information which is specific to the problem being solved, and which is obtained or provided in order to solve the problem. For example, if we are determining whether to lend a customer some money, then the problem data might include such elements as the customer's salary, credit history and tangible assets, as well as the interest rate and the amount of credit requested.

Knowledge is information at our disposal which is to some degree problem independent. In our credit-rating example, knowledge would include the method of determining the customer's ability to pay back the loan, the method of determining the risks involved, and the method of balancing the risks against the benefits of granting credit.

Reasoning is the application of knowledge to knowledge or data so as to produce new knowledge or data. This can be viewed as the *active* part of the problem-solving process: you know that a customer can pay back a loan; you know that the risks are low; and you know that if the customer can pay back the loan and the risks are low then credit should be approved. Reasoning is the part of the process which takes these pieces of knowledge or data and puts them together to give a new piece of information: credit should be approved. (This process of deriving new information from old is also known as *inference*.)

Control is a matter of determining at all stages in the problem-solving process what to do next. Should we apply the knowledge we have which enables us to determine risk from credit histories at this stage? Or should we be working out whether the customer will have sufficient income to pay back the loan in question? Reasoning is an unguided process: at any stage there may be many ways of deriving new knowledge from old. Some of these inferences may be relevant, others may not. Control tells us which of these inferences we can or should make next.

It would be nice if, having given names to the four elements of a problem-solving system, we could simply build a knowledge-based system (KBS) accordingly with one module called "data", another "knowledge", a third "reasoning" and a fourth "control". Unfortunately such pristine distinctions are for philosophers and theoreticians. In practice, it is not always possible, practical, or desirable to distinguish these elements. Each element interacts with the others: the reasoning system must understand the knowledge and data representations; the control mechanism must understand the reasoning and the current problem state; knowledge is not always separable from data.

The effect of this is that the choice of (say) knowledge representation technique will limit the choice of reasoning and control mechanisms, and vice versa. It is therefore necessary to have a basic understanding of all the elements in order to fully understand the issues involved in the design of any particular one.

1.3 Predicate logic

One of the earliest, and certainly the best-known method of representing knowledge and then reasoning with it is predicate logic. Logic also forms the basis of many other reasoning methods and representations, and therefore is a particularly good place to start in our explorations of representation and reasoning methods.

A logical system provides us with two things:

- A set of symbols which can be assigned meanings and built into sentences to reflect "truths" about the world.

- A set of rules for manipulating these sentences which will preserve such "truths", *if the original sentences were truthful and consistent.*

Note that logic does not tell us *how* to assign meanings to symbols or which truth-preserving manipulation we should apply at any point: all it tells us is that *if* the original sentences were true and consistent, and *if* the manipulation rules were followed, *then* the resulting sentences will also be true. Logic therefore provides a perfect example of the programming maxim "garbage in — garbage out".

Note that there are many different ways of formulating a logical system. This introduction is more pragmatic than most. Do not be surprised if there are minor areas of disagreement between this description and those of other authors.

The logical world is described by what we shall term *well-formed sentences.* By well-formed, we signify that the sentence obeys our rules for the formation of sentences, not that the sentence is true. Using an English language analogy:

```
The cat is sitting on the mat eating a rat.
```

is a well-formed sentence since it obeys the rules of grammar regardless of whether there is a cat sitting on a mat or not. However,

```
Sitting the cat rat on is the mat a eating.
```

is not well-formed, since it is totally ungrammatical. How do we determine if a sentence is well-formed? The answer lies in a set of rules which enable larger sentences to be constructed from smaller ones. Assuming **x** and **y** are already well-formed sentences, then the following are also well-formed:

```
1.  (and x y)
2.  (or  x y)
3.  (if  x y)
4.  (not x)
```

Thus, if we have these well-formed sentences:

```
(the price of gold falls)
(the dollar rises)
(exports decline)
```

then each of the following is also well-formed:

```
(not (the price of gold falls))

(and (the dollar rises)
     (exports decline))

(if (the dollar rises)
    (exports decline))

(or (the dollar rises)
    (and (exports decline) (the price of gold falls))
```

Meanings can now be ascribed to most of the above: the interpretation of the final example is "**either** the dollar rises **or both** exports decline **and** the price of gold falls". As you can see, quite complex concepts can be formulated in this way.

The **if** connective in predicate logic differs slightly in semantics from the English "if". For example, in predicate calculus the sentence

```
(if x y)
```

means that if the sentence **x** is held to be true, then **y** must be true also. If **x** is not true, then it implies nothing about the state of **y**. This differs from an English **if**, where a notion of causality is usually implied. So, in predicate logic, we could say:

```
(if (the grass is pink) (the Visigoths are wonderful people))
```

without saying anything about the Visigoths, since the grass is not pink.

Now that we have established a formal language with which to describe things held to be true, what truth-preserving manipulations can we perform on it? The following set of manipulations is commonly used:

Rewriting rules:

The following pairs of sentences are interchangeable.

```
1. (not (not x))          and     x.
2. (and x y)              and     (and y x).
3. (or  x y)              and     (or  y x).
4. (and (not x) (not y))  and     (not (or x y)).
```

Inference rules:

In the following pairs of sentences, the second sentence follows if the first sentence is true.

```
1. (and x y))             implies   x,  y.
2. x                      implies   (or x y).
3. x, (if x y)            implies   y.
4. (not y), (if x y)      implies   (not x).
```

The last two of these rules have special names. Rule 3 is what most people think of when they consider inference. For example, one view of the British-American politics might be:

```
If the US invades a Latin-American country,
then the British prime minister will praise the US.
```

If we then learn that the US has invaded a Latin-American country, we will deduce that the British prime minister will praise the US invasion. This form of reasoning (as shown in rule 3) is known as *modus ponens.*

However, if we learn that the British prime minister is not praising the US, then we can instead deduce that the US has not invaded any Latin-American countries, because if it had, then the British prime minister would be praising it. This form of inference is known as *modus tolens.* This form of reasoning (as shown in rule 4) is common in diagnostic tasks, where we are often trying to eliminate possible causes of observed symptoms.

A final inference rule, which is extremely rare in knowledge-based systems but common in mathematics, allows us to construct sentences of the (**if x y**) form. Informally we might write it:

```
5. If, by assuming x, we can prove y
     then  (if x y)  is true.
```

Quantifiers and variables

So far, so good. We have a language in which quite complex facts can be described, and which we can manipulate while preserving truthfulness. Quite a few expert system shells are content to work at precisely this level, and indeed, if the problem being solved fits entirely into this kind of structure, such expert system shells may prove suitable.

However, brief experimentation with this language will show that there are various ideas that we cannot express. In particular, we cannot express a chain of reasoning such as:

```
All Computer Scientists are Brilliant
Mike is a Computer Scientist
Therefore, Mike is Brilliant.
```

Furthermore, we cannot express ideas like:

```
My tie should be of the same colour as my suit.
```

without drawing up a set of sentences for every known colour of the form:

```
(if (my suit is coloured green)
     (my tie should be coloured green)
(if (my suit is coloured brown)
     (my tie should be coloured brown)
...
```

which would be tedious in the extreme, especially if we had an artist friend who kept on inventing new colours. Now if there was just a way we could let some symbol **x** stand for any colour...

And therein lies the solution of our representation problem, with the introduction of the notion of a *variable*. A variable is quite simply a symbol which is used to represent any well-formed sentence. To enable us to distinguish variables from other symbols in our notation we will prefix them with the symbol "?".

Since a variable can stand for anything, it follows that if we introduce a variable into our sentences above, the resulting *formula* is neither true nor false. For example:

```
(?x likes being stroked)
```

might be true if **?x** were "Tigger" our pet cat, but would not be true if **?x** were "Jaws" our pet shark. In such a formula, **?x** is referred to as a *free variable*, and the formula itself is referred to as a *predicate* or *property*, since it represents some quality of **?x** which can be tested for truth or falsity.

However, to apply this notion of variables to reasoning (rather than inventing sentences which might either be true or false) we need to *quantify* the variables

— in other words, specify how they are being used. To quantify a variable, we place the quantifier before the formula containing the variable. There are two quantifiers: the *universal quantifier*, and the *existential quantifier*.

The *universal quantifier* states that if the specified variable is replaced by *any* well-formed sentence, the following formula will be true. The universal quantifier is often written as **forall** since its usual mathematical notation (∀), is not representable in most computer character sets. The suit and tie matching requirement described previously can be represented using the universal quantifier as follows:

```
(forall (?x)
        (if (my suit is coloured ?x)
            (my tie should be coloured ?x)))
```

The brackets after the **forall** quantifier contain a list of all the variables which the quantifier applies to — in this case, just **?x**.

The other quantifier is the *existential quantifier*. The existential quantifier states that, for *some* value of the specified variable, the following formula is true. The existential quantifier is generally written as **exists**, since (once again) the mathematical notation (∃) is not available on most computers. The existential quantifier is often quite useful in its negated form. For example, we might express the idea that no sane person eats fish by the sentence:

```
(not (exists (?p)
        (and (?p is a person)
             (and (?p is sane)
                  (?p eats fish)))))
```

Note the way an extra clause **(?p is a person)** was introduced here. This turns out to be a particularly common (and important) technique in knowledge representation. We had to ensure that the variable **?p** referred only to people here: some perfectly sane cats eat fish, and if we had not restricted the values **?p** could take in this way, we might have cast undeserved aspersions on their sanity.

The universal and existential quantifiers, therefore, add two new forms to our list of well-formed sentences, to give:

```
1.  (and x y)
2.  (or  x y)
3.  (if  x y)
4.  (not x)
5.  (forall (?v) x)   where x is a sentence containing ?v
6.  (exists (?v) x)   where x is a sentence containing ?v
```

We also need some additional inference and re-writing rules to cope with these new forms. The most important of these are:

The specification rule

This simply states that if we see a formula containing the universal quantifier, then we can substitute a sentence for each occurrence of the variable.

The interchange rule

```
(forall (x) (not ...))
     can be re-written as
(not (exists (x) ...))
     whenever it occurs.
```

There are other inference rules; however, these are used comparatively rarely in knowledge-based system toolkits, and the reader is referred to the literature on logic for more information.

1.4 Where logic fails...

It might seem at this point that we have solved all the problems of knowledge representation: we can represent facts or truths about the world by sentences of symbols in our computer; we can manipulate those sentences in a number of ways while preserving truth (i.e. only deducing facts for which a proper basis exists); finally, we can interpret the resulting sentences as inferred truths about the real world. Unfortunately, life is not that simple.

A number of problems emerge when we try to map real-life situations into logical systems: some of these are because logic does not tell us everything we need to know or do; others are because the real world does not match the perfect world of logic; and some problems emerge from the sheer effort required to translate the required knowledge into the logic formalism. These problems limit the scope of logical (and other) systems, and are worth examining in some detail.

The main problems with logical representations can be identified by asking a number of questions:

1. How do I represent something?

2. How do I prove something?

3. What if one of the facts is wrong?

4. What if we do not have all the facts?

5. What happens if a fact changes?

6. How do we handle mathematical facts?

Let us examine each of these in turn.

Problem 1: How do I represent something?

A major problem when translating a real world problem into its logic form is that there is no rigorous formalism for converting real world facts into logic. In the examples above, we made many arbitrary decisions about how to translate a real world fact into a logic sentence. This is a strength of logic — we have considerable discretion in choosing symbols — but also a major weakness. Since there is no fixed and formal methodology of translating knowledge into logic, each knowledge engineer must invent or adopt suitable conventions. For example, to express the idea that a door is painted red, we might write:

```
(painted red door)
```

or

```
(colour-of door red)
```

or

```
(door
     (painted red-paint)
     (height 2 meters)
     (width 1.5 meters)
      ...
)
```

and so on. Each of these is near enough equivalent to the others to be a plausible expression of the idea that a door is painted red. However, each can be interpreted differently, and none is equivalent according to our rules of inference.

This is a difficult enough problem when a single person is working on a project of significant size: it is obviously compounded greatly when more than one person is involved.

A second problem related to representation is that of ambiguity. To take a simple example, it would seem quite safe to write:

```
(John hit Mary)

(forall (?x, ?y)
        (if (?x hit ?y)
            (?x does not like ?y)))
```

However, when John's career as a singer takes off, we might also write:

```
(John hit the big time)
(John hit the high notes)
```

from which the unintended conclusions would follow:

```
(John does not like the big time)
(John does not like the high notes)
```

In natural languages, words have many meanings: we generally select the correct meaning from the context in which they are used, and from our general knowledge about the world. Logical systems have a very limited notion of context, and no general knowledge: when we use words as logical symbols we need to specify precisely what they mean, and ensure that they are only used with that meaning. Often it is better to invent new symbols, such as **hit-person**, **make-a-hit**, and **musical-reach**, rather than rely on the overworked and overloaded English language.

Problem 2: How do I prove something?

Logic only tells us what transformations we *can* make: it does not tell us which transformation we *should* make. This is rather like reading for the first time the rules to the game of chess, and then being expected to be able to play. We know what moves we can make at any stage — we have the rules — what we do not know is how to assemble those moves to produce a useful or winning sequence.

Referring back to the introduction, this is the problem of *control*. We shall address this problem (which is not unique to logic) in a later section.

Problem 3: What if one of the facts is wrong?

Suppose that we make a mistake in entering our logical facts into the system — not an unlikely eventuality. Obviously we can no longer expect all our inferences to be correct. However, a rather surprising consequence of logical inference is that if somehow we manage to arrive at both a fact and its negation, it becomes theoretically possible to deduce (literally) *anything* from a contradiction. Proof of this is beyond the scope of this book, see [Dowsing et al.].

In practice, the situation is never as bad as this, primarily because knowledge-based systems are generally incapable of exploiting the full power of mathematical logic. Problems are therefore normally restricted to direct or indirect inferences from the erroneous or contradictory facts. However, even these may be considerable when universal quantifiers are being used.

(An intriguing speculation here is that as knowledge-based systems begin to exploit more and more of the power of logic, so the likelihood of introducing an inconsistency increases, and the consequences of errors will become more extensive and unpredictable. Perhaps a case of power corrupts?)

Problem 4: What if we do not have all the facts?

We can distinguish between two cases here.

1. We know what the facts might be, but cannot determine whether they are true or false;

2. We have not modelled all the facts in our knowledge base.

Case 1 is the simpler of the two cases to deal with. The simple true/false distinction of logic can be extended to include a third state "don't know". Inference rules can then be written to exploit this third state. For example, if we know **X** is true, but we do not know whether **Y** is true, then

```
(and X Y)
```

is in the "don't know" state. It is more complicated, but workable systems have been built which utilize this intermediate state.

Case 2 is more complicated, and more fundamental. There is a principle in knowledge engineering which ought to be documented somewhere:

In any inference, there is always one more loophole.

Consider, for instance, the simple question of whether I should put up my umbrella. It might seem that the inference rule:

```
(if (it is raining)
    (put up umbrella))
```

is a perfectly reasonable thing to have in a knowledge base. However, this is is a generalization and, as Alexandre Dumas (fils) put it,

All generalizations are dangerous, even this one.

What if it is windy? What if I am indoors? In a crowd? Am about to fend off a group of Ninja assassins? Eating a hot-dog? Have a broken umbrella? The umbrella belongs to someone else? I already have an umbrella up?

Life is only simple when we choose to make it so. A real-life inference is normally only true to some degree: there will remain an element of doubt in the conclusion. Facts are often less straightforward than they seem. Is a four-foot high man short or tall? A five-foot man? A six-footer? A seven-footer? At what height does a man cease to be short, or become tall? Outside of the world of logic, the truth or falsity of a fact is not always distinct.

One approach to this problem is to simply argue that we should be more precise. We could, for example, have defined "short" to be "less than five-foot", and tall to be "greater than six-foot". But this approach has its limitations. An abrupt transition between "short" and "not short" will probably have undesirable effects in the knowledge base. Even if this is acceptable, we are not yet out of the mire: a physical measurement has associated with it a statistical error, meaning that a true measurement which is near a boundary may be measured as being either side of that boundary. Furthermore, there are some concepts (such as "living" or "reasonable") which defy such precise definition.

A common solution to this problem is to adopt a logical system which does not make a binary distinction between truth and falsity, but instead has a range of values in-between. This approach is often referred to as *fuzzy logic*, to distinguish it from its boolean counterpart.

Problem 5: What happens if a fact changes?

The simple logic described above is not good at handling changing data. For example, if we have the fact in our knowledge base:

```
(religion Nigel sun-worship)
```

then this may enable us to make all sorts of useful inferences about Nigel. For instance, we will be able to deduce that he (probably) gets up at dawn, attends ceremonies at Stonehenge, has a notable sun-tan, and does all those things which sun-worshippers are known to do. These new facts will be added to our knowledge base.

However, if one fateful day we discover that Nigel has been converted to moon-worship, we have a problem: all the facts we deduced from Nigel's sun-worshipping activities may now have been invalidated. And the facts deduced from those facts, and so on...

If our knowledge base is large, and the facts in it are subject to change, then we can have problems. There are three possible approaches to this problem:

1. Remove (or do not maintain) deduced facts or knowledge in the knowledge base. This is workable if the knowledge base is relatively small.

2. Maintain dependency information in the knowledge base (i.e. which fact was deduced from which other facts). Use this to work out which facts should be retracted if a fact is removed or altered. This approach comes under the general heading of *truth maintenance* or *reason maintenance*, and is supported by several of the large toolkits.

3. Ignore the problem, and assume that facts never change.

All three approaches have been used in the past to address this problem.

Problem 6: How do we handle mathematical facts?

The point to be made here is that logic is not particularly wonderful for representing many kinds of interesting problems, such as those involving mathematical relationships or geometrical reasoning. Employing logic to solve problems in areas such as these is generally best left for the student (or the professor). Pragmatic approaches are often called for, and a system based on logic should allow some kind of interface to more *ad hoc* systems.

1.5 Object-oriented representations

In the previous discussion of logic-based systems we identified a number of problems with "just" logic. One of these problems was the lack of any formal methodology for converting real world information into logic statements. Other areas of concern which we did not discuss include the potential lack of structure in the resulting system, and the tendency towards repetitiveness in the knowledge base. Clearly this is unsatisfactory, and something more is needed. The major current contender to be this "something" is object-oriented or object-based representations, which are currently enjoying a remarkable vogue in most areas of the software industry.

The basic idea behind an object-oriented representation is that information should be clustered around "objects" — an object corresponding to some conceptual entity in the real world.

The easiest way to understand this is to consider an example. Let us suppose that we are setting up a customer classification system for the Ultimate Novelty Mail Order Company. The system will advise us on mailing a customer with information about a particular new product. The objects in this situation might represent:

- Each individual customer
- Each particular product
- Groups of products, such as "Executive Toys" or "Naughty Novelties".
- Groups of customers, such as "Business Customers" or "Occasional Purchasers". This segmentation might be made on buying habits, information about the customer's business or profession, or anything else we know about the customer.
- Market seasons, such as "Valentine's day madness", "Christmas Rush", and so on.
- Types of mailing: "personal appeal", "mini-catalogue", etc.

Obviously there are many other aspects to the mail order novelty business which we could include. However, these will serve as examples.

Whereas in predicate logic the information about an individual entity (such as a customer) might be scattered among a number of facts, in an object-oriented representation these will be grouped together. Thus we might have a fact about a customer "Jane Doe" which contained the following information:

```
(customer
        (number 506783)
        (name   ''Jane Doe'')
        (date-of-birth  ''24 March 1963'')
        (job-title advertising-manager)
        ...
)
```

Each category of simple fact in this compound fact (**date-of-birth**, for example) is called a *slot* or an *attribute*. Each grouped set of facts (each **customer** in this case) is called an *object* or an *instance*.

In this example, there will be an instance for each customer containing similar information, and it will be useful to us to have a fact describing the information which could be known about a customer. We can describe this in the form of a *schema* (also known as a *class*, *generic*, or *meta record*, and confusingly as an *object* or a *schema object*). This is essentially a fact which describes another fact. Thus we might have a fact of the form:

```
(generic-personal-customer
        (number integer)
        (name   string)
        (date-of-birth date)
        (job-title profession)
        ...
)
```

This has a number of advantages: it allows us to "check" a customer record to ensure that it has the correct fields with acceptable values, and it gives us a convenient place to attach knowledge which is not specific to an individual customer but applies to all customers. As a simple example, we may wish to target products according to the age group of the customer: this can be deduced from the customer's date of birth. A similar deduction can be made for every personal customer (note the need to distinguish between personal and business customers), and thus the knowledge required to make this deduction can quite conveniently be structured by attaching it to the **generic-personal-customer** schema.

Obviously for this knowledge to be used the reasoning mechanism must know where to look to find the relevant knowledge. The development of the reasoning mechanism must therefore proceed hand-in-hand with the development of the representation.

In toolkits, there seem to be two main ways of declaring how to infer new facts from existing knowledge.

The objects can be fairly passive in nature, linked together in *frames* or *semantic nets* of knowledge, with global rules that can be used to infer attribute values from the values of other attributes in the object, or from the attributes of other objects.

Alternatively, schema objects can contain not just facts, but also pieces of code as attributes. These *procedural attachments* or *methods* can be invoked either via a message from outside the object or invoked from another method within the object. This rather more active style of object allows object-oriented *programming* rather than just object-oriented representation.

An extra feature that is often provided with object-oriented programming, is the ability to invoke a method automatically when an attribute's value is accessed or evaluated. This feature is referred to in various ways — sometimes the attached procedure or rule is called a *demon*, or sometimes the attention is focussed on the attribute to which the attachment has been made, calling it an *active value*.

An interesting (and not uncommon) occurrence in our customer database will be for information to be unknown. For example, our modest advertising manager Jane Doe may have neglected to supply her date of birth when filling out a reply-paid form, or the mailing list may simply not contain all the information we desire. To allow us to reason in the absence of such information, we will need to make default assumptions about Jane Doe. These can range from the simple:

```
If a customer's age is unknown, assume it is 32.
```

to the more complex:

```
If a customer's age is unknown,
and the customer is an Advertising Manager,
   assume the customer's age is 43
(since this is the average age of Advertising Managers
according to the latest census).
```

Where should these inference rules concerning the handling of unknown information and defaults reside? In the first case in the **personal-customer** schema, since the knowledge does not refer to any other object. In the second case, however, the ideal location of the knowledge is less obvious: the average age of advertising managers should clearly be a property or attribute of an **advertising-manager** object. The **advertising-manager** is presumably an instance of an object of the **profession** schema. However, the method of handling the default (looking for the average age of the customer's profession) is best attached to the **personal-customer** schema.

1.5.1 Relationships between objects

There are two ways of viewing (and expressing) the fact that Jane Doe is an advertising manager. The first of these, which we used above, was to give Jane Doe an attribute (**job-title**) which had a value (**advertising-manager**) which referred to an object containing information about advertising managers in general. An alternative we might also have considered was to introduce the notion of *relation* or relationship between objects. For example, we might say that there is a relationship **job-category** which links personal customers to profession, and that there is an instance of this relationship which links **Jane Doe** to her profession of **advertising manager**. This gives us another set of places where we can potentially attach knowledge.

For this type of relationship, the decision as to whether to model it as a relation which links objects or as an attribute which "points" to another object will depend upon a number of factors, including the usefulness of these extra objects, the complexity added by introducing them, and the underlying representation in which the bulk of the data is available — which is likely to either be a semantic network or a relational database.

The **job-category** relationship was special in that it was specific to the particular application. However, there are other relationships which are commonly supplied in order to structure knowledge, which are of a more general utility.

The following is a non-comprehensive list of common relationships:

Is-an-instance-of This is the relationship between Jane Doe and the schema object **personal-customer**. The schema object will contain knowledge about personal customers: the permissible attributes; the permissible values attributes can take; default attribute values; knowledge which allows attribute values to be deduced from other attributes; etc.

Is-a-member-of An individual object may also acquire attribute values or characteristics by being a member of (or related to) some other object. For example, Jane Doe may be a member of the group **Impulse-Buyers**, from which we can deduce something of her buying characteristics.

Is-like-a This relationship is useful if two objects have a large number of characteristics in common, but differ in other respects. Consider, for example, the problem of describing a dog to someone who has never seen a dog, but has seen a cat. We might then say that "a dog is like a cat, but it does not meow, and..." continuing with a list of changed or additional attributes which are important in the context. In our example, we might say (for example) that **Valentine's-Day-Madness** is like the **Christmas-Rush** except that it is shorter, takes place in February, and only involves adults of a romantic disposition.

Is-a-kind-of This is distinct from **is-like-a** in that one object acquires *all* the other objects characteristics unchanged, plus some additional ones. The **is-a-kind-of** relationship is commonly found in taxonomies, particularly of the "invented" sort. For example, a **Rubber-Duck** is a kind of **Children's-Product**. It has all the attributes associated with a children's product, but also additional attributes associated with its rubber-duckness. The important point here is that anything that is true of a **Children's-Product** is also true of a **Rubber-Duck**, without exceptions.

These common relationships are often supported in the more comprehensive knowledge-based system toolkits, although the names (and precise semantics) will generally differ, making comparison difficult. Confusingly, most of these relationships have at one time or another been compounded into a single **is-a** relationship. On the other hand, some powerful toolkits will allow the definition of novel types of relationships with different semantics.[1]

This acquisition of attributes or characteristics through a relationship is known as *inheritance*. Typically (but not exclusively) the term is used to describe an **is-a-kind-of** relationship or an **is-an-instance-of** relationship. The objects (or schemas) from which characteristics are inherited are referred to as *ancestors* or *parents*, and the object (or schema) acquiring the characteristics is termed a *descendant* or *child*.

Having defined inheritance, and the key relationships which may hold between objects, we can now summarize the ways in which an object can acquire a value for one of its attributes:

- The value can be assigned or given.
- It can be deduced from the values of other attributes.
- The attribute can default to a value given in the schema, or to a value deduced from the values of other attributes.
- The value can be deduced through some relationship with another object.
- The attribute can default to a value derived from some relationship with another object.
- The object can acquire a value for the attribute through some complex inference from many objects.

---

[1] We can compare this situation with that of a man who enters a bespoke tailor's shop and asks to buy a suit. The tailor offers to make a suit to whatever design the customer desires, all at the same low price. At first the customer is pleased, because the tailor can provide the suit he wants. However, the customer swiftly becomes disillusioned when he realizes that although the tailor can provide the suit he wants, the customer will have to design it first!

1.5.2 Object-oriented representation methodology

It should be realized that an object oriented representation has not given us any additional expressive power over predicate logic: every concept that can be included in an object-oriented representation can also be expressed in predicate logic. However, what it has given us is a far more coherent conceptual structure with which to attack the problem.[2]

This gives an underlying methodology for developing a knowledge representation:

1. Identify an initial set of conceptual objects.
2. Identify the relationships between those objects in terms of **is-an-instance-of**, **is-a-member-of**, **is-a-kind-of**, and **is-like-a**. (If other relationships are used, then their semantics should be rigorously defined at this point.)
3. Identify the attributes of the objects, being careful to distinguish inherited attributes. Determine how the values of these attributes will be determined.
4. Identify (and encode) the knowledge required to solve the application problem, making sure that each piece of knowledge is expressed in the most general terms appropriate, and is associated with the appropriate object or relation.

During stages (3) and (4) the list of conceptual objects will generally be revised and restructured. In practice, this methodology will need to be adapted to fit in with the methodology for engineering the entire solution. Customer data, for example, will probably be maintained in an external database, as will product data — and only the more complex representations of deduced characteristics will be entirely defined and managed within the knowledge-based system.

1.6 Further reading

Logic. [Dowsing et al.] is a very good text on the use of logic in Computer Science. Many of the better textbooks on Artificial Intelligence, such as those by [Charniak & McDermott] and [Luger and Stubblefield] contain a great deal of more specific material on the use of logic in knowledge-based systems.

[2] This is analogous to the assembler/high level language debate. Assemblers can do everything. Therefore high level languages are logically superfluous. However, the abilities to structure information and manage complexity are such that larger programs can be written in high-level languages, and the programs are easier to write.

Object-oriented programming. AI textbooks like the two referenced above contain a reasonable amount of detail about inheritance and the origins and usage of terms such as frames and schemata. However, they do not have much detail about the use of such representations in practical knowledge-based systems. [Price and Hunt 89a] tries to give the feel of using an object-oriented representation for KBS work, but the most detailed exploration of the use of object-oriented programming is in software engineering books like [Meyer] and [Cox].

Chapter 2

Controlling the system

Michael Z. Bell

Knowledge, when wisdom is too weak to guide her,
Is like a headstrong horse, that throws the rider.
Miscellanies, Francis Quarles.

2.1 Basic control strategies

When we try and solve a difficult problem, we generally use one of three methods:

1. We consider what we are trying to find out — the goals of our problem — and look at what we need to know in order to determine these goals. If each piece of relevant knowledge or data exists, we can immediately draw the required conclusions. If not, we can examine the data required to infer this data, and so on, until finally we find the information that we need and can make the inferences necessary to determine our goals. This process is generally known as *backward chaining* or *goal-directed* reasoning.

2. We consider what we know, and determine what conclusions (new data or knowledge) can be drawn from that which we know. We repeat this process until we find that we know the answer to the problem. This is often termed *forward chaining* or *data-driven* reasoning.

3. We ask someone or something what the answer is! This is ultimately what any problem-solving system (humans included) must do if the required knowledge or data is not already known. It may, however, be a sensible

approach even if the data is known: why go to the effort of solving a problem if you can get somebody or something to tell you the answer?

Let us consider how these reasoning mechanisms work in practice in the context of a simple example. Suppose that we wish to determine whether to lend some money to an individual: what do we need in order to solve this problem?

An initial analysis of the problem might produce something like figure 2.1. In this simplified analysis, an individual is **Worthy of credit** if he/she has both the **Ability to pay** and a low **Risk of default**. The **Ability to pay** is determined from the individual's **Outgoings** and **Income**, the **Amount** being sought, and the current **Interest rate**. A low **Risk of default** is likewise determined by the quality of the individual's **Credit history**, the availability of a **Guarantor**, and the individual's **Fixed assets** — which presumably could be seized in the event of default on the debt.

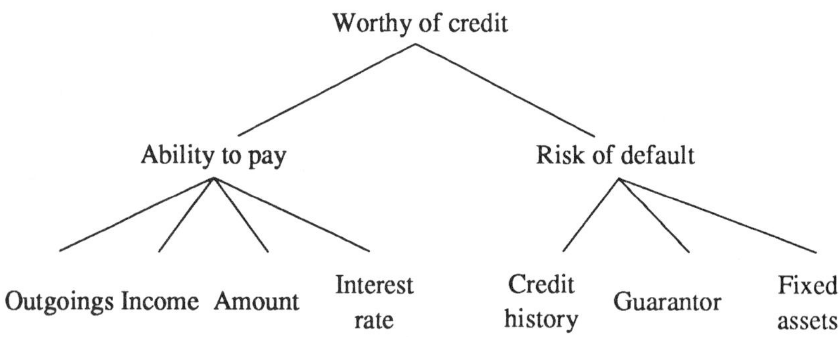

Figure 2.1: Knowledge for loan assessment

In this example, *backward chaining* would work as follows:

Initially the problem would be presented as determining whether or not the individual was **Worthy of credit**. The system would first of all check to see if it already knew this. Assuming it did not, it would recognize that it needed to determine **Ability to pay** and **Risk of default**. If it did not know the **Risk of default**, it would identify that it needed to determine **Credit history**, **Guarantor**, and **Fixed assets**.

The system would continue descending the dependency tree in this manner until either it found a piece of data which it already knew, or one which could be determined by asking some other system or person. Once it reached a point where (say) **Credit history**, **Guarantor**, and **Fixed assets** had been determined, it would use its knowledge to determine **Risk of default** and so on, working back up the tree until the solution to the problem had been determined.

Forward chaining starts at the other end of the problem, using facts that are known, and working forward towards the solution. In the above example, this would happen as follows:

The system would examine the facts which it knew (assume that it knows all the facts at the bottom of the dependency tree), and identify a piece of knowledge that would allow it to determine a new fact. In this example, there is a piece of knowledge relating **Outgoings, Income, Amount** and **Interest rate** which allows us to determine **Ability to Pay**. It would then apply this knowledge, and look for another piece of knowledge it could apply. In our simple example, this would be the knowledge relating **Credit history, Guarantor**, and **Fixed assets** to **Risk of default.**

The system would continue in this process of identifying pieces of knowledge to apply and then applying them until it finally determined **Worthy of credit**, at which point it should recognize that it has now solved the problem and stop.

It should be noted that both these strategies are to a large extent independent of the type of knowledge contained in the system: our method of determining **Ability to pay** would typically be a complex mathematical function of the various factors identified; **Risk of default** might, however, be a simple logical "or" function requiring only that one of **Credit history, Guarantor**, and **Fixed assets** be true.

On their own, both forward and backward chaining are adequate for solving many types of problems. However, neither is without its problems, and for more complex problems a more complex strategy is often called for — as we shall see in the following sections.

2.2 The trouble with control

Imagine that I start to tell you a story, and I begin the story by explaining that it was about someone called Jake, and the problem was why he was hanged. At this point, using your common-sense knowledge, there were a number of possible inferences you could make:

- There is some reason why I am telling you this story.
- It is probably either an old or fictional story, because Jake is no longer a common name.
- Jake is probably human, since few animals are called Jake.
- Jake is probably a man, since Jake is typically a man's name.
- Jake had at some stage a mother and father.
- Jake's mother had, at some stage, a mother and father.

- Jake's mother's mother had, at some stage, a mother and father.
- Jake's mother's mother's mother...

Undoubtedly these and a lot of other similar inferences flashed through your mind the moment I gave you this single fragment of data. They didn't? Why not? Why did you not make every inference that could be made? Why did you not work out that, barring interbreeding, Jake had 4 grandparents, 8 great grandparents, 16 great great grandparents, 32...Clearly you are not a great fan of forward chaining if you are not still working out that Jake must have had 128 great great great great great grandparents!

Nor did you bombard me with a list of questions about Jake: Why was he hanged? Was he hanged "judicially"? Lynched by a mob? Did he commit suicide? How old was he? Did he play the guitar badly? What did Jake do for a living? You felt no particular urge to bombard me with such questions? You considered one or two? Then perhaps there is some evidence of backward chaining.

Most likely, however, you waited for me to continue: realizing that there was too little information given for you to be able to make any interesting or relevant inferences.

This example serves to introduce some of the main problems with the control of the reasoning process. We can generally regard control as containing three main steps:

- Deciding when or whether to do any reasoning.
- Determining the possible inferences.
- Deciding which inference to make next.

We will look at each of these areas in turn in the following sections.

2.2.1 Deciding when to reason

Deciding when to perform reasoning is rarely a problem — although when it is a problem, it is not easy to solve. If the data is available, and the problem goals are known, then the problem is only to determine the goals given the data and the knowledge base. However, when partial data is available (and more expected), or when reasoning has cost implications (perhaps denying computing resources to other processes) then the decision as to whether to do any reasoning or not can be quite complex. Generally, however, it is a decision tied closely to the specific application and, apart from pointing out that it is a potential problem area, it will not be discussed here.

2.2.2 Determining the possible inferences

There are two major problems with deciding what are all the possible inferences that can be made at any point in the reasoning:

1. The knowledge is structured in such a way that enumeration of all possible inferences is either impossible or not practical.

2. It may be computationally infeasible to enumerate a list of possible inferences.

An inappropriately structured knowledge base will make (1) the case. For example, if I sent you into a public library and asked you to identify from the knowledge contained in the library all the ways you could make someone happy, it would not be an easy task. The knowledge in a library, although extensive, is not indexed in such a way as to render it accessible for this type of query.

The alternative problem — that the number of possible inferences is too numerous to list — is perhaps more common. Suppose I have ten very general inference rules each of which can be applied to ten items of data. That gives 100 possible inferences — which is probably manageable. However, if I scale each of these by a factor of ten, it gives 10,000 possible inferences — which is probably excessive given the frequent need to enumerate these inferences. Additionally each inference will presumably yield more knowledge or data — adding to the computational complexity. A naive collection of inference rules coupled with a small knowledge base can quite easily get out of hand.

Obviously any time spent enumerating a list of potential inferences is wasted if most of those inferences are not going to be made. Although our separation of control into distinct processes of listing options and deciding which one to pick is convenient when determining potential problem areas, in practice the determination of possible inferences is therefore often closely combined with the decision of what to do next.

2.2.3 Deciding which inference to make

Some knowledge-based systems make this process visible — having a data structure (often called an *agenda*) holding a list of possible inferences (it may, alternatively, hold a list of possible inference rules to apply). In other cases the control strategy is buried more deeply in procedural code.

In either case, the intent is the same. Each inference should take us nearer our goals — the desired areas of knowledge which we wish to reach — without causing us to digress into areas which are not currently of any relevance or interest.

The backward-chaining strategy, described earlier, is one method of ensuring that inferences made are in some way relevant to the final outcome. We are still, however, faced with a choice as to which knowledge relevant to the outcome of our problem we should seek to determine or obtain.

The forward-chaining strategy has no such sense of direction or relevancy enforcement. Each inference yields new, potentially irrelevant knowledge, and this new irrelevant knowledge may in turn trigger a series of further irrelevant inferences. The decision as to which inference to make next is therefore of crucial importance in any but the simplest forward-chaining system.

There is no single superior approach to this problem. A large variety of tactics are therefore employed, and here we will restrict ourselves to discussing some of the main or more interesting methods. Many of these methods do not have any accepted name: the names given here should simply be regarded as convenient "tags" for remembering or discussing the methods. Remember that methods encountered in practice may well be a hybrid of the schemes discussed here.

2.3 Ways of choosing which inference to make

2.3.1 First possible inference

In this method, the first possible inference found is used. In backward chaining, this corresponds to always investigating the leftmost (or rightmost) unknown and looking for the first inference rule which will allow this unknown to be resolved. In forward chaining, the first inference rule found which can be used is used. Depending upon how the knowledge base is structured, this can lead to some disastrous behaviour. Suppose our knowledge base contains a first rule that allows us to infer that every person has a mother. Suppose we then add a person to our knowledge base. We will immediately infer the existence of that person's mother. We can then infer the existence of the mother's mother, and so on which is unlikely to achieve any useful ends.

Despite this disadvantage, first possible inference remains an important and common method. It is generally viable for backward chaining. It is sometimes viable for forward chaining when the number of potential inferences is limited. It is simple and easy to implement, and is therefore a method of choice for problems where it will work.

2.3.2 The meta-knowledge approach

At the opposite extreme to the "first possible" approach is the meta-knowledge approach. In this approach a second knowledge base is used to decide which possible inference to pursue. The reasoning behind this is that choosing which inference to make is an intelligent decision. Knowledge-based systems are designed to make intelligent decisions. Therefore, why not use a knowledge-based system to make the control or scheduling decision. This second level of knowledge — the knowledge about reasoning — is termed *meta-knowledge.*

The full power of a knowledge-based system can therefore be made available at this second or meta-level, controlling the first. There are no limits to the number of subtle factors that can be introduced to control the reasoning of the first level, including heuristic estimates of the likely benefit of a particular inference measured against the computational effort required to generate that inference.

How, you should ask, is the second level itself controlled? Although it would be possible to introduce another — a third level — in practice this is rarely attempted. After all, this process of adding extra levels cannot continue indefinitely — where would it end? In addition, while we can envisage quite a large amount of heuristic meta-knowledge regarding the control of the first knowledge-based system, it is less easy to identify any knowledge at a higher level: we are not used to controlling the control of the solution of a problem. The meta-level is therefore generally controlled by one of the other mechanisms discussed here.

2.3.3 Breadth-first

Suppose when we generated a list of possible inferences we decided to do each of them in turn, adding new possible inferences to the end of our list. This characterizes the breadth-first approach which, as the name implies, tries to extend our knowledge in all directions simultaneously. (If you are familiar with shortest-path algorithms you may also be familiar with this approach.)

This method has the advantage that it always finds the shortest series of inferences which will reach between two points: its disadvantage is that in finding this series it will always have explored all possible combinations of inferences of that same length — which may be an excessive number.

Breadth-first may well be the default strategy of an agenda-based system where no prioritization decisions are made since, as noted above, it consists essentially of a first-in first-out ordering of possible inferences.

2.3.4 Scoring approaches

Scoring approaches can be simple to implement, and are therefore quite a common way of deciding what to do next. Essentially each inference rule is given a numeric priority by the knowledge-based system designer, and the rule with the highest priority that is capable of being applied is used next.

Despite its simplicity, it can be useful. It is an easy way of incorporating some limited human intelligence into the control decision, while avoiding the complexity (and speed implications) of utilizing a full-blown meta-level.

Variations on this method include the system learning the scores for the rules (by examining which rules were most helpful in solving earlier or similar problems), and modifying the rule scores according to the problem stage.

2.3.5 Procedural approach

Conventional programs achieve their performance using *procedural* or *imperative* control: explicitly working how and in what order things should happen. Similar approaches are sometimes useful in the higher-level control of reasoning systems. For example, if you were performing a diagnostic task you might have the following sequence of steps in your reasoning process:

- Identify the symptoms.
- Hypothesize underlying causes for the symptoms.
- Eliminate implausible causes by further reasoning, by observation, or by experiment.

This, coupled with the use of a few program control structures to give conditional or iterated steps, is procedural control. Its primary disadvantage is its dependency on problem knowledge (if you change the knowledge base, you must change the procedural control). However, as indicated here, it can be particularly useful for imposing an overall structure on a reasoning process, and is best used in combination with other methods.

2.4 The coherent dialogue (and other) problems

One important factor to consider when deciding between possible control approaches (including those outlined above) is whether the sophistication employed here can have undesirable or unexpected consequences. Several early expert systems made some crucial errors along these lines.

One particular backward-chaining system used an ingenious method (based on information-theoretic measures and estimated probabilities) of determining which single inference would be of most assistance in solving the overall problem. The advantage that the designers intended to achieve by this means was that the system should ask the user (who supplied the problem data) the minimum number of questions to solve the problem.

Undoubtedly the system did meet this objective. However, the resulting user dialogue was horrendous. As the information-theoretic measures were updated, the system would flit from subject to subject — giving the unfortunate user the feeling of being interrogated by some irrational inquisitor. It was not a pleasant system to use, but it was not alone in its neglect of human factors considerations in the pursuit of more efficient reasoning.

Another classic error relates to the failure by many inference control mechanisms to take into account the ease with which required information can be obtained. The (hopefully apocryphal) tale of a car engine diagnosis system which asked "Is there evidence of carbon build-up on the cylinder heads?" before asking "Is there any fuel in the tank?" perhaps best exemplifies the problem.

All these serve to emphasize that the decision as to what to do next should not always rely purely on the state of the inference process, but should take into account the external systems (or people) with which the system interacts.

2.5 Hard questions on representation and reasoning

This section aims to help you apply what you know so far in order to assess knowledge-based system toolkits. No book can reasonably be expected to describe more than a representative selection of currently available systems and their variants and, even if it did, it is doubtful whether the book would ever be up-to-date. The following guidelines are therefore intended to assist in examining the "unknown" system. You might look on them as a first level of KBS Toolkit Checklist (more detailed questions about issues other than representation and reasoning are explored in chapter 12).

The first rule is that there are no rules

The first thing to remember is that there are no cast-iron generalities: only you understand the application, and therefore understand what trade-offs can sensibly be made. Just because Frederick Bloggs used an ASAD[1] toolkit for his successful application it does not mean you should necessarily use it for yours.

Ignore the name: look at the functionality

Since knowledge-based systems represent a young technology, the terminology in use is still fluid. The accepted meaning of some words has changed considerably, and the terminology in some toolkits is now rather archaic.[2] It is important, therefore, to establish what the author means by, say, inheritance, rather than to assume that the author's meaning is the same as your own.

Try to identify the features of a toolkit by functionality. Regard the name of each feature as a detective might regard a clue: often it will lead you in the right direction, but sometimes it will turn out to be a red herring.

---

[1] ASAD = all-singing, all-dancing

[2] This is not a new phenomenon. See *Burnt Norton, V, 13-17*, T.S.Eliot for a philosophical discussion of this point.

Do not assume that the authors of the documentation will tell you what is missing from their toolkit: they are interested in telling you what it *can* do, not what you cannot.

What forms of knowledge representation does it support?

Is it object-based? Or logic-based? Does it support the whole of predicate logic (unlikely)? What does it leave out? Are you likely to need the things which are omitted? Does it support a particular methodology? Or is the designer so non-committal that everything is left to the user to design?

Assuming it is object-based, what are the available inheritance mechanisms? Does it distinguish between different types of inheritance relationships? Is the inheritance method too general? Or too restricted?

Does it support approximate reasoning schemes, such as fuzzy logic or Bayesian reasoning? What are the characteristics of the scheme it supports? Is it required for your application? Does it require you to supply information which you will never have (e.g. accurate conditional probability estimates)?

What forms of control strategy are supported?

Do the available control strategies include backward chaining? Forward chaining? Can the two be mixed? Can the same inference rules be used for both? Is there a meta-level where additional knowledge can be used to control inference? Is it needed?

Are there special features which solve problems identified here?

Nearly every toolkit designer incorporates novel features designed to address some of the potential problems described here. What features have been added? Are they required? Are they realistic solutions?

Will the toolkit interface to my existing software and systems?

Look very carefully at the interfaces provided by the toolkit to the outside world. Early toolkit designers were rather arrogant and tended to assume that their toolkit was the centre of the universe, around which all other software would fit. Specific wrong-headed assumptions to watch out for are:

All knowledge and data must be represented in the toolkit. Some toolkits do not allow knowledge and data to reside in external systems or files, or if there is external data, then it must be in a format determined by the toolkit.

This is (arguably) a valid assumption for small systems: however, when a database starts to contain hundreds, thousands, or millions of entries or to interact with numerous other systems, this is clearly an unhelpful assumption to make.

The toolkit is "in charge". The toolkit is the primary program, and all other programs providing information to the toolkit or using data supplied by the toolkit are subroutines.

This is a distressingly common assumption. The control flow is entirely driven by the toolkit, probably pessimizing the performance of every system to which it is interfaced. A toolkit should allow the development or reasoning modules which can be built into a larger system.

All other systems are programmed in LISP **or C.** Some toolkit designers pretend never to have heard of FORTRAN, COBOL, or Ada. Consequently, they only provide limited interfaces to the toolkit in the languages of their choice — which may not include the language of your choice.

The user interface of the toolkit is perfect. In keeping with the principle that the toolkit is the centre of the universe, some designers seek to ensure that any interaction with the toolkit must be through their user interface. Want to make the system have the same "look and feel" as other systems that your users will be familiar with? Tough. Want to provide a low-bandwidth interface suited for a modem connection? Tough.

The end-user must be allowed to update the knowledge base. And so, when the office junior is given the job of using the program, he or she can quite happily browse through the knowledge base amending the odd detail here or there. If a toolkit application is to be put into an environment where the end-user is not the developer, it had better be suitably protected against changes — well-intentioned or otherwise.

If you don't know how to handle an error, don't test for it. This maxim was provoked by a well-known operating system, but it applies equally well to some KBS toolkits. Toolkit designers often give little thought to the handling of incorrect information, circular reasoning structures, storage limitations, etc. They are also careless about providing hooks so that user can redefine the behaviour of the system in the event of an error being detected. "What? You didn't want the system to print out a message and abort if it detected an error? It stops your *entire* production line? Oh..."

We all have unlimited budget. Every user has an unlimited budget for computer memory and disk space. Furthermore, there is unlimited time available for the problem to be solved.

Strangely enough, few vendors offer any hard performance figures. In fact, few vendors offer much in the way of performance estimates. Yet performance (Can it do this task within this time and bounded by this amount of memory?) is an important issue. A system providing support to telephone sales staff may be useless if it cannot guarantee a response in a second or two. It may be too costly to widely distribute an end-user system if it requires the purchase of additional memory boards for each computer.

Be careful here: memory and time will rarely scale linearly with problem size. Processes may scale $O(N^2)$, $O(k^N)$, or $O(N!)$. If you are lucky, it may be relatively easy to guess how the toolkit works, and gain a feeling for how the problem will scale up. It may even be documented. But some home-brewed benchmarks may be advisable — preferably while the toolkit is still on evaluation, rather than when it is paid for. (You might consider trying to add a performance clause to any purchase or licence agreement.)

What testing, validation, and maintenance facilities are there?

This is an important question to ask if intending to develop a system of any size, complexity, or criticality. Features to particularly watch out for here are those to support known test case and regression testing, and the provision of diagnostic trace or explanation facilities.

To support test cases and regression testing the toolkit must provide some means whereby the results can be compared with expected or previous results. Simple manual comparison, although slow and unreliable, may suffice if the application is sufficiently small. For larger systems, however, it will be unworkable, and some means to provide for automated testing is essential.

Diagnostic trace is required to determine why the system is not working correctly. As a minimum, it must be possible to determine why the system reached a particular conclusion. A better system may allow the user to ask why a specified conclusion was not reached. If the system is in a critical application and has an expert end-user, then this facility can also form a useful part of the end-user's interface. For example, imagine a system which has produced a "Buy $1M IBM stock now" type of decision. Before staking the company's future on it, you might just like to know why!

The other side of the maintenance equation is modification: how easy is it modify the knowledge base? And how likely is it that the new knowledge will introduce a fault? Are there cross-reference and documentation utilities? And does the size of the development justify their use?

Is there expertise available for using this toolkit?

There is not (judging from current recruitment advertisements) a significant pool of expertise readily available for any toolkit, so the presence of in-house expertise may be a significant factor in choosing a toolkit. Learning curves for some of the larger toolkits can be long, and in-house familiarity (choosing the known against the unknown) may well dictate the choice of toolkit.

How much does it cost?

Although everyone would like to think otherwise, money — in the form of price / performance and cost / benefit has to enter into the equation. Apart from the obvious question of "how much does the toolkit cost?", critical questions to ask include:

- What is the cost of any specialized hardware required?
- What is the cost of support/maintenance for that hardware?
- What is the cost of any toolkit support?
- What is the likely learning period for the hardware and the toolkit? — With some LISP-based systems, this can be considerable.
- What is the cost of any specialized staff required to develop or maintain the system? The skills required for this function will differ from those required for more mainstream developments, and it may not be possible or desirable to use the same staff for support of this and other systems.
- How long will the development take? This is often difficult to predict — knowledge-based system developments are quite prone to the 90% syndrome.
- Is partial performance acceptable? If the system is not performing too critical a function, it may be of use when only partially completed. Conversely, if it is of no use until it is 100% complete and validated, then the pay-back period is delayed.

What are the benefits?

This is the other side of the cost equation. The development may save time, save money, or both. It may allow less skilled staff to perform some function, or reduce the effort required by skilled staff to tackle some problem. It may improve the quality or consistency of performance. It may enable the capture of expertise which will one day no longer be available due to staff retirement or turnover. The formalization of knowledge can often lead to an improvement in expert performance, since the task becomes better understood. It may allow some task to be undertaken which would otherwise be impracticable or uneconomic. It may improve staff morale (and decrease staff turnover), or destroy it.

The point to make here is that, as with most business investment decisions, the benefits to be obtained must be carefully examined. They will depend on the specific situation, and may be both tangible and intangible. Only you can decide whether the benefits justify the costs.

2.6 Further reading

Control strategies. Standard AI textbooks have quite a lot of material about controlling reasoning — [Winston 84] is particularly good on this subject.

The LISP book jointly written by the same author [Winston and Horn] contains Lisp code which performs some of these control regimes, although [Charniak et al.] contains rather more detail on how to implement reasoning systems. However, while the implementation information contained in those books may be of interest, most developers would be ill-advised to build their own representation and reasoning systems, for reasons which are explored in chapter 6.

Chapter 3

Human–computer interfaces for knowledge-based systems

John Hunt

> Evil communications corrupt good manners.
> 1 Corinthians 15:33, Authorized Version.

3.1 Introduction

Most modern computer systems provide facilities for more than the basic text-only style interface — even humble home computers now possess at least a simple graphics interface. As workstations fall to accessible price levels and personal computers grow more powerful, a revolution is occurring in the way in which humans and computers interact. The days of almost hieroglyphic single line text commands, whose meanings were virtually incomprehensible, are fast disappearing. Today, many computer systems provide mechanisms for displaying graphic images, associated either with system operations or objects such as files, which can be directly manipulated by the user. These techniques present possibilities for the human–computer interface which were unthought of ten years ago, but which are now becoming considered the norm by users.

This chapter considers the human–computer interface (HCI), from the viewpoint of the developer as a user of a toolkit and as a designer of an interface. It is structured in the following way:

Section 3.2 provides an overview of HCIs, presenting the main classes of interface currently available.

Section 3.3 considers the type of development tools required, examining both the formats used to display information and the facilities they provide.

Section 3.4 presents the facilities required to support the construction of user interfaces, and describes what a developer should expect from a window-based interface construction toolkit. It also discusses the additional facilities often available within a knowledge-based system development toolkit, presenting an example to illustrate these points.

Section 3.5 discusses some future directions for HCIs.

3.2 Human–computer interfaces

Every interactive software system has a human–computer interface, whether it be a single text line system or an advanced graphic display. It is the vehicle used by developers for obtaining information from their user(s), and in turn, every user has to face some form of computer interface in order to perform any desired computer operation. When selecting a toolkit for building knowledge-based systems, it is important to consider the interface provided. This interface can be divided into two areas, the development interface and the user interface. The development interface, is the interface between the developer and the system development tools such as the editors, compilers and debuggers. The user interface is the interface between the user and the application system, which is designed by the developer using the facilities provided in the toolkit.

If the toolkit has a friendly, easy-to-use development interface, not only will the developer make better use of his time, but it is likely that the quality of work produced will be higher. If the user interface is friendly and easy to use, then the potential users will be encouraged to use the system. This is particularly important where a prototype system is being built which is intended to convince sceptical management. It is a sad fact of life that people are always impressed by a "pretty" graphical interface, no matter what the underlying system is like. However, if the system is to be a delivery system used day-in day-out, it is more important that the user interface is usable, rather than pretty.

Any toolkit must provide a flexible set of facilities, allowing a developer to design a wide variety of interfaces, from within an easy-to-use development environment. The set of facilities provided by the tool chosen will, to some extent, depend on the cost of the tool — expect a more comprehensive range of facilities with an expensive toolkit than with a cheaper one.

The remainder of this section considers the main categories of HCI and what features are required by knowledge-based systems in particular.

3.2.1 Classes of human–computer interface

In many situations where the relationships between large amounts of information must be conveyed, it is much easier for the user to assimilate this graphically than textually. Similarly, it is often easier to convey some meaning by manipulating some system entities on screen, than by combinations of text commands. This has led to the emergence of at least two metaphors that describe the ways in which humans interact with computers. These two main classes of interface are *the conversational world* and *multi-thread dialogue*.

In the conversational world, the user describes each step which the computer should execute in turn (often using a command language or networks of menus), or the system specifies the order by request↔response interaction. Either way, the system moves, in a predictable manner, from one part of the dialogue to the next.

Multi-thread dialogue is a task-oriented concept referring to the multiple task paths available to the user at any given instant. For example, the *dialogue box*, illustrated in figure 3.1, is an example of such interaction. The options open to the user from this box include the creation of a new file, scrolling through a list of file names, changing directories, changing disc drives, and ejecting a disc.

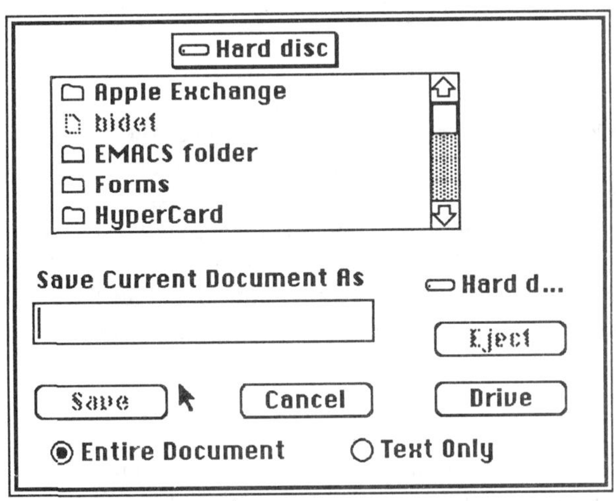

Figure 3.1: An example dialogue box

The main difference between the conversational world and multi-thread dialogue is that, during conversational dialogue the system presents the user with the ability to perform one task at a time, while multi-thread dialogue presents many tasks to the user at a time. Typically most systems will exhibit both conversational and multi-thread modes of dialogue, for example, commands might be typed in via the keyboard or selected off menus, which might cause dialogue boxes to be displayed allowing the user to manipulate the tasks presented via a mouse.

In the remainder of this subsection the three styles of interface most often found are discussed, they are command languages, form fill interfaces, and window environments.

Command languages

Command languages typically provide only facilities to support the conversational world, allowing the user to issue a set of commands, sequentially to the system, requesting it to perform some operation or execute some action. Even so, they can be relatively flexible and can allow users to use their own initiative. They have the potential to allow the user to issue commands in advance, and to combine commands together to form new commands. In some cases they allow the user to chain commands together to avoid the need for intermediate files. For example, the UNIX *pipe* command allows the output of one command to act as the input to another enabling the user to "string" a series of commands together. In the following example, a listing of a directory has been requested (using ls -la). This is then *piped* (the UNIX pipe symbol is |) into the grep command which searches its input for any sequence of characters containing the string "jjh". The output of the grep command is then *piped* to the print command lpr:

```
ls -la | grep 'jjh' | lpr
```

Command languages, for all their power and flexibility, can be intimidating even for experienced computer users if they are not familiar with that particular language. This is due to the variety and flexibility which they provide, and to the substantial training and retention required to use them. The counter-intuitive nature of many of the commands and the poor error handling compounds the situation. For example, a user wishing to list all the entries within a directory along with the size, date of last modification, and the files' owners would have to type something like:

```
ls -la ~otheruser/projdir/libdir/srcdir/execdir
```

Not only does this long sequence have to be entered with no mistakes in order to be accepted; it has to be remembered by the user. For those unused to UNIX, the command **ls -la** may have no relationship to its function: that of fully listing the contents of a directory. Even where systems attempt to provide command reuse through features like command histories and aliases for commands, much typing of arrow keys and filenames is typically needed.

One of the most significant changes which has occurred in the development of new computer systems (from the point of view of the user at least) has been the introduction of graphic-based interfaces. Knowledge-based systems have been at the forefront of this revolution, often pioneering many of the features which are now prerequisites of most new user interfaces.

Form filling

Command languages are not suitable for entering large amounts of data, as their use becomes cumbersome and error prone. However, if a user is able to enter data into a "form", which visually resembles a traditional paper form, many of the problems of data entry can be eased. Users will see a display of related fields, into which data can be entered. Usually a user can move the cursor between the fields using cursor control keys or a mouse, then when a desired field is reached, data is entered by typing. One useful side effect of the form filling interaction style is that users feel that they have a modicum of control over what is happening. They can usually move to different fields, modify data they have already entered etc., as they wish, rather than in some predefined manner.

Form filling, as a single style of interface, has a very limited domain — mainly that of data entry. However, when combined with other interaction styles, particularly window environments, it can augment the other facilities to the benefit of both developer and user.

Window environments

Window-based environments, which allow both the conversational world and the multi-thread dialogue style of interface, have become very widely used. One of the best known is the WIMP style environment. WIMP stands for Windows (or Window Managers), Icons, Mice and Pop-up menus — the main elements of any WIMP interface. The WIMP environment relies on a pictorial representation of the system which is ideally based upon a concept to which the user can relate.

The essence of a WIMP interface can be summarized by the following characteristics:

- the whole screen represents a working surface (often a desktop),
- graphic windows represent sheets of paper on that desktop,
- graphic objects are used for specific concepts, for example filing cabinets for discs or a waste bin for file disposal (these could be regarded as desk accessories),
- various application programs are displayed on the screen. These stand for tools that you might use on your desktop.

In order to interact with this display, the WIMP user is provided with a mouse (or occasionally a light-pen), which can be used to select icons and menus or to manipulate windows.

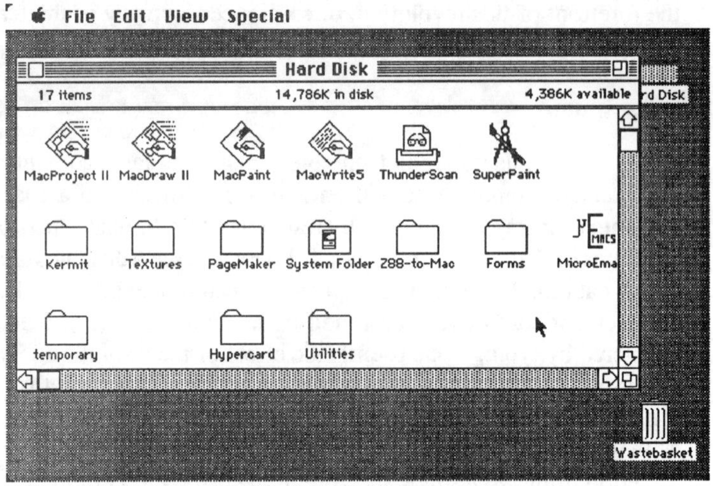

Figure 3.2: An example of the Macintosh interface

The main advantage of any window-based system, and particularly of a WIMP environment, is that it requires only a small amount of user training. There is no need to learn complex commands, as most operations are available either as icons, operations on icons, or from menu options, and are easy to use. (An icon is a small graphic object that is usually symbolic of an operation or of a larger entity such as an application program or a file.) In general, WIMP-based systems are simple to learn, intuitive to use, easy to retain and straightforward to work with.

These WIMP systems are exemplified by the Macintosh interface and the Smalltalk-80 interface, both of which were influenced by the pioneering work done at the Palo Alto Research Center on the Xerox Star Machine. It was, however, the Macintosh which brought such interfaces to the mass market, and first gained acceptance for them as tools for business, home and industry. This interface has transformed the way in which humans expect to interact with their computers, becoming a de facto standard, which has forced other manufacturers to provide similar interfaces on their own machines, for example, Microsoft Windows for the IBM PC.

This type of interface can be augmented by providing direct manipulation graphics. These are graphics which can be "grabbed" and manipulated by the user, using a mouse, to perform some operation or action. Icons are a simple version of this, the "opening" of an icon causes either the associated application to execute or the associated window to be displayed. More complex direct manipulation graphics are active images such as sliders and dials. These are like icons in that they have an associated action or operation, but the method used to "activate" them is generally more complex, allowing the user greater manipulation of the interface.

Window-based environments do have their disadvantages however. In general they require a greater level of system support or programmer effort than command languages. It is also possible to get carried away with WIMPs, providing heavily nested menu trees, multiple overlaying windows and a plethora of icons across the user's screen. Not only does this leave the user bewildered and lost, but also very frustrated. Even when "good interface guide-lines" are followed, the resulting systems can be so menu / icon / mouse oriented that they encourage many frequent, yet slow, users. For example, if all system commands are available only as menus, then every time a user wishes to execute some command they will have to select the appropriate menu(s). This can be time consuming. If keyboard options are available as well, frequent users can take short cuts quickly performing the same operation in one key stroke.

A more pragmatic restriction on the use of window environments is that they require screen space. On large, high resolution, bit-mapped screens this might not be much of an issue, but on small PC screens (often used as the delivery platform, if not the development platform) this is of rather more importance. A final point about window environments is that it is harder to record a history of the user's interaction with the system, using WIMPs and active images in particular, than for command languages. This is important if it is necessary to maintain an audit trail of user–computer interaction.

3.3 Tools for developers

Toolkits for building knowledge-based systems are complex systems in their own right and usually have complex interfaces. If the system is difficult to use or is counter-intuitive, developers will not want to be bothered with it and the toolkit will become counter-productive. This section examines what classes of tool should be provided and how such tools should present their information. The classes considered are: inspectors, editors, debugging tools, the command system itself and hypertext facilities.

3.3.1 Inspectors

An inspector allows the developer to *inspect* some information available in either the application or development system. Information cannot be entered or modified using an inspector. The information displayed can vary from the structure of a frame-based system to the contents of a knowledge base and will depend on the knowledge representation provided by the system.

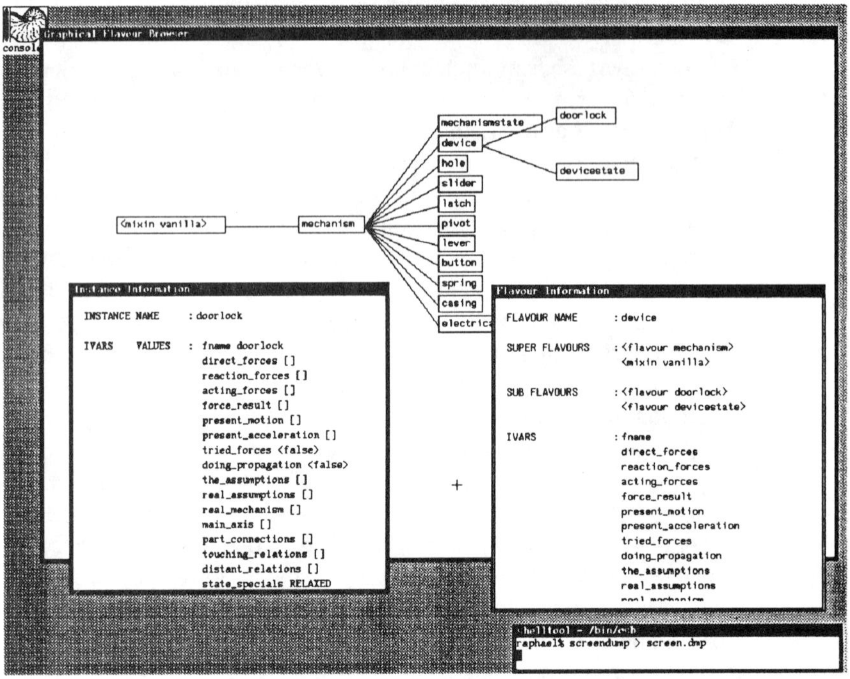

Figure 3.3: An example inspector

When considering the facilities provided by an inspector it is important to ask the following questions:

What information is displayed? For each important system feature, there should be an appropriate inspector. For example, if the system being developed is a rule-based system, facilities should be provided for inspecting not only the rules available for consideration but also the dynamic state of the application, including the current contents of working memory, and the current rules being considered.

Inspectors within a hybrid system, containing for example both rules and objects, should be integrated in such away as to allow a developer to inspect one type of representation easily from another, possibly still displaying the first. The line between some inspectors and some debuggers can be rather vague, and it is often desirable having "inspected" a value, to be able to "edit" that value. It is therefore advantageous to have inspectors, debuggers and editors integrated in a unified system.

How is information displayed? Some methods of displaying information are easier to assimilate than others, for example, when inspecting frames, objects or hierarchies of schemata it is easier to view the connectivity between items as a graphic tree. However, information within a rule might be best displayed in a textual form, therefore the method used to display information should match the type of information being inspected. Figure 3.3 illustrates an inspector for the POPLOG Flavours library, an object oriented extension to the POP-11 language. Three windows are displayed, the largest window graphically displays the relationships between the objects currently available in the system and their relationships. The two smaller windows textually display information about a particular instance and a particular flavour definition. This mixture of graphics and text enables the information available to be displayed in the appropriate manner.

Can the inspector be manipulated? Some inspectors are limited in the amount of information which can be displayed at any one time. For example, if an inspector is of fixed window size and the information display of fixed format, then it can quickly become unmanageable and unusable for anything but very small networks of information. Scrollable, or selective inspectors, allow the developer to manipulate how much information and what information is displayed. This allows large quantities of data to be displayed in a relatively meaningful manner.

3.3.2 Editors

Editors are the means by which the developer can define (and refine) the application system. Editors can range from relatively simple text-based editors, such as *vi*, through powerful, text-based editors such as EMACS, to more graphical editors such as the PALM Network Editor[1]. Some text-based editors are context sensitive providing either syntax validation facilities or automatic generation of language structures. Graphic-based editors allow a developer to traverse a complex network of information easily and quickly.

Editors can be divided into two classes — structure editors and dynamic editors. This section will only consider structure editors, dynamic editors will be discussed under section 3.3.3.

Structure editors enable the user to edit the structural features of the system, i.e., class definitions, schemata, rules etc. For example, the PALM Network Editor allows hierarchies of schemata linked by various relationships, to be displayed graphically on the screen in a tree format. New schemata can be added or deleted from the hierarchy. Schemata themselves, are modified within the PALM Schema Editor which can be invoked from within the Network Editor. As this example illustrates, there need to be multiple structure editors, one for each class and level

[1]The PALM Network Editor is part of the Knowledge Craft toolkit.

of structure. If a common "text editor" is used to define the structures, this can be time consuming and error prone.

The way in which information is displayed within the editor is almost as important as the types of editor available. Graphic-based editors are best suited to complex knowledge structures which have many links between different "objects" in that structure. However, text-based or form fill-based editors provide better facilities for the entry and modification of rules and schema etc. Such editors allow information to be entered in a manner which is natural for the structure it edits. For example, the GoldWorks II rule editor allows the developer to enter rules with a menu-driven interface which performs syntax validation on the input. Not only does this speed up rule entry and avoid syntax errors at compile time, it can also buffer the developer from the underlying language used to represent the knowledge, in this case LISP.

Finally, the method used to incorporate edits into the dynamic system is important. That is, how does the editor interact with the rest of the system? For example, does it use an edit-compile-execute cycle, or is the editor integrated with the whole system as in the case of **VED**, the POPLOG editor? One of the advantages of having an integrated editor is that as soon as a change is made and compiled, within the editor, the executing system will contain that change — very useful for quick prototyping.

3.3.3 Debugging tools

Debugging tools enable a developer to monitor, modify, or control the execution of the application system. They could be based on a WIMP interface or on a command language, and could display their information graphically or textually. For example, the rules being considered in a rule-based system, can be displayed textually as a text rule trace, or graphically as a tree in which those being considered are highlighted; see figure 3.4 for an example of both. The monitoring facilities, such as single stepping through the program and trace facilities, can either be controlled by a command language or by use of the mouse. Control facilities, such as break points can also be extremely useful debugging facilities. A further class of debugging tools are dynamic editors, which allow a user to monitor and modify the applications dynamic data during system execution. If facilities are provided for inspecting the dynamic data, such inspectors should update automatically whenever an item being displayed changes.

When evaluating the utility of a debugger it is important to consider which features of the system to be built can be monitored, whether these are the pertinent features and what facilities are provided to effect control, modification and monitoring of system execution. These facilities can be considered under two main headings — dynamic execution and dynamic state:

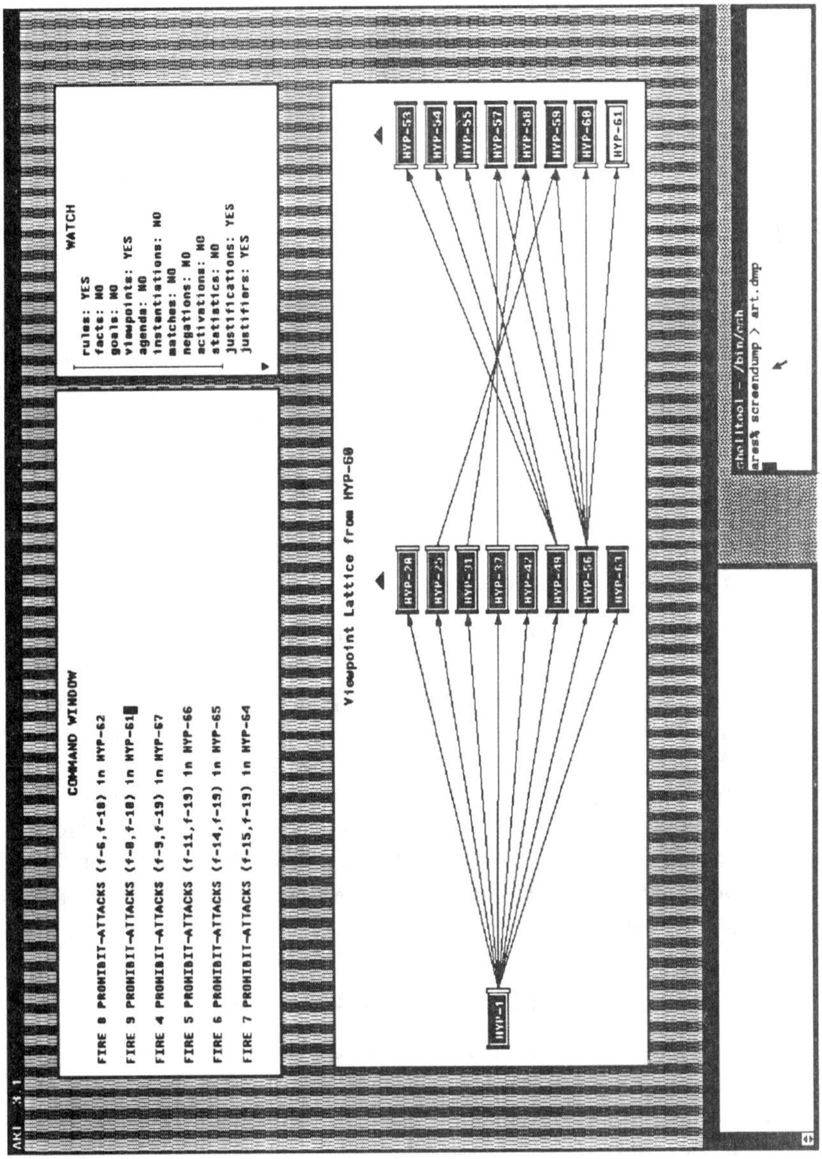

Figure 3.4: Examples of both a textual and a graphical rule trace

Dynamic execution This class of facility usually displays information on the control structures which are processed during the system execution. Some systems list these textually while others illustrate them graphically. Examples of these type of debugging facilities include:

- Rule Tracing — display the rules that fire during the system execution.
- Goal Tracing — displays the goals which are being satisfied during system execution.
- Method Tracing — displays the methods that are being executed for a particular object.

Dynamic state Dynamic editors enable the developer to monitor and modify the current contents of the dynamic state of the system, for example, slots and values in schemata. Dynamic traces allow the facts being considered and the objects being manipulated to be monitored. In either case, the dynamic information being displayed should be updated dynamically and automatically. Some systems, however, require the developer to explicitly request an update.

3.3.4 Command system

The command system is the glue of the whole development environment, it can be a command language system, or a WIMP-based environment. In some cases the developer has the choice. The most important feature of the command system is how integrated are the tools available within it. If the developer has to exit from one tool before entering another, then the environment is poorly integrated. Today no developer of a complex system should have to leave an editor to execute a compilation etc. Indeed, it should be possible to invoke inspectors, debuggers and editors with the minimum of effort. A highly integrated environment allows one tool to be directly invoked from within another and can greatly improve the productivity of the developer.

3.3.5 Hypertext / hypermedia facilities

With a hierarchical document system, the structure of a document is well-defined. If a user is at one terminal node in the structure but wishes to reference another, often he/she has to retrace his/her steps up the hierarchy and then descend down to the desired node. The advantage of hypertext is that it avoids this. Hypertext systems feature links — both within and between documents — which allow the user to move around a network of interconnected nodes. Windows on the screen are associated with nodes, and links are represented graphically as labelled tokens or icons.

3.4 Interfaces for users

There are numerous techniques available to allow a developer to design and implement a user interface. Among the simplest are user written programs, while the most powerful include advanced interactive interface design / prototyping tools.

This section explores the requirements of any toolkit that will be useful for building HCIs. This will enable the evaluation of different toolkits in the light of these requirements. This is followed by a consideration of the facilities needed to support the construction of window-based interfaces. Features particularly useful for the construction of knowledge-based systems are then presented. Finally an example interface is discussed.

3.4.1 Requirements for user interface development

When appraising a toolkit's facilities for building user interfaces, it is worth considering some of the desirable features of interface development systems in general. These requirements are becoming better understood and fall mainly into the following six categories:

Usability If the interface building facilities provided by the toolkit are easy to use, well-documented and integrated into the existing development environment (that is, a separate graphic environment is not required), developers will be encouraged to use them. This will improve developer productivity through the utilization of the existing facilities.

Functionality This refers to the styles of interface that the system can be used to build, for example, window-based interfaces, form-fill interfaces etc. This is particularly important for knowledge-based systems, as they often require very complex multi-mode interfaces, needing facilities for a variety of input/output devices.

Extensibility Even given that most user interface design tools will have a reasonable level of functionality, it is unlikely that they will be able to cover all of a knowledge-based system's requirements. Therefore, it must be possible to extend the facilities provided by the toolkit.

Escapability It may be necessary on occasions to abandon the toolkits facilities completely and develop part of the interface externally. This may be desirable for a particular feature which cannot be implemented within the toolkit, but which is vital for a particular application.

WIMP-style interface A WIMP-style interface provides a single interface standard for the various facilities provided by the application. Facilities for building WIMP interfaces should be available to the developer.

Interface construction tools As most developers of user interfaces think visually about their interfaces, the toolkit should allow the user to generate an interface graphically. This enables the developer to view the same interface as the user would see while designing it. Such tools are only just becoming available.

3.4.2 Window-based interfaces

This subsection considers what windowing facilities are required by the developer of a HCI for a knowledge-based system.

Windows

Most development software today provides facilities for window-based interfaces, and knowledge engineering toolkits should be no exception. In general the development toolkit should provide support for the creation, manipulation and deletion of windows. The windowing system should allow programmatic control of window resizing, scrolling, text display, graph and graphics display. The level of this support, however, is as important a consideration as the style of interface provided. If one toolkit provides fewer windowing facilities than another, but packages those facilities together in such away that they are easier to use, then it might well be the preferable system.

Information suppliers

An information supplier is used to present some information to the user. It is a general term covering anything from the drawing of a line, to the generation of a box to tell the user about some system operation. In order to support this, facilities need to be provided for generating the graphic display, managing transient displays and supporting help systems. These are considered below:

Graphic building facilities There has been a steady movement towards high-level interface generation facilities. These facilities insulate the developer from the implementation details of graphic programming on a particular system, often providing instead a pseudo graphics language in which to describe the interface required. Some systems provide additional tools to simplify this process. These high-level languages also promote the portability of the interface, as only the low-level, platform specific routines, must be reimplemented.

If lower-level graphic facilities are to be used, it is important to ensure that a graphics standard, supported across the delivery platforms, is used. A platform specific standard will require that a new interface be implemented when the system is to be delivered on a new platform.

Information display facilities Most interactive systems need to be able to display information to the user without corrupting the existing display. Such facilities should be provided by the development system. Typical examples of information displays are prompt boxes, which are displayed on the screen on top of the existing display, as a graphic box containing some message.

Support for an integrated help system Features should be provided to support on-line help facilities in the delivery system, these can range from simple pop-up prompts to hypertext-style environments. In knowledge-based systems these facilities need to be integrated with explanation facilities.

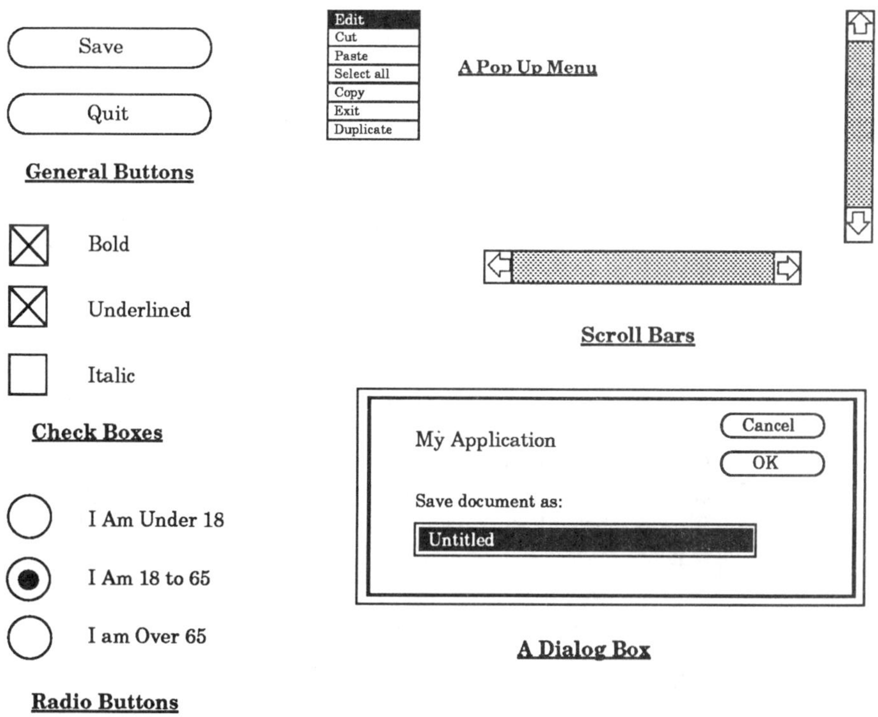

Figure 3.5: Example information gatherers

Information gatherers

Information gatherers provide facilities for obtaining information from the user, either through the keyboard or from the mouse. The facilities include menus, command windows and icons. Examples of information gatherers are illustrated in figure 3.5. These are discussed in greater detail below:

Selections Any WIMP environment should provide at least a minimum level of menu and pop-up item support. When considering a WIMP-style interface, it is important to know what facilities are directly supported by the development system. A full set of menu facilities could include the ability to define menu bars, pop-up menus, walking menus, selection menus and multiple choice menus. It should also be possible to associate keyboard commands with menu options, allowing experienced users to take shortcuts. Direct support for control objects such as button options, check boxes, dialogue boxes and scroll bars, should also be provided.

Forms If large amounts of data are required by the application system then direct support for data entry, using form filling techniques, should be provided by the development environment. These should allow the developer to specify the format of the form and the valid entries for fields.

Command windows This is really a broader issue about the ability to combine different interface styles. WIMPs are sufficient for many application operations, but it is often necessary for a user to enter some text, for example, when entering a new filename. It is therefore useful if the developer is supplied with facilities for easily combining text-based command windows / items with WIMP-style interfaces.

ICON support Icons are an effective way of providing a simple to use command interface. Tools to support the development of icons, such as icon editors (which allow an icon to be graphically designed), can simplify the generation and manipulation of icons. The development environment should therefore provide such facilities, if the application is to utilize any iconic features.

3.4.3 Catering for knowledge-based systems

Knowledge-based system construction toolkits often provide facilities to simplify the generation of the complex, highly interactive, user interfaces which are typical of knowledge-based systems. The most important of these include: mouse-sensitive items, hypertext facilities and active values.

Mouse-sensitive items Mouse-sensitive objects are screen items, or areas of the screen, which are sensitive to the mouse. This means that when the mouse is moved over such an item it is highlighted, or over such an area then it is boxed. If a mouse button is clicked, while over either, some action (defined by the developer) is invoked.

Hypertext help interfaces Advanced help facilities can be developed using hypertext systems. It should be possible to define the relationships between documents and sub-documents via links and relationships. The system should include browsers to view these nodes and links, allowing the user to select any node, or move along links to find nodes. Advanced systems will also provide facilities for including graphics and occasionally sound.

Active values Many knowledge-based systems require a graphic image to alter as an associated system parameter (or parameters) changes. For example, an expert system performing a monitoring role might require a set of dials or sliders that would reflect the dynamic system state. One easy-to-use facility, provided by many toolkits, can be termed an *active graphic*. This is a simple access-oriented programming technique for handling values and associated graphic objects which alter at run-time.

An active graphic is attached to an attribute of an object. When the attribute's value is accessed or stored, then the graphic display is updated if the active value is changed. Active graphics can also provide facilities for updating the attribute's value directly from the iconic screen object. For example, if a dial is an active graphic, then when the user changes the position of the pointer in the dial, using the mouse, the associated active value is updated in the appropriate manner.

Active graphics can be used to integrate the underlying representation, reasoning process and graphic display, by associating actions, such that, whenever an active value or active graphic is changed, the appropriate graphical or symbolic representation is updated.

3.4.4 An example interface

This example illustrates a control panel for a very simple car simulation system. Figure 3.6 presents the user interface containing a speedometer, a temperature gauge, and rev counter as output only displays. The user can interact with the simulation by turning the engine button on and off, the handbrake button on and off, selecting the appropriate gear and setting the amount of accelerator or footbrake being applied. The system has been implemented in POP-11, using the Flavours library language extension and the Window Flavours library of facilities.

The designer has made the attributes of the car components "active", so that a set of POP-11 Flavour methods are called whenever those attributes are changed. The active values and associated active graphics are illustrated in figure 3.7. Each active value has one active graphic with which it is directly associated (represented by an arrow indicating the direction of dependency). For example, the contents of the active value **the_speed** is displayed directly in the active graphic speedometer.

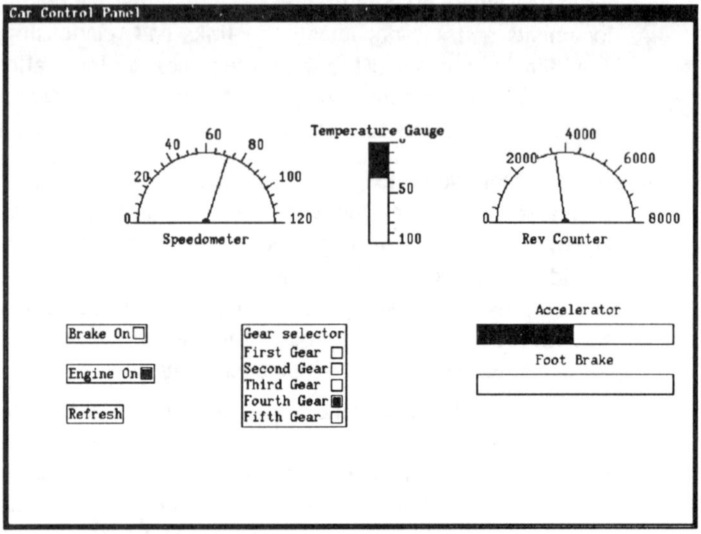

Figure 3.6: The interface to the car control simulator

However, there are additional "relationships" between active values, for example, the status of the footbrake influences the contents of **the_speed.**

To generate this simple simulation system, all that was required was the definition of the window, positioning of the graphic items, linking of the active values with their active graphics and specification of the relationships between the active values. The remaining windowing facilities, for example, handling the mouse, handling the updating of an active graphic when its value changed, were all provided by the Window Flavours library.

In order to illustrate how the user interacts with the interface, and what effect such interaction has, an example session is now considered. The numbered points refer to the sequence of arrows shown in figure 3.8.

1. To determine the effect of accelerating on the status of the car simulation, the user indicates the level of the accelerator by dragging the slider level to the correct position.

2. This causes the active value **accelerator_position** to be updated.

3. A relationship exists between the **accelerator_position** and the **rev_count**, such that the **rev_count** is modified by a function of the value of **accelerator_position**. This function, however, is also influenced by the current gear

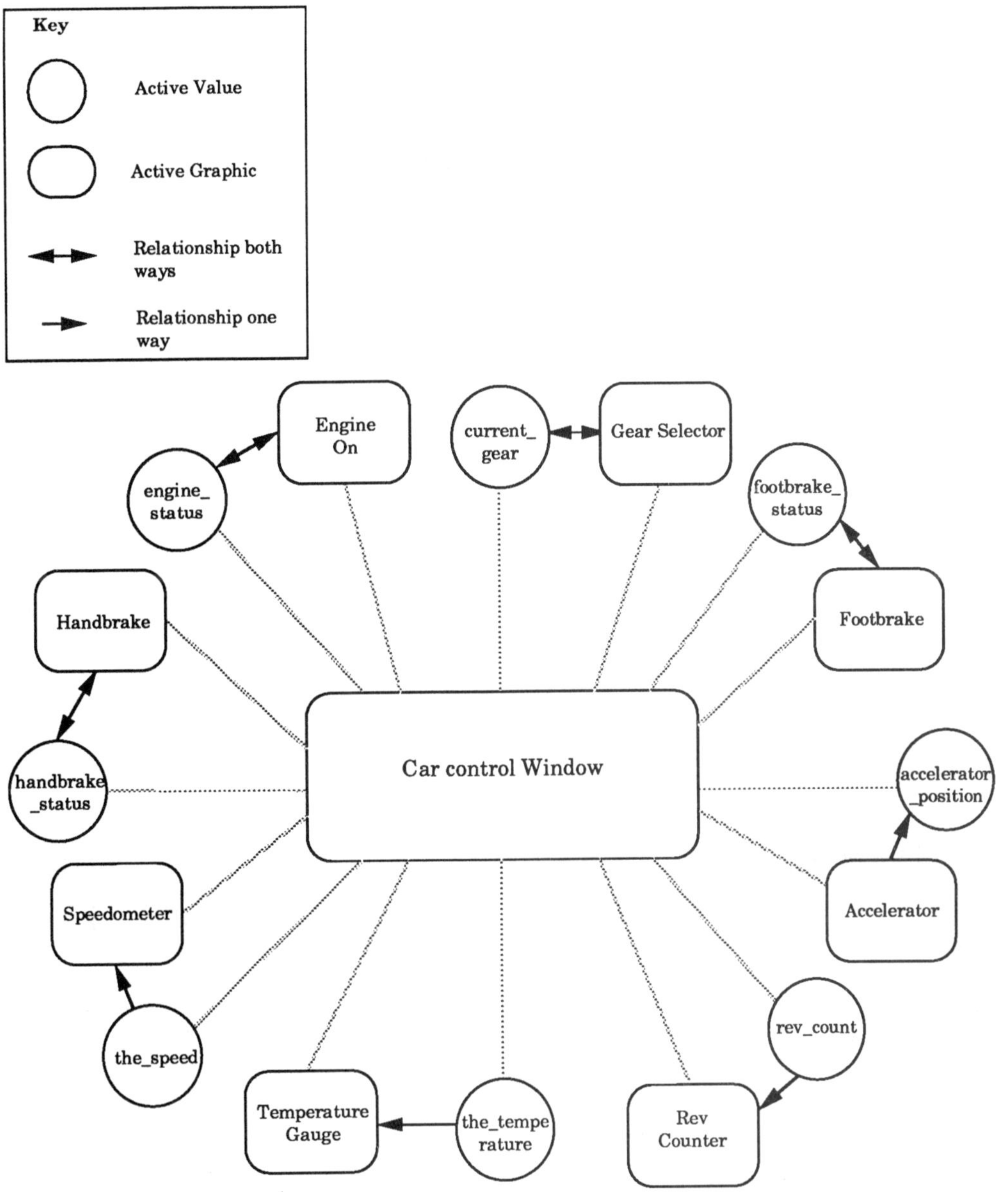

Figure 3.7: The relationships between the interface objects

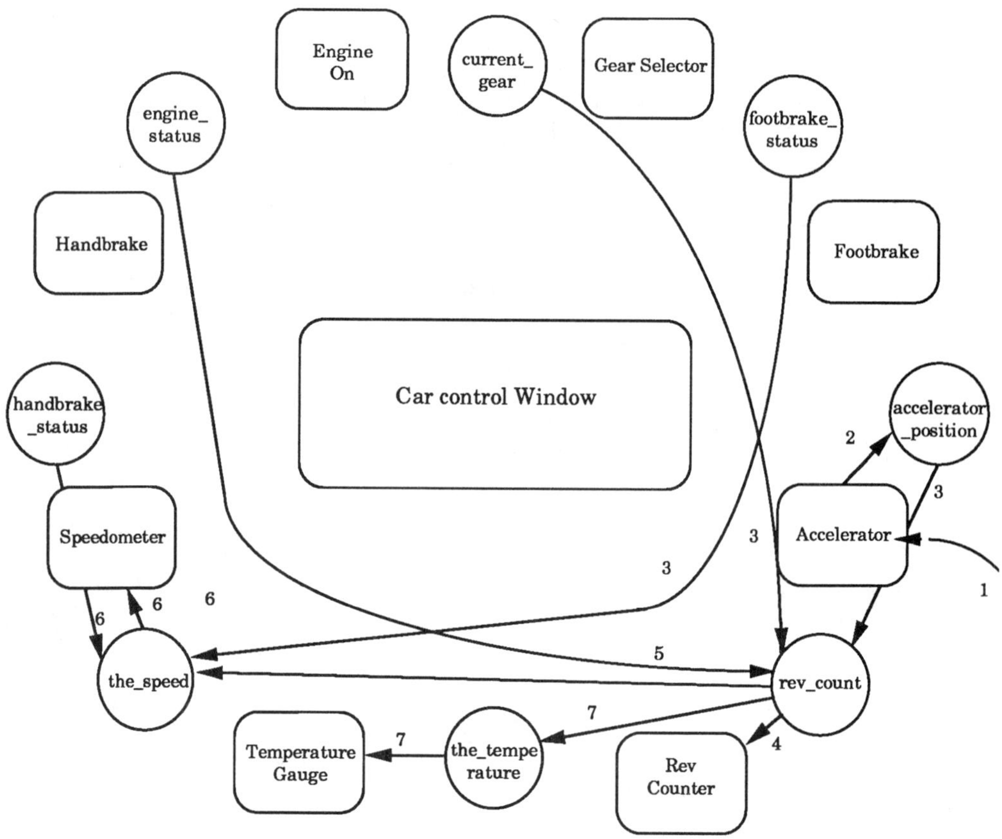

Figure 3.8: The effect of increasing the accelerator

selected and the current status of the engine. For example, if the engine is switched off then no matter what the **accelerator_position**, the **rev_count** will be zero.

4. Once the **rev_count** value is determined, the graphic icon rev counter is updated to display the new value.
5. **the_speed** active value is then updated because it is associated with the **rev_count** active value.
6. However, as well as **rev_count**, the contents of **the_speed** depends on the values of **footbrake_status** and **handbrake_status**. Once **the_speed** value has been calculated, the associated dial graphic, speedometer, is updated.
7. Finally, **the_temperature** active value is also modified whenever **rev_count** is modified. The temperature is a function of the current **rev_count**. This is then displayed in the associated temperature gauge icon.

3.5 Future interfaces

In the future, the use of the graphics facilities provided by high power workstations will continue to influence user interface development. For example, the much acclaimed NeXT Machine has a highly graphic interface to the UNIX operating system and provides an application builder toolkit. As even more powerful workstations become available, this trend will continue.

The current research into numerous kinds of interactive tools for HCI development will begin to filter through to the market place, freeing the developer from much of the tedium of "coding" the user interface. It will provide facilities for machine independence and standardization. Further work on prototyping systems for developing user interfaces will provide facilities for the early observation of the behaviour / suitability of user interfaces. This will result in improved interfaces due to the possible communication between system designers, developers, and users — they will be able to view how the user interface will work long before the actual system is available. Work is progressing in these areas, for example RAPID/USE.

Research is also considering the use of very high-level support systems. For example, Peridot is an experimental interface construction tool. It differs from previous systems because, instead of explicitly defining the whole interface, the user of Peridot demonstrates how the interface should look and act. This is accomplished by requesting the developer to draw the screen display, then allowing them to manipulate the interface in the same way as the user would.

There is also likely to be an increase in the use of hypermedia-style help systems. Hypermedia is a more general concept than hypertext, encompassing text, graphics, digitized speech and animation. Much research work is currently being expended on hypermedia systems.

In general, there will be much greater support for the developers of HCIs, not only for the construction and maintenance, but also for design, evaluation and prototyping of complex, graphical, highly interactive user interfaces.

3.6 Further reading

Human–computer interfaces A discussion of the WIMP-style interfaces can also be found in [Hunt and Price]. This paper presents the WIMP-style interface and the development of such interfaces using POP-11.

[Hutchins et al.] provides a detailed discussion of the two main metaphors that describe the ways in which humans and computers interact — *the conversational world* and *multi-thread dialogue*.

The pioneering Xerox Star machine has been documented in [Smith et al.]. The Smalltalk system itself has been extensively documented. Two good references are [Goldberg and Robson] and [Tesler].

The influence of hypertext systems on the design of user interfaces is likely to increase in the future, [Conklin] provides a good introduction to hypertext in general and presents a survey of existing hypertext-style systems.

Developing user interfaces Guide-lines are slowly emerging which will help to direct the developer when designing and implementing a user interface. They mainly address the issue of usability; see [Shneiderman] for a detailed discussion on this topic.

Future advances [Harston and Hix] provide a very detailed and comprehensive discussion of the current state of research in HCIs. This paper also includes a review of a number of advanced user interface development systems (including the RAPID/USE system, which is more comprehensively documented in [Wasserman and Shewmake]).

[Myers] documents the Peridot system, providing a detailed discussion of the system, its design and numerous examples.

Chapter 4

The knowledge engineering lifecycle

Chris Price

Between the idea
And the reality
Between the motion
And the act
Falls the Shadow
The Hollow Men, T. S. Eliot

4.1 Introduction

A knowledge-based system (KBS) is a complex piece of computer software, and so it should come as no surprise that many of the problems involved in engineering knowledge-based systems can be encountered when constructing any other complex piece of software (lack of experience, badly specified projects, inappropriate applications of the technology). However, the nature of knowledge-based systems emphasizes certain difficulties in addition to those which occur in any software engineering endeavour:

Specifying the scope of the system. Human experts are very flexible in their response to problems. Specifying realistic limits to how much of their expertise can be reproduced by a knowledge-based system is not always easy.

Implementing the requirements. Analysing the content of human expertise, it often appears that the knowledge which distinguishes the expert from the novice is not the structured theoretical knowledge of the domain, but rather more haphazard knowledge about when it is appropriate to apply the more theoretical knowledge. It can be hard to organise this knowledge into a coherent form in order to express it in a knowledge-based system.

Designing the human–computer interface. Where a knowledge-based system obtains its information through interaction with a user, it can be important for the system to provide the impression that it is behaving in the way that a human expert would behave. This means that the system needs to imitate the expert's information gathering techniques as well as his expertise. This often increases the complexity of the system.

Ensuring the system meets the specification. Validating expert systems is made harder because such systems often reflect the haphazard appearance of the original expertise. Maintaining them can often seem an impossible task.

These extra problems, inherent in constructing knowledge-based systems, make it imperative that anyone building them should apply software engineering principles to the construction and maintenance of the systems that they build, and should use any and all the tools that are available to make their task easier.

This chapter examines the complete software engineering system development lifecycle, indicating the points which are especially critical for KBS development. The important parts of the lifecycle are then examined in detail. Relevant tools to help the knowledge engineer are explored in chapter 5.

Unfortunately, it must be pointed out that presently available commercial toolkits do not provide tools to cover the complete development and maintenance of KBSs. Some people even claim that the lifecycle concept is irrelevant to knowledge engineering. There are two ways of attempting to justify such claims:

Artificial intelligence is not the same as programming. The basic idea behind this justification is that truly intelligent systems must have an incremental learning component, and so it will be impossible to completely specify the behaviour of such systems before they have been built.

This objection does not apply to the sorts of system that can be built today for industrial applications. Very few of them have any automatic learning component, let alone a learning capacity which updates the system while it is running. In addition, one could argue that the level of specification for such systems needs to be greater, not less, than that provided for less intelligent systems. In the same way that a little learning is a dangerous thing, a semi-intelligent system is likely to be more dangerous than one you know to be stupid.

Extrapolation from simple systems. This justification for the lack of lifecycle support can be blamed on the newness of knowledge engineering as a discipline. Many people are making the same mistakes that were made in the earlier days of software engineering.

Having successfully built (and possibly even have in use) some fairly simple prototype expert systems, they claim that prototyping is a sufficient methodology for the construction of much larger systems. As was the case in software engineering in general, there are likely to be some notable failures before this view is entirely discredited.

Present-day toolkits tend to reflect a belief in the sufficiency of prototyping as a knowledge engineering methodology. They provide the equivalent of code generation tools plus some system debugging help. While this is sufficient for exploratory system building, the serious system builder needs more tools than just a compiler and a debugger. A complete knowledge engineering toolkit would contain tools to support the whole of the knowledge engineering lifecycle.

It is ironic that the products of knowledge engineering are helping to support the work of other types of engineer, and yet very few applications of knowledge engineering have been built to help the knowledge engineers themselves.

The fact that toolkits do not support the whole of the knowledge engineering lifecycle needs to be borne in mind when looking at the case studies in part two of the book. Implicit in the case studies is significant amounts of effort on the part of the implementors which might have been unnecessary if the right sorts of tools had been available.

Several of the case study systems are only prototypes or research systems, whereas the engineering of KBSs only becomes of vital importance when building delivery systems. Scaling up from a prototype to a large delivery system is a very difficult and expensive process — one reason why many expert systems never go beyond the prototype stage.

4.2 The proposed lifecycle

Many KBSs have been constructed to be as independent as possible of any other software development. To some extent, the stand-alone nature of most present-day KBSs stems from the fact that the output from many of the tools used for constructing expert systems cannot be embedded in larger applications — the tools have been built with the assumption that they are 'in charge' of the application, perhaps calling other software as subroutines in order to obtain information or to perform complex calculations, but never being called as subroutines themselves.

The stand-alone nature of many KBSs can be compared with using a database only as a system for users to type in direct queries. It severely limits their usefulness. The most powerful applications of database technology occur when they are integrated into larger systems. There is a symbiosis within such systems, some other components of the larger system providing further information for the database, and some components making use of the information that is already present in the database. Similarly, some of the most useful applications of KBS technology will be as adjuncts to much larger systems. Some of the possibilities for KBS components of more complex systems are:

- intelligent front-ends to large numerical simulations;
- personal money management advice for employees provided as part of the company payroll system;
- intelligent monitoring software embedded in process control systems;
- knowledge-based hardware fault diagnosis software over communications networks;
- knowledge bases as the kernel of the next generation of IPSEs.

Some of these applications are being built or researched at the moment, and such systems emphasize the importance of specifying exactly what a knowledge-based system does. When a KBS component is built into a more complex system, it is not sufficient to say that the KBS component is for advisory purposes only. It becomes necessary to guarantee performance under a specified set of circumstances and to explicit identify failed cases.

In software engineering, a general methodology has evolved over many years based on the concept of a software engineering lifecycle. While it has some limitations when constructing any complex software, it can be adapted so that knowledge-based systems, of the sort that are commercially feasible today, can be built within the standard software lifecycle.

The software engineering lifecycle takes a software project from the conception of an idea to the completion of the system (and beyond). It splits the lifetime of a software project into *phases*, with identifiable *deliverables* produced by each phase. The deliverables are intended to ensure that the objectives of each phase have been achieved. There are many variations on it, but a fairly typical set of lifecycle phases are:

Feasibility study. The purpose of this phase of the project is to decide whether the proposed system is technically feasible, and whether it is worth the effort of building it. For some types of project, the feasibility study will be a very minor part of the project, but for more ambitious systems of the kind likely to need KBS components, it is a vital exercise. The deliverable from this phase of the project is a report which says whether the proposed system should be built.

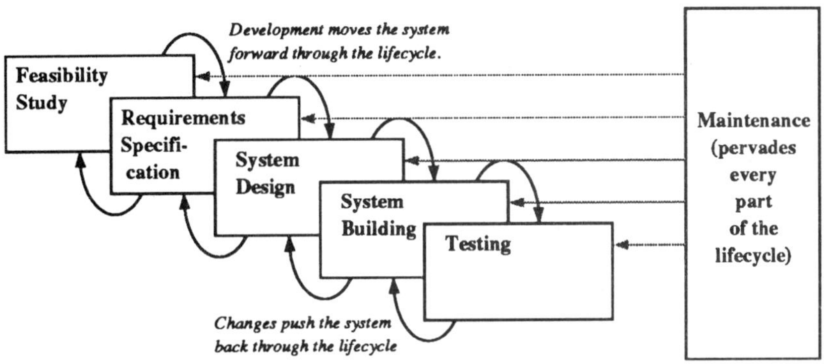

Figure 4.1: Typical software engineering lifecycle model

Requirements definition This phase of the project produces a document which sets out in detail what the system will do and how it will appear. This document, produced in collaboration with the users of the proposed system, commits the system builders to providing a particular system which is capable of a specified level of performance.

System specification and design. The specification phase examines the details of how the promised system will be built. Typically, the system specification will occur in a top-down manner — the system designers will modularize the complete system into a set of subsystems. Where those subsystems are still of a significant size, they will be broken down further into modules. The system specification document (the deliverable from this phase) will describe all these units, and the interactions between the units.

System implementation. During this phase, the actual implementation of the system takes place. The main deliverable should be a system which meets the requirements definition and which matches the design in the system specification document.

Testing. By the time that the system reaches the stage of complete system testing, much of the testing should have already happened. This phase tests that the complete system does indeed meets its requirement definition.

Maintenance. This is usually the most neglected phase of the software engineering lifecycle. This is regrettable, because for most successful systems, it will be the longest phase and will take the most manpower. The maintenance phase attempts to keep the system useful despite the inadequacies of the previous phases.

The rest of chapter 4 examines each of the phases of this typical life-cycle model and shows how they can be applied to a large application system that includes one (or possibly more) KBS component. It highlights where special care needs to be taken for the KBS component and where specific knowledge engineering tools can help. Chapter 5 explores the identified tools more deeply.

The construction of stand-alone expert systems can be looked on as a subset of this larger problem, with the issue of integration having reduced importance. Even for such stand-alone systems, the discipline of an engineering methodology should result in a more robust, a more reliable, a more maintainable — in short, a *better engineered* — product.

4.3 Feasibility study

The feasibility study phase of the software lifecycle can include the construction of prototypes for some parts of the knowledge-based system, but this is not mandatory. It may be unnecessary if there is previous experience of similar applications. There may be good reasons for prototyping during a feasibility study, but it should only be done if some of those reasons hold:

To find out if the application can be built. Experience of knowledge-based systems is at a fairly early stage, and for many applications it is difficult to judge whether they are possible without actually trying to build the difficult parts of them. For an application which contains a novel KBS component, the feasibility study will examine what knowledge is needed and what reasoning is to be performed by that component. A prototype may be constructed to ensure that the proposed representation and reasoning are capable of performing their intended task. Some knowledge analysis tools (see section 5.1) may be employed during this prototyping exercise.

To test possible user interfaces. Human–computer interface issues are often difficult to resolve for knowledge-based systems without experimentation. If the proposed system does need to interface to end-users, then human factors experiments using a prototype of the system will aid the correct design of the interface. Such a prototype does not need to address difficult knowledge representation issues, only how the system will appear to the end-user.

To convince others that the application can be built. It is often necessary to demonstrate to one's management the ability of the proposed system to meet its needs. Except for this last reason, there is no need for the prototype to ever be robust or to cover the complete problem addressed by the proposed KBS component.

A commonly held opinion is that the development of a knowledge-based system should progress from a prototype to a final system by continual refinement. Applying this policy to a KBS component of a large system is likely to prove disastrous.

The most important issue in any system which is to be delivered to (possibly many) users is reliability. Incremental prototyping produces inherently unreliable systems. Because of the need for reliability, prototypes should be thrown away, although the ideas and experience gained through building them should be fed into the system development.

Feasibility questions that need to be answered for the KBS component will also cover the conventional parts of the proposed system:

- Do we want it?
- Can we afford it?
- Can it be done?
- Will people use it?

Prototyping of other components of the proposed system may also be necessary in order to answer all of these questions satisfactorily. In essence, the final output from the feasibility study is either a "Yes" or a "No".

Yes means that the system can conceivably be built and that the ratio of the cost of building the system to the benefit gained from the system is such that it is worth the effort of building the system, and the project should proceed.

No means that it is impossible or too costly to build the system, so the idea should be shelved. Good feasibility studies are likely to result in a higher proportion of "Noes" than bad ones. Badly done feasibility studies will fail to predict significant costs and serious problems that will arise during the process of building the system, and are likely to result in a higher proportion of failed projects.

4.4 Requirements definition

Having demonstrated that the whole system can and should be built, the next task is to describe what the system will look like. This task is addressed by the requirements definition phase of the software lifecycle.

In general, requirements for a system tend to be system-wide criteria, but there should be a closer focus on those parts of the system which are particularly important and/or difficult. KBS components of a larger system will often need this more detailed examination.

The outcome of the requirements definition phase of the lifecycle is a requirements document for the system. This document will specify both goals for and requirements of the system, and needs to make plain the difference between these two things:

Goals are general characteristics for the system to aim at. A goal of the system might be *The system should not ask the user to make any input requiring expert judgement.*

Requirements are aspects of the system that can be tested. *The system must run on a Spectrum with 16K of memory* would be a (very stiff) requirement.

For a KBS component which is to perform some task currently performed by a human expert, the performance of the human expert gives some pointers to the sort of expertise that can be required of the new system. The requirements for the KBS component will probably focus on the nature of the task which it must perform and the level at which it must perform that task.

As well as specifying broadly the task that the KBS component will perform, there are two main areas of performance that should be addressed as requirements.

Case-based performance. Examples of all categories of problem which the KBS component should handle correctly can be given. For problems that are not safety-critical, the acceptance requirement might only be that the system should deal correctly with a large (specified) percentage of such cases. It should also be required that all unmanageable cases are indicated as such. This is especially important when results from the KBS component are being handed back to more conventional software.

In addition to these requirements, it is often useful for the requirements specification to indicate the boundaries of the KBS component by giving examples of cases outside its scope.

Response time performance. If this is relevant (and it usually is), then timing trials should be done during the feasibility study. Estimates of the final size of the knowledge base and extrapolations of search time should allow estimates of response time, at least within an order of magnitude.

It should be noted at this point that complex, rapid, real-time tasks are beyond the scope of present KBS technology for a number of reasons (garbage collection problems; system architectures). In general, it would be a brave knowledge engineer who would commit the KBS component of a heavily loaded system to requirements like:

> *Upon receiving a high-priority interrupt, the system must evaluate the situation and make the correct response within 40 milliseconds whatever else is happening at the time.*

Further information about the KBS component should be recorded in the requirements document to assist the task of maintenance. There will be fundamental assumptions behind the design of the system, and they should be recorded (e.g. *The system will deal correctly with all loan risks for a rate of inflation lower than 5%*).

Anticipated changes to the system such as *Any change in income tax rates will mean that the system's results are invalid* can also be recorded, but knowledge-based systems have an advantage here over conventional systems. Many such anticipated changes can be handled by extra rules and facts. Where that is the case, the ability to cope with such a change should be recorded as a requirement instead, for example: *The system should work for any basic rate of income tax between 15% and 35%.*

4.5 System specification and design

During this phase of the development lifecycle, the specification of the complete system is modularized into subsystems, one of which will be the KBS component of the system. It is worth repeating at this point that large systems may have more than one separate KBS component — for simplicity, we are presently considering the case of a single KBS component.

The first task during this phase of the lifecycle is to specify each of the parts of the whole system, to decide what component parts will comprise the system, what task each part will perform and how. This modularization is followed by specification of the interfaces between the parts.

The interface between the KBS component and the rest of the system will need to be most rigorously defined. There are three sorts of interface which need to be addressed:

Obtaining information from the rest of the system. This should specify what information will be available to the KBS component within the system, from which other components it obtains that information and how. This sort of interface will include invocation of other subsystems, database accesses and simple routines written in conventional languages.

Interface with the user. If a user needs to answer questions, then this section should state the level of competence and the breadth of information expected from the user. It should also state what information the user expects from the KBS component, and at what level of expertise that information should be pitched.

Providing information for the rest of the system If the KBS component is invoked to perform a specific task, then this section should specify what information will be passed to it on startup, what results are to be returned and how, and what information should be returned when the KBS component is unable to reach any result.

After clear and complete interfaces between the different parts of the system have been defined, the development of the KBS component can be divorced from the development of the rest of the system. The internals of the KBS component are irrelevant to the rest of the system — it could be implemented in FORTRAN IV as long as it meets the performance requirements and the specified interfaces (although it should be noted that FORTRAN is not the language of choice for the implementation of most knowledge-based systems).

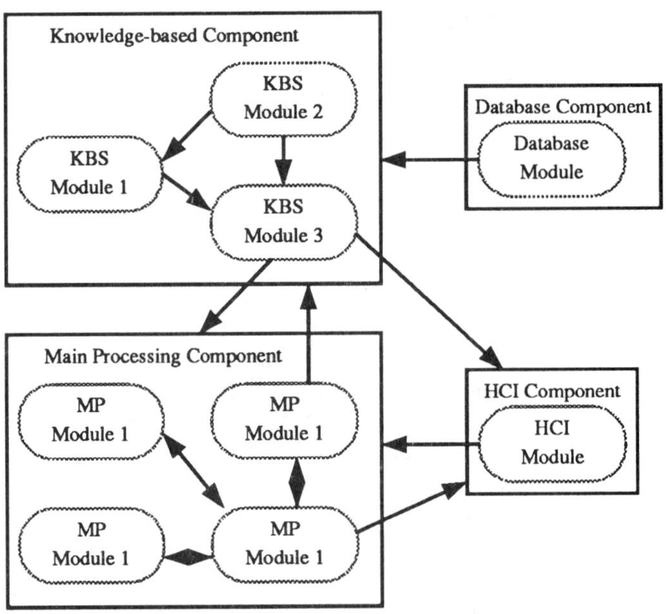

Figure 4.2: Modularization of the system

If the KBS component is itself a large system, it will be advisable to perform further modularization of it. Another level of design will be necessary, specifying the functionality of the modules and the interfaces between them and perhaps a top-level control module. It is also a good idea to specify what tests of the functionality of each module can be made, in order to reduce the problems of system integration.

For large knowledge bases, the ability to implement sensible modularization of the knowledge base is vital. See section 5.2 for further discussion of this topic.

4.6 System implementation

The task of implementing the modules that make up the KBS component of the system is done under the same constraints that are applied to the implementation of any other subsystem of the final system. Modules need to be constructed to meet the fixed interfaces laid down in the system specification, and should also meet the requirements and aim for the goals specified in the requirements document.

Some people quote the restrictiveness of this regime as the reason why KBSs should not be developed under this sort of methodology, but it should be noted that changes are a fairly frequent occurrence in any complex software system, and the methodology does make allowance for them to be handled, but in a controlled way.

When the implementor needs to cross the specified boundaries of a module, then there need to be changes to one of the documents produced earlier in the lifecycle. For example, a change of the interface between two modules would mean a change to the system specification document, and would have to be done in consultation with other implementors. Other infringements (e.g. an inability to meet performance requirements) are more serious, as they mean changes to the requirements definition, and would need to be agreed with the system's eventual users.

Within these limits, the implementor is free to experiment with different ways of structuring the knowledge within modules. It is possible to use such techniques as rule induction to generate the knowledge used within a module (see section 5.1). Knowledge base checkers (see section 5.3) can also be used to ensure that the KBS component has been built correctly.

4.7 Testing

The requirements and system specification documents each constrain the produced KBS component. Those constraints can be turned into tests with expected outcomes, and such tests should be specified during those phases (while the problems are fresh in the minds of the designers). Further tests will need to be added (as they would for any software). If the KBS component is designed and built as a set of modules, then each module should be tested during the implementation phase, before integration into the KBS component. The KBS component can then be rigorously tested as a subsystem, using a test harness to simulate all of its interfaces.

If any of the tests fail, then the testers need to decide whether it is the KBS component which is at fault and should be changed, or whether the test is wrong and needs to be changed, or whether a requirement or a part of the system specification is wrong and must be changed. If a requirement or part of the system specification is changed, then the earlier phases of the lifecycle will have to be retraced in order to look for knock-on effects in other parts of the system.

A knowledge-based IPSE (section 5.4) could help this process of iteration through the lifecycle stages. This is true whether the iteration is needed during implementation, testing or maintenance.

During subsystem testing, the KBS component is, in effect, a black box. We are testing that the correct set of inputs produce the correct outputs. When the KBS component passes these tests, it is ready to be integrated into the complete system. This top-level integration should be no different from that necessary for any other top-level subsystem, and the full system testing is the same as for any large piece of software.

4.8 Maintenance

This is a phase of the system's lifecycle that can be ignored when building a small prototype expert system. Typically, if they are used at all, they are used by one or two people and can be updated in an ad hoc manner. A significant delivery system might be distributed to several hundred sites, and all those sites should have the same system.

This means that the knowledge base maintenance, like all other maintenance, must be centralized, and that there must be some method by which users can report errors. Reported errors should be examined by the maintenance team, and classified as one of:

Error. There is something wrong with the system which must be fixed.

Restriction/feature. There is something wrong with the system, but it is unimportant compared with the cost of fixing it.

Change to specification. The system did not behave according to its specification, but its behaviour was correct. This will result in a change to the specification, but no other action.

User misunderstanding While the system does not behave as the user expected, it did behave according to its specification.

For a genuine error, the subsystem(s) responsible should be identified and a fix made, going back as far in the lifecycle as necessary. For example, a change to an interface may need to be specified in order to correct the wrong behaviour.

Once the error has been fixed, all tests on relevant subsystems and on the full system should be carried out again, including a new test which distinguishes between the old and new versions of the system.

This description of a sound testing procedure is identical to that which should be performed for any large system, but is doubly vital for a knowledge-based system, because of the flexible way in which the knowledge in such systems is used.

4.9 Summary of knowledge engineering lifecycle

Over many years, the software engineering lifecycle has shown itself to be adaptable to the development of many different sorts of software systems. It would be foolish to abandon this methodology without first discovering something better with which it could be replaced.

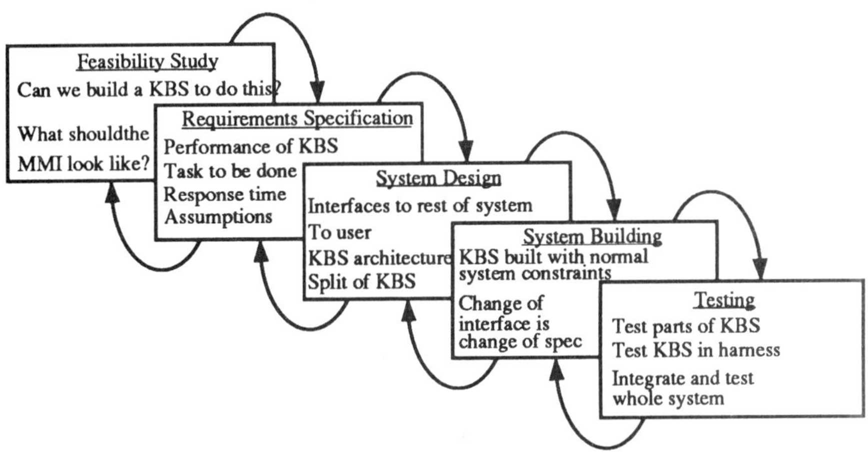

Figure 4.3: Lifecycle model annotated with KBS issues

We have pointed out that rapid prototyping is an inadequate and dangerous replacement as a knowledge engineering methodology. We have also demonstrated how the standard lifecycle can be adapted to take into account the special needs of KBS development. Figure 4.3 sums this up.

In the next chapter, we will look at what software tools are available at the moment to aid the knowledge engineer with the different parts of the KBS lifecycle outlined in this chapter.

4.10 Further reading

Software engineering. [Somerville] provides a good introduction to software engineering issues and methodology. [Gilb] is an interesting attempt to bring more of the advantages of rapid prototyping into software engineering.

Knowledge engineering lifecycle. There has not been a great deal of work published that attempts to examine seriously the idea of a knowledge engineering lifecycle. Among the best are [O'Keefe] and [Born 88]. Each of these papers considers the issue of validation, and in doing so has to consider much of the rest of the knowledge engineering lifecycle, at least indirectly.

Knowledge acquisition. A major knowledge engineering topic that is beyond the scope of this book is that of knowledge acquisition (with the exception of tools to aid the knowledge elicitation process). However, it is clearly of relevance to any debate about the knowledge engineering lifecycle.

[Welbank] or [Hart] provides a good, simple introduction to the subject. [Greenwell] is better than either of the other books, although not as generally applicable as it claims to be.

[Kidd 87] gives a more varied picture of the subject.

Chapter 5

Improving present-day toolkits

Chris Price

> Ah, but a man's reach should exceed his grasp,
> Or what's a heaven for?
> *Andrea del Sarto*, Robert Browning.

The main observation of the previous chapter was that knowledge engineers need more help in building their systems than is normally the case when software systems are being constructed. Methodologies like the one outlined in chapter 4 provide some help in controlling the complexity of knowledge-based systems, and they need to be employed when building large KBSs, but they are not sufficient given the complexity of the task. Computer-based tools to support the KBS building process are vital.

This chapter examines the implications for commercial toolkits of the knowledge engineering lifecycle outlined in the last chapter. This includes considering the limitations of the features that are available in the toolkits, and an examination of tools available to support the areas of the knowledge engineering lifecycle that are ignored by most toolkits. There has been an attempt to restrict the consideration of extra tools to those that are well enough developed to be of general use today — a longer range view of what tools will emerge from research over the next five to ten years is given in Appendix A.

It is a condemnation of most present-day toolkits that very few of the facilities outlined in this chapter have yet found their way into the majority of commercially available toolkits. Knowledge-based systems building will continue to be an art rather than an engineering discipline until tools become available to make the system builder's life easier.

5.1 Knowledge acquisition tools

One of the clichés of knowledge engineering is that knowledge acquisition constitutes the main bottleneck in obtaining and representing knowledge. For heuristic expert systems — ones based on the rule-of-thumb type of knowledge that experts use for much of their work — there is a lot of truth in the stereotype.

A common experience when building rule-based systems is that it is difficult to extract the large numbers of rules necessary to encapsulate the important knowledge held by an expert. This means that any tools which can provide help for this complex task are very welcome. There are two main sorts of tool that are proving useful for knowledge acquisition:

- Knowledge elicitation support tools

  A number of different techniques have proved useful for acquiring knowledge from human experts — repertory grids; problem decomposition; transcription analysis. Most variations on these techniques can be augmented with computer-based aids, although very few such elicitation tools are commercially available. We will look at a repertory grid tool in slightly more detail to give some idea of how this automation can be performed. We will also look at a knowledge acquisition tool which is being used to elicit diagnostic knowledge from experts.

- Rule induction tools

  These tools can automatically generate rules from well-presented cases. Commercial rule induction tools do not always state their theoretical basis, but many of them seem to be similar to the ID3 work of Quinlan [Quinlan]. In essence, this type of tool needs to be given a large number of example cases, each split into the example data and the result. ID3 uses the examples to build a decision tree which is capable of performing the classification of cases to results. An example of the sort of problem which is tractable using this type of tool will be explored later in this section.

5.1.1 Repertory grid tools

The repertory grid can be used to identify *constructs* which differentiate between a set of items and then to rank all items in the set against that construct. This activity is repeated for different constructs, and eventually it should prove possible to discriminate between all the items in the set.

A simple example would be the construction of an expert system to choose an apt computer language for different types of application. The user would have to type in all the possible language choices, and the automated repertory grid would typically select 3 elements from the set at random and prompt:

```
What differentiates one of ADA, PASCAL, ASSEMBLER
from the other two?
```

If the user answered **run-time speed**, then the system would ask him to classify all items against **run-time speed** on a range 1-5 (having established that 1 meant SLOW and 5 meant FAST).

Three more members of the set of languages would be chosen, and the question reasked:

```
What differentiates one of SMALLTALK, PASCAL, PROLOG
from the other two?
```

This elicitation process would continue until it was possible to distinguish between all the languages. The information which had been elicited could then be used as the basis of an expert system with questions like:

```
How important is run-time speed in your application?
Answer in the range 1 to 5:
```

The usefulness of grid techniques depends on the user choosing sensible constructs. If, for example, the user answered the question:

```
What differentiates one of ADA, Modula-2, PASCAL
from the other two?
```

with **not designed by Wirth**, then it would be hard to use such a construct in a meaningful manner.

Repertory grids are being built into sophisticated knowledge acquisition tools such as AQUINAS [Boose 88], which has been used for knowledge acquisition in many different problem domains.

Other knowledge acquisition tools are becoming available which are only applicable to a more restricted range of tasks than the repertory grid tools, but which are very useful for specific types of representation problems. One example of such a problem-specific knowledge acquisition tool is MORE [Kahn 85] from Carnegie Mellon University. MORE is specifically designed to help with the acquisition of knowledge for diagnostic tasks.

MORE elicits knowledge about what can cause particular symptoms, and builds a domain model which links causes to different effects. This model can be used to acquire further information about how to differentiate between different causes and about their relative likelihood. All of the knowledge can be used to generate a rule-based system to perform the diagnosis. These techniques seem to provide a relatively painless way of building a simple diagnostic expert system. It seems likely that such problem-specific knowledge acquisition tools will become more widely used over the next year or two.

5.1.2 Rule induction tools

Rule induction tools should be included in knowledge engineering toolkits more often than they are. Most of the ones that are available are based on Quinlan's ID3 algorithm [Quinlan], which takes a set of example cases and turns them into a decision tree to differentiate between the cases.

Consider the problem of a financial institution deciding whether to grant an application for a loan. Using a large set of example decisions similar to the ones in table 5.1, an induction tool might come up with the decision tree illustrated in figure 5.1.

loan-secured	good-credit	loan-size	loan-reason	verdict
yes	yes	< 3 * yearly_salary	house	Give loan
yes	no	< yearly_salary	car	Give loan
no	no	< yearly_salary	house	Refuse loan
no	no	< 0.1 * yearly_salary	car	Give loan
no	no	< yearly_salary	party	Refuse loan

Table 5.1: Possible example credit decisions

This can be expressed as a rule in the following way:

```
IF loan_is_secured
OR (good_credit
   AND (loan_size < yearly_salary)
   OR ( (loan_size < 3 * yearly_salary) AND (loan_reason = house) ) )
OR (not(good_credit)
   AND (loan_size < 0.1 * yearly_salary) AND (loan_reason = car) )
THEN give_loan;
ELSE refuse_loan;
```

If we were really trying to induce rules in order to use them to decide whether to give someone a loan, we would need much more information about each example case. Loan risk evaluation is an application area where rule induction has been used successfully to generate an outline set of rules that can then be refined.

Deriving rules for running a chemical process plant is another area where an induction tool might be used. A single example given to the induction tool might

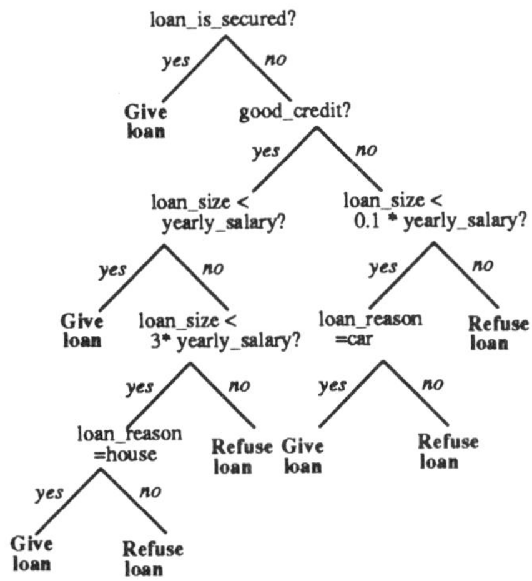

Figure 5.1: Example credit decision tree

consisting of inputs (all the significant readings on the process plant), plus the correct action to take when those inputs were observed. A training set of such examples would be supplied, from which a rule (or set of rules) to decide the correct action in each example case would be induced.

Rule induction can be very successful in highlighting significant criteria in a plethora of detail — such clarification is vital when there are many example cases available, but no clear idea of what the rules are which give correct answers. Problems occur with induction when some of the significant factors are not included in the training examples. In the process plant example, if the history of the plant over several hours was important, but only immediate readings were given in the examples, then the rules derived would not be generally applicable to running the plant. Rule induction can be powerful, but needs to be used with care.

As we have observed, the output of a rule induction tool is basically a decision tree for distinguishing between cases. With early tools, that tree was transformed into a rule written in Pascal or FORTRAN. A much better idea that is gaining credence is to produce rules for consumption by a particular expert systems shell. The reasons for doing this are the same for using a shell rather than a procedural language in the first place — it separates the knowledge from how you use it. The expert system rules produced will be easier to edit and to append with explanation than would be the case with Pascal or FORTRAN code.

In summary, rules generated through induction might be usable, but may well not be explainable to the user or justifiable by the developer. Care must be taken to ensure that the problem is suitable for induction techniques, that complete examples have been provided, and that reasonable coverage of the problem area has been achieved.

5.2 Implementation issues

5.2.1 Interfacing to knowledge engineering toolkits

As has already been observed earlier in the chapter, the existence of interfaces from knowledge-based systems to other computing systems is vital for more widespread and powerful use of the technology. There are several possible levels of interface:

Procedural calls to other systems. At least this level of interface will be provided by most knowledge engineering toolkits. One way in which toolkits can make up for the limitations of their representations is to allow the system builder to call outside routines to do processing that they find difficult. Such calls are also used to bring back information from other software, e.g. to obtain records from a database.

Mutual exchange of data. Sometimes a knowledge-based system and another system each produces data that the other processes. In such a case, one solution is for the two systems to run in parallel and communicate via message-passing. This producer–consumer relationship is often the easiest to implement, but is regrettably not sufficient for all sorts of interaction. Sometimes, a system really wants the information NOW, not when the other system feels like providing it.

Embedding the expert system. In the final level of relationship between the systems, the knowledge-based system is a module of another system, invoked to make a specific decision. When it returns its judgement, the other system uses the information. This type of use will increase as more tools are able to support it, and as more conventional system builders see the need for knowledge-based enhancements to their systems.

Happily, after years when the only possible interaction with a knowledge-based system was through it making a procedure call, more tool builders are seeing that their tools must interface more flexibly with large systems, and tools are appearing that allow all of these types of interaction. Nexpert-Object, KES, and NEXUS are among the growing list of systems that stress the importance of such interaction.

5.2.2 Modularization

Modularization was established long ago in software engineering circles as "a good thing", and it seems remarkable that this lesson has not yet permeated into knowledge engineering circles. Very few toolkits limit the scope of facts or rules. Ideally, one should be able to localize knowledge in a knowledge base and specify a subset of that knowledge for general use by other knowledge bases.

Blackboard systems (see [Engelmore and Morgan 88] for more details) provide a research example of one type of system architecture where this occurs, although their use of global data structures for communication between knowledge bases has equally worrying implications for the production of robust systems.

5.2.3 Real-time systems

The most important characteristic of real-time systems is that they must operate within fixed time constraints. These constraints will vary with the task which the real-time system is carrying out, but the system will need to produce the best result possible within a guaranteed response time.

Some knowledge-based architectures seem more reassuring for meeting fixed performance requirements than others. While backward chaining systems are less flexible in general than forward chaining ones, it is easier to control them in such a way that they will converge to a solution (or to an acknowledgement that they have failed to find a solution). This makes it much easier to perform maximum response time calculations.

Blackboard systems seem to provide a promising approach to real-time problems as well as modularization, but their flexible control strategies have frightening implications for fixed performance requirements — given little control over how inference happens, how do you constrain it? While blackboard systems can be very powerful for prototyping solutions to tough problems, using a blackboard architecture will not usually be the best way to implement these solutions in a real-time delivery system where performance must be guaranteed.

The presence or absence of a frame-based representation on top of the basic reasoning architecture seems immaterial to this discussion. A much more difficult question is whether the architecture should allow the implementor to indulge in object-oriented programming. It would be advisable to impose some sort of convention on the interaction between objects in the knowledge-based system, or the system design tends to collapse into anarchy (interesting and potentially powerful, but unconstrainable).

A second characteristic of real-time systems, which probably takes most of them out of the scope of ordinary knowledge engineering toolkits and into a specialist area is the way in which knowledge changes over time. Most real-time systems operate continuously and as information becomes older, it becomes less valuable, because its potential for having been superseded by changing events increases. Real-time toolkits need to be able to reason about the passage of time in order to deal with this issue.

A third issue of significance to real-time systems is the ability to react to changing external circumstances — as an alarm occurs on a process plant, a knowledge-based system monitoring the plant should react immediately. What happens to the reasoning being carried out when such an event occurs? One solution (which assumes that any important new information such as an alarm must enter the system via an interrupt) is just to throw away any uncompleted reasoning whenever an interrupt occurs. A second solution is for the system to sample possible alarm inputs at convenient breaks in processing and react as necessary. Neither solution is ideal, and either solution points to a specialized real-time toolkit as the right solution for implementing a real-time KBS.

5.2.4 Compile-time checking

Many of the more complex knowledge engineering toolkits have made a decision which increases the speed of prototyping, but which is dangerous if it is carried through into a delivery system. Many syntactic checks that could be made at compile time are left until run-time. This is a classic mistake in software engineering. For example, one part of a program that is unlikely to work is any error-handling code that exists. If the error handling code is executed for a real error, and falls over with an error that could have been detected at compile-time, then a bad situation has been needlessly compounded. In fact, the general principle is that it is less costly to detect problems at compile-time wherever that is possible.

This subsection will list some of the major pitfalls of run-time compilation, and indicate how they can be avoided. In some cases, the toolkits do provide enough information to get rid of errors at compile-time. In other cases, improvements to the toolkits are needed in order to provide robust run-time systems. Examples are from some of the toolkits examined in the case studies later in the book.

It must be stressed that the drawbacks should not be seen as criticisms of the specific example tools given — these types of problems occur in many of the knowledge-based tools that are currently available.

Automatic definition

In ART for example, it is possible to define a schema `Page` containing an attribute `PageDimension`. If the system builder writes a rule intended to give a value to this attribute, but using a new (wrong) name `PageSize`, then ART will add a new attribute `PageSize` to the schema, rather than flagging an error and not compiling the rule.

In POP-11, any variable that is referenced will be automatically declared if it does not exist. The situation is made even worse by another feature of POP-11:

variable names are different if the letters of the variable names are in different case. So `PageSize`, `Pagesize` and `pagesize` are all different variables. As is the case with UNIX users, POP-11 users learn the hard way to restrict themselves to lower-case names only.

In these languages (and many others with similar characteristics), it is very easy to think that a value that was set in one place should be available in another, only to discover that the two places are using different variables.

Both ART and POP-11 provide enough facilities for the strong-willed to avoid the problems caused by this feature. In both cases, the knowledge engineer is informed that this auto-declaration is taking place. The solution is to find all occurrences of such auto-declaration, and either make the declaration explicit or replace the variable usage with the correct variable name. However, one of my colleagues was generously given a POP-11 library file developed elsewhere, and intended as a deliverable piece of software to perform a particular task. When loaded into the POP-11 system, it produced over a hundred warning messages for different auto-declarations. That software has remained unused.

Weak typing

POP-11 is a powerful language for rapid prototyping because it does not force the prototyper to make explicit decisions about how knowledge will be represented. It is possible to write a procedure which will sensibly handle a parameter which is a boolean or an integer or a real number or a list of pointers to other facts.

This flexibility allows rapid changing of the system to experiment with different representations or reasoning strategies. Unfortunately, this flexibility has negative implications for the robustness of the systems being constructed. The user has to check that all possible invocations of his procedures pass sensible parameters in all cases. When wrong types of parameter are passed, the system will only detect it at run-time. In a system with strong typing, these checks can be performed at compile-time, at the cost of the rapid experimentation possible with a weakly typed language.

Ideally, one would implement an exploratory prototype in a weakly typed system, and restrict the complexity of the delivery system by declaring the types which matched the final implementation decisions. No toolkit supports both weak-typing for development and the option of enforcing strong typing for delivery systems, but it is time that users started demanding such features.

Object-oriented programming

Object-oriented systems are a more complex example of run-time binding — they have run-time binding of procedure calls as well as run-time binding of variables.

Again, the implication for delivery systems is that checking which should be performed at compile-time is left until run-time, when it can cause the system to break — a woeful state of affairs.

Depending on the object-oriented language being used, several actions may be needed to improve the situation. For languages where such checks can be performed at compile-time, users need to start demanding true compilers that are able to perform these checks. More complex languages may have to be restricted to a subset with less flexibility in order for compile-time checking to become feasible.

5.3 Verification and validation tools

Much verification and validation at the very lowest level will happen automatically if the sort of features outlined in section 5.2.4 are added to toolkits. A higher level verification of a rule-base is also possible by using rule-checking tools.

Such tools are feasible for most rule-based languages, although the details will vary from language to language. Again, it must be observed that rule checkers are another useful tool that is not commonly distributed with shells or toolkits.

Several years ago, researchers at Lockheed identified and listed some of the obvious ways in which rule-based systems could be automatically checked for errors or omissions. The errors that they identified were:

Rule redundancy If two rules have the same conditions and the same effects, then one of the two rules must be superfluous, and should be deleted.

For example, with the rules:

```
RULE 1: IF a THEN b
RULE 2: IF a THEN b
```

then either `RULE 1` or `RULE 2` can be deleted.

Effect conflict This happens when two rules have the same conditions but contradictory effects. In this case, either one of the rules is wrong, or extra conditions are needed to differentiate between the cases.

```
RULE 1: IF patient has spots THEN disease IS chicken pox
RULE 2: IF patient has spots THEN disease IS measles
```

The conflict in the rules above might be resolved by adding the clause `AND skin itches` to `RULE 1`.

Condition conflict This occurs when two rules have the same effect, and the conditions of one are a subset of the conditions of the other. One of the rules is superfluous, and the system builder needs to determine which of the rules it is.

```
RULE 1: IF car won't start THEN battery IS flat
RULE 2: IF car won't start AND headlights don't work
        THEN battery IS flat
```

In this case, `RULE 2` seems more comprehensive than `RULE 1`, so the sensible action is to delete `RULE 1`.

Circular dependency It is possible to write rules where each of the rules depends on the result of the others. A simple example of this is:

```
RULE 1: IF a THEN b
RULE 2: IF b THEN c
RULE 3: IF c THEN a
```

If a system chains backwards from goal `a`, then it will try to satisfy goal `b` and then goal `c`, and then goal `a` again, and so on ad infinitum.

This is one check that many present-day toolkits do often make. However, it is typically dealt with at run-time (when you can check for circular dependency by looking at what goals have been stacked).

Like many other checks we have mentioned in this chapter, each of the error checks above should be possible at compile-time, and doing the checks then rather than at run-time should result in more robust and possibly more efficient systems.

The Lockheed researchers also pointed out areas of potential omission in a rule-base. These items are not necessarily errors in the rule-base, but are places in the rule-base that deserve closer examination.

Missing values Most facts can take on a range of values. If there are not rules for assigning all allowable values to a fact, then perhaps some rules are missing. For example, a boolean fact can usually take on the value *TRUE* or *FALSE* (or possibly *UNKNOWN* in some systems).

If there are rules to assign *FALSE* to a particular fact, but no rule to assign *TRUE*, then perhaps the rules giving the conditions under which that fact is *TRUE* have been inadvertently omitted.

Unused facts If the value of a fact is never used in the *IF* part of any rule, or as a top-level goal for backward-chaining, then it is not being properly used. Probably the system builder defined it for some reason and then forgot about it. It should be utilized or deleted.

Undefined facts If there are no means of assigning any value to a fact (for example using rules, questions or default values), then it will remain undefined at run-time. The ways in which facts can be assigned values vary from system to system, and so this may not be relevant to all systems.

This error typically occurs when facts are defined as stubs, with the intention of expanding on those stubs later on. The system builder then forgets to fill out some stubs. A good rule checker can draw the attention of the system builder to this sort of problem.

The seven problems listed above occur quite often when building a rule-based system. In part, the occurrence of these problems can be attributed to the incremental way in which expert systems are frequently built, so it is vital that the system builder has as much help as possible in tracking these faults down.

The research described above has only been applied to rule-based systems. The automated checking of more complex representations is an unsolved research issue, although some of the errors and omissions outlined above should be detectable in more complex representations.

5.4 KBS project support tools

The main project support tools that are available for KBS projects are the same as those for any computer-aided software engineering (CASE). As we observed at the start of the chapter, the complexity of KBSs makes the management of KBS projects harder even than for a normal software project, and the need for computer-based support even greater. Fortunately, KBS technology is also helping to build better CASE software. Knowledge-based systems can be built to accomplish different levels of project support:

Stand-alone expert systems Expert systems to support project management tasks can be built and are being built now. They are limited in scope because they are not integrated with all available project information. Usually, all project relevant information must be entered directly to the system, and any updates must be prompted by the user.

The knowledge-based IPSE Software engineers and knowledge engineers spend much of their time performing secretarial or housekeeping tasks — making sure that somebody else has updated a module, or recompiling and linking a number of modules because of changes that have been made. Integrated project support environments (IPSEs) take some of the burden of these tasks away from the engineer. With richer knowledge structures, an intelligent IPSE has the potential to take even more of this burden.

Automatic programming The most successful efforts at automatic programming have really been knowledge-based software libraries where programming *clichés* can be reused in different programs [Waters 86]. These appear to be of most use in areas where the applications are well-understood and clichés can be easily identified, and so they seem unlikely to affect knowledge engineering just yet. More promising (although even longer term) are systems where a formal specification of the system is automatically turned into a program [Green et al.], [Marcosian et al.].

In order to illustrate the sort of tools that are presently possible, we will look in slightly more detail at a stand-alone system for project estimation, and a research prototype of an intelligent IPSE.

5.4.1 The GUESSTIMATOR system

This system is a good example of a useful stand-alone expert system to support project management. It helps a manager to decide how long a project will take to carry out, and is based on the standard project lifecycle inside the company that built it (a software house).

It prompts the user to break a project down into all the tasks that need to be designed and programmed, and to give an estimate of the difficulty of each task. It provides a checklist of extra features that might need to be planned in to a project, such as interfacing to a database.

Combining this information with details of standard times for different tasks, and the number of people working on each phase of the project and their level of experience, GUESSTIMATOR calculates the effort and elapsed time for the whole project, and even fills in a barchart which covers the whole lifecycle of the proposed project. The user is allowed to change some figures (he is likely to have knowledge of specific circumstances like "Jane is so talented that she can easily do that six months worth of estimated work in three months"), and GUESSTIMATOR will recalculate the project plan. This example illustrates an important feature of many successful expert systems: instead of replacing the expert, it enhances the expert's abilities. The human and the computer each perform the tasks for which they are best suited.

Stand-alone tools like GUESSTIMATOR can be (and are being) built to aid engineers with many aspects of knowledge-based system project support. Notable areas are: assessing applications for their suitability for expert system assistance; selecting tools for simple applications; planning effort for expert systems applications where there is sufficient experience of building similar systems.

5.4.2 Intelligent System Manager project

The Intelligent System Manager (ISM) project (part of the UK Government's Alvey Research Programme) is aiming to automate many of the project control tasks associated with large software projects. Here is an example of one task that ISM aims to perform which is beyond the scope of present IPSEs. It is the set of procedures that ISM will initiate when an error is discovered as a system is being developed.

- A test uncovers a bug in a module.
- The severity of error is automatically assessed.
- The author of the module is informed by electronic mail of the nature of the problem.
- ISM automatically invokes contingency planning to estimate the consequences of the fault, and the project is provisionally replanned using knowledge based on past experience of such problems.
- Users of the module where the problem lies are automatically notified about it.
- The project manager is sent a summary report detailing the error and the changes to the project plan.

From this example, it is possible to guess the sorts of knowledge that an ISM system would need in order to carry out this level of project support. We are still several years away from such intelligent IPSEs. It must be stressed that ISM is really an aid to the Project Manager, making sure that important information reaches the top of the organization so that the Project Manager can then judge whether any further action needs to be taken.

For knowledge-based systems, the most significant advantage of an intelligent IPSE will not occur during the development phase of the project. The dynamic nature of an expert's knowledge will mean that the ability to track changes to the knowledge base, and to make inferences from their type and frequency will be an invaluable aid to the maintenance team.

5.5 Conclusions

This chapter has been somewhat wide-ranging in its concerns — knowledge acquisition systems; implementation issues; tools for validation and for project support. Many of these issues need to be addressed by vendors of tools rather than by users. Yet it is only as the users ask,

"How will your toolkit help my knowledge acquisition problems?"

that vendors will be driven to provide reasonable knowledge acquisition tools, and it is only as the users show their concern for the whole of the development lifecycle that the vendors will join them in that concern.

5.6 Further reading

Knowledge acquisition tools. Further details of the use of automated tools based on repertory grid techniques can be obtained from [Boose 88].

There are two excellent compilations of papers dealing with current research work on knowledge elicitation [Boose and Gaines], [Gaines and Boose]. This research should eventually filter through to the marketplace. Those books and the new journal *Knowledge Acquisition* from Academic Press are good places to look for more detailed information on future trends in knowledge acquisition tools.

The academic reference for a description of the ID3 work is [Quinlan]. An article in *BYTE* magazine [Thompson and Thompson] is more approachable by the non-expert who wishes to learn more about ID3.

Real-time expert systems. There are no definitive works on real-time expert systems as yet. [Leitch and Dulieu 88] and [Odette and Dress] both outline the main issues.

Verification and validation tools. [Nguyen et al.] describes the Lockheed system in some detail. [Preece 89] gives a slightly more general perspective on the problem.

KBS project support tools. [Vaughn] describes the ISM system discussed in this chapter, and a more ambitious project support system with some similar characteristics is described in [Green et al.].

Chapter 6

Putting the pieces together

Chris Price, Baggy Shah, Dave Wilson, Chris Orgill

> Eye of newt and toe of frog,
> Wool of bat and tongue of dog,
> Adder's fork and blind worm's sting,
> Lizard's leg and howlet's wing...
> *Macbeth, Act 4, Scene 1*, W. Shakespeare.

6.1 Introduction

This chapter will examine the assembly of the representation and reasoning features that have been discussed in previous chapters into the different types of knowledge engineering tools that are commercially available. The tools are separated into five classes, and the characteristics of each class are considered. The four case studies in later chapters will put some flesh on the bones exposed in this chapter. Each of the case studies deals in detail with an example of one type of tool, and gives an impression of the sorts of problem that it can be used for, and how easy it is to use.

6.2 Making a toolkit

We have already noted that no commercial toolkit of any type covers the whole of the knowledge engineering lifecycle, and so the case studies will mainly consider the ease and efficacy with which applications can be built using different types of toolkit.

In general, a toolkit is a mixture of representation and reasoning features, so this chapter builds on the material in the first part of the book. For example, it is possible to describe many simple expert system shells as a set of boolean facts and rules, plus a backward-chaining mechanism which can be used to produce conclusions.

Unfortunately, even for a simple shell, that level of description is not all that needs to be given. There are design decisions that separate the good shells from the mediocre ones, for example:

- What do questions look like to the user?
- How easy is it to retract wrong answers?
- What top-level control exists to focus the backward-chaining?

For more complex types of toolkit, direct comparison between superficially similar toolkits becomes even harder. Not only is there a range of usefulness within each class of toolkit, but there will be overlap between the classes whatever classification is chosen. This makes it hard to distinguish accurately between the various toolkit types, but in fairly general terms, the following classification of toolkits seems reasonable for minimising unnecessary overlap:

Artificial Intelligence languages. This is the lowest level of tool for writing knowledge-based systems — rather analogous to writing a conventional system in machine code. What often happens is that the system builder first constructs a reasoning and representation framework in the basic language before implementing the application.

Loosely coupled toolkits. These toolkits were originally developed in large AI research centres, where people became fed up with re-inventing the wheel in an AI language, and started reusing their representation solutions on new applications. The next step was to build libraries of available components from which solutions can be developed. Some of these libraries have been packaged and sold commercially together with the underlying language.

It could be argued that these packages are more deserving of the "toolkit" title than the tighter coupled systems that we will consider next, as they do resemble a bag of tools from which you build a solution.

High-end integrated toolkits. These toolkits also evolved out of work done in the major AI research centres (and out of the loosely coupled toolkits). A much greater effort was made to select only the features that were of widespread use, and develop and integrate them with a graphical user interface. These toolkits were first developed on Symbolics LISP machines. $50,000 was originally the right ballpark figure for buying one of these systems to run on a Symbolics computer costing at least a similar amount of money. Cheaper Symbolics machines are now available, and these toolkits have also been ported to general-purpose workstations (Suns) giving similar performance, but they are still among the most expensive knowledge engineering toolkits.

Medium-priced integrated toolkits. These are more recent developments than the high-end toolkits, and aim to capture much of the toolkit market. Both the facilities available and the prices are lower. Some of them are implemented in C rather than LISP, and they run on Sun and VAX workstations, on the Macintosh, and on the large 386-based computers rather than Symbolics. While they do have fewer facilities, and the graphics are sometimes less polished, the distinction between high-end and medium-priced toolkits is becoming blurred. The high-end toolkits are dropping in price and becoming available on smaller machines, and the medium-priced toolkits are improving their facilities.

Expert system shells. The early shells were systems whose representation consisted of simple facts, rules about those facts, perhaps a little top-level control and a simple user interface. This is no longer true, and it can be hard to keep up with the changing facilities offered by a number of the more popular shells. Again, there is a blurring of the distinction between some shells and the simpler toolkits. Several of the shells have started to add frame-like or object-oriented features. Others have added more powerful control structures, facilities for integrating the shell within a larger system or pretty graphical interfaces.

We will now explore each of these five classifications in more detail, outlining the main features, advantages and disadvantages of each type of toolkit.

6.3 AI languages

The two best known artificial intelligence languages are LISP and Prolog. In the United Kingdom at least, POP-11 is also popular enough to deserve a mention. The features provided by OPS5 are so rudimentary that it should probably be classified as a language rather than a shell.

AI languages have the power of a conventional computer language, plus some features that are very useful for AI work, such as more powerful list processing facilities, built-in inferencing or pattern matching, or the ability to treat pieces of program in the same way as pieces of data.

A large proportion of the knowledge-based systems that have been built in the United States have been implemented either in LISP or in a toolkit that has been built using LISP, so it is certainly possible to build knowledge-based systems using such a language. However, it is not the easiest way to build most systems.

The level of representation provided in an AI language (e.g. a list structure) is too general for knowledge representation for a particular application, and so the system builder will usually need to construct a specialized representation. It will also be necessary to reason with the knowledge in the system, so reasoning strategies will also have to be built (Prolog includes a simple reasoning strategy, but it often needs doctoring for use in a particular application).

For many applications, this representation and reasoning development work is the wrong thing to do, because an existing toolkit could fit the problem adequately. To some extent, it is yet another example of the not-invented-here syndrome in action.

As well as the significant amount of extra work implied by the construction of a special representation for the problem, there are other drawbacks of such custom-built toolkits. The representation usually does not read as well as one that has been developed for a commercial toolkit, which will have soaked up significant effort. One of the main integrated toolkits has quoted *seven million dollars* of development effort to build the toolkit — how many one-off projects can spend that much on putting together a representation? The custom-built toolkit will also tend to have bugs in it that will only become apparent during use on the application. Commercial toolkits will have eradicated many of these bugs through the effort and patience of the application developers that use them.

Development from scratch in an AI language is almost invariably a bad idea (unless you are a developing a toolkit that will be used by many people over a long period of time). The representation building blocks provided by a loosely coupled toolkit speed up development for almost all applications.

Because of the narrowness of this field of interest, there is no case study of such work in this book. The loosely coupled toolkit case study covers much of the same ground — construction of a specialized representation — but starts from a toolkit which provides many primitive tools to help in the construction. That is a much better solution when what is wanted is an experiment in novel representation.

6.4 Loosely coupled toolkits

This is a much more varied category than any of the other three types of tool that we will go on to discuss in the rest of the chapter. The main thing that these systems have in common is that they do not pretend that all of the features that they have are both necessary and sufficient for all applications.

Both POPLOG and Knowledge Craft have more features than are likely to be needed on any application. The object-oriented LISP toolkits, on the other hand, tend not to have any serious rule-based facilities, so reasoning control has to be implemented by the developer.

Each of the toolkits that we will consider in this category has at least some representation features, some reasoning capability and some graphical user interface. The most profitable thing that can be done is to consider each one in detail.

6.4.1 POPLOG

POPLOG has a large number of features, not all of them relevant for any single application. We will try to give some idea of the scope of the POPLOG system, and an impression of which of its many features are the most useful for building knowledge-based systems.

The POPLOG system contains the languages POP-11, Prolog and COMMON LISP, all implemented to be interactive, and integrated by a screen editor VED. A good implementation of standard ML is also available to run under POPLOG, but needs to be purchased separately. Numerous additional facilities that have been implemented in the three main languages are supplied as libraries, and these will be considered in more detail later in this subsection.

POPLOG is a complete programming environment where a programmer can edit, compile, debug and document programs in the different languages without leaving the system. The main advantages of this are:

- Speed of development. It really is possible to build rapid prototypes and to make and try out small changes to such prototypes very quickly.
- Communication between editor and compilers. The screen editor VED interfaces directly to the different language compilers, and so the developer can edit some LISP in one window and some Prolog in another, and recompile small parts of each file interactively and have them processed by the correct compiler/interpreter.
- Ease of communication between different languages. As well as compiling different languages through VED, the newly-changed code in the different languages can then be made to run together through one of the pieces of code invoking the others, without any extra work (e.g. a linking phase) on the part of the developer.

The way in which the languages are integrated means that it is feasible to write the main part of your program in LISP, implement your knowledge base representation and search in Prolog, and then interface your program to some of the libraries written in POP-11. It is also possible to interface to routines written in other languages such as C or Pascal, but such routines need to be previously compiled, rather than interactively constructed like a routine in any of the POPLOG languages.

The VED screen editor

This is the glue that holds the POPLOG system together. In POPLOG, instead of interacting separately with the editor and the compiler, the developer almost always communicates with the system through VED.

VED is more powerful than most screen editors — perhaps the only reasonable parallel is one of the larger Emacs editors, such as GNU-Emacs. It has knowledge of the syntax of programs in different languages, which enables the automatic reformatting of programs (and of text too). VED allows the developer to compile single procedures (or even single lines of code!) from the editor. This makes the development of programs through VED a highly interactive process.

VED is written in POP-11, and all the editor routines are POP-11 system procedures and are available to the user. This allows developers to tailor the editor to their own requirements, and to integrate its facilities into their application programs.

This re-use of VED features is illustrated in POPLOG's comprehensive help facilities. Several types of help file are provided by the POPLOG system, and each of them is accessed via the VED interface. There are TEACH files to aid in learning about using different features of the POPLOG system, HELP files for reminding experienced users about the features, and REF files for giving system-level details. Users can browse these information files as if they were ordinary text files. Most information files contain links to other, related files. An extension of VED for the help system allows the user to browse from file to file across these links. The integrated nature of the VED interface means that it is also possible from the help system to compile and run small pieces of example code in the information files in order to understand the examples better.

VED supports both simple terminals with cursor keys, as well as workstations that allow multiple windows, menus and mice. The latter are supported using a set of routines collectively known as the POPLOG Window Manager (PWM), which we will describe next.

The POPLOG Window Manager

The PWM supports the manipulation of multiple windows on a workstation screen, with associated graphics drawing routines and mouse-handling facilities. It has basically the same interface on a variety of workstations, making it simple for a developer to port applications from one machine to another.

Program developers are provided with PWM facilities that enable application programs to create, manipulate and delete windows. These windows can be used to display text and graphics and to obtain input from the keyboard or the mouse. Pop-up menus, dialogue boxes and raster graphics operations are also supported by the primitives supplied.

The PWM provides all the facilities necessary to enable a developer to build a WIMP-style interface to an application program. Further window-handling features are implemented in Flavours, the object-oriented extension to POP-11, and provide support for advanced graphics, for example, graphic objects that can be manipulated using the mouse. Having said that, building a sophisticated interface in POPLOG is much more work than building the same interface in KEE or ART.

Program development features of POPLOG

As we have observed, the POPLOG system can be used to build programs which employ the most effective aspects of each of the main languages used for knowledge-based systems work. In practice, hardly any programs directly use code written in all three of the languages. Rather more frequent is the use of one of LISP or POP-11, plus some Prolog code if the application would benefit from it.

Apart from all the interface facilities provided by VED and by the PWM, and the advantages for program development of integrating several different languages, there are two main reasons for choosing POPLOG for implementing advanced knowledge-based systems:

Extensive libraries. The POPLOG LIB facility allows the developer to load into his program a variety of features, which are provided in a large collection of libraries. These are mostly provided as source code (allowing customization for particular applications), and cover a wide range of topics related to knowledge-based systems and artificial intelligence. For example, there are libraries dealing with:

- Simple natural language processing.
- Object-oriented programming.
- Pattern recognition.
- Production rule systems.
- Database searching facilities.
- Simple discrete event handling systems.

Evidently, some of the libraries mentioned above will be irrelevant to the needs of any particular developer. However, when a library contains material of use, then it can save much development time. For instance, the

Flavours object-oriented library provides similar facilities to those in the object-oriented LISP systems discussed in section 6.4.3, and can be used to construct powerful knowledge-based systems [Price and Hunt 89a].

The rule-based system libraries are fairly weak, and rule-based programming is probably better implemented with an application specific language, perhaps based on the example libraries provided.

Implementing user languages. The ability to implement with comparative ease an application specific language as an extension to POP-11 is one of the most powerful features of the POPLOG system. POP-11 provides excellent language primitives to declare new language keywords and to act on them. The LISP system was originally implemented in this way, although it has since been recoded for efficiency reasons. The Flavours library, like many others, is also implemented by means of POP-11's language-building primitives.

Several other powerful KBS tools have been built using the general features provided by POPLOG:

- RULES, an advanced rule induction tool.
- POPKEATS, a portable re-implementation of a knowledge acquisition system originally built on the Symbolics machine by British Telecom and the Open University.
- KERIS, a medium-priced integrated toolkit.
- BLOBS, an object-oriented blackboard system.
- FLEX, a rule-based system.

The distributors of POPLOG also supply RULES, KERIS and FLEX to POPLOG users who need want such tools for specific applications.

Summary of POPLOG

POPLOG is a superb tool for knowledge-based systems research, for rapid prototyping of all KBSs, and for the development of systems that are out of the ordinary. However, for applications where an impressive interface is vital, and where suitable representation and reasoning facilities are provided by a simpler toolkit, building in POPLOG could mean rather more work than was strictly necessary.

6.4.2 Knowledge Craft

Knowledge Craft has often been grouped with ART and KEE as one of the "big three" knowledge engineering toolkits. The decision to place it in this section rather than in the high-end integrated toolkit section was made on the grounds that its features are much less integrated than those of ART or KEE. That means that a greater degree of experience is needed to use it to its full capacity. It should be stressed here that less integration is not necessarily a bad thing — in the hands of an experienced user, Knowledge Craft may well be a more powerful tool.

Representation and reasoning

The representational aspects of Knowledge Craft are based around CRL (Carnegie Representation Language), originally developed as SRL at Carnegie Mellon University. It is a frame-based language which contains the sort of features that would be expected — object-oriented programming, slot inheritance, access-oriented programming, user-defined relations.

CRL stands out as a particularly powerful and elegant representational tool because of its orthogonality. Its single frame is called a *schema*, and almost everything is defined in terms of schemata. A slot in a schema is also a schema, and inherits its characteristics from the definition of a Slot schema. As well as inheritance, it is possible for the developer to define his own application-specific relations, and to define actions to be taken when those relations occur. For example, a *has-components* relation between a device and its constituent parts might maintain the mass of the whole device as the sum of the masses of its constituent parts. Relations (including system ones like inheritance) are represented as schemata that inherit properties from a Relation schema.

Rule-based programming in Knowledge Craft is a choice between CRL-OPS for forward chaining and CRL-Prolog for backward chaining. CRL-OPS is an extended version of OPS5. Given that OPS5 is not a very pretty language in which to write, the extensions to allow CRL-OPS programmers to talk about schema details (both for a single schema and for classes of schemata) have been well done. It is more powerful and more expressive than OPS5 itself, and coupled with schemata, it allows the developer to implement many knowledge-based applications with significantly less rules. CRL-Prolog, on the other hand, is a disappointing implementation of Prolog, and not of as high a standard as CRL-OPS. It should also be noted that compared with the more 'wordy' representation of many expert system shells, neither OPS5 nor Prolog are particularly readable languages.

Knowledge Craft provides a feature called *Contexts* for performing hypothetical reasoning. This only provides a subset of the features of a full truth maintenance system. If more is needed, then it has to be implemented by the developer.

Graphics interfaces

The developer is provided with several tools to help him in building Knowledge Craft applications. There are 'workbenches' for CRL-OPS and CRL-Prolog. These allow the developer access to trace and debugging information as his programs are running. It is possible to display different information about the running program in different windows, and to control these different displays with mouse-based commands. Both workbenches interface to the EMACS editor, making development an interactive process.

A class browser is supplied with CRL, which allows the developer to manipulate a hierarchy of schemata. It is possible to create and delete schemata via mouse commands, and to alter them through a link to a text-based editor which works on a single schema definition.

Window-handling and graphics primitives supplied in the Knowledge Craft toolkit enable the user to build complex graphical interfaces. In a published comparison [Laurent 86] with the interface development features provided by ART and KEE, Knowledge Craft loses out to the other two. The specific criticisms are that it is less easy to use, and has less features (predefined graphics such as gauges; 'active' graphics) than KEE or ART.

Summary of Knowledge Craft

CRL gives a flexibility to Knowledge Craft which makes it powerful enough to use for advanced knowledge-based systems research applications. Two specific criticisms which would be relevant if one tried to classify Knowledge Craft as a high-end integrated toolkit are that it does not include a full truth maintenance system, and the graphical features could be improved. Both of these features could save the developer significant effort for some applications.

6.4.3 Object-oriented LISP toolkits

The extended LISP environment available on LISP machines like the Symbolics and the Texas Instruments Explorer was one of the main reasons why they were originally used to develop toolkits such as ART, KEE and Knowledge Craft. The most common LISP systems on engineering workstations like the Sun and the MicroVAX are being improved until they are beginning to resemble the more powerful LISP environments available on LISP machines. The main features of this enhancement are:

- Integration of the LISP interpreters with Emacs editors, providing the sort of integrated development that was described between VED and the POPLOG languages.

- The addition of object-oriented programming features with capabilities that are similar to Flavors on the Symbolics.
- Provision of primitives for building WIMP interfaces. These primitives make it much easier to build impressive-looking user interfaces for applications.
- Enhancement of the symbolic debugging capabilities. The improved debugging tools speed up development by providing the developer with information about what is happening inside a faulty application.

A second trend among these toolkits is towards greater conformity in the main features available for constructing application programs. This began with the standardization on a COMMON LISP dialect (it came as no surprise to anyone that this was somewhat of a compromise between the main dialects then in use). For some years, the LISP community has been waiting for a standardization of object-oriented extensions to COMMON LISP, and more recently, a standard set of window-handling primitives has been expected. Both the object-oriented and the window-handling extensions seem to be reaching some consensus. Standardization in these areas will have definite benefits for those who choose to develop using LISP systems adhering to all of these standards.

It should soon become possible, with careful programming, to build a system which uses all of the standard extensions, and to be able to port that system, not just to different computers, but to computers supported only by a different LISP system vendor who also adheres to the standards.

Object-oriented extensions

There is strong evidence of general agreement on this extension to the language. When COMMON LISP becomes an ANSI standard ("real soon now"), then the COMMON LISP Object System (CLOS) is intended to be included as part of that standard. It provides the sort of functionality that Flavours gives on a LISP workstation — a full object-oriented system. More importantly, as part of the COMMON LISP standard, it should be genuinely portable.

Windowing extensions

Windowing interfaces are further from agreement by all of the main players than object-oriented extensions, although the problem is too many choices of standard, rather than no standard at all. Common Windows was proposed by Intellicorp as a standard interface, but has never become an expected part of a LISP toolkit.

One reason for the lack of any general enthusiasm for Common Windows on UNIX-based engineering workstations is the emergence of a higher level standard. X-Windows, despite some problems, appears to be in the process of adoption by many of the engineering workstation manufacturers (or sometimes in spite of the manufacturers) as a workstation windowing system. CLX and CLUE were beginning to constitute an unofficial pair of related standards on UNIX workstations, but very recently a broader initiative has been gaining significant support. A new standard called CLIM (COMMON LISP Interface Manager) has been proposed, which would present the same interface to machines running UNIX and X-Windows, to machines running OS/2 and Presentation Manager, or to machines running DOS and Microsoft Windows. Several vendors have endorsed it, but it remains to be seen whether it will overcome both the technical difficulty of implementing a common interface across such different systems, and the political difficulty of persuading all of the major vendors to back the initiative with genuine enthusiasm.

Developer's interface

Most LISP toolkits supply browsers which allow the display and manipulation of a class hierarchy — similar in function to the network editor described for Knowledge Craft.

The better toolkits now have excellent symbolic debuggers, allowing single stepping through evaluation of programs, interactive examination of all data in the environment, and display of functions on the stack at time of examination with their argument values. All of this information is provided at the level of the original LISP code.

Building knowledge-based systems in LISP

The ANSI standard COMMON LISP will form a good foundation for knowledge-based systems work, but lacks several useful features for many applications. One obvious one is the absence of any rule-based paradigm. If you need to do rule-based programming in this sort of system, then you have to implement your own.

As time goes on, however, enhancements to the LISP toolkits will emerge. Already, additional tools such as truth maintenance systems are available under COMMON LISP, some of them in the public domain. A simple forward chaining rule-based system is also available through a public domain version of OPS5 that has been implemented in COMMON LISP. Better graphical tools will become available as add-ons, as standards emerge for graphical extensions to COMMON LISP, because it will be worth the effort of producing them if they will run on a wide range of machines with no extra effort.

6.5 High-end integrated toolkits

The two toolkits in this category, ART and KEE, have each been commercially available for more than five years. They have undergone radical changes and extensions in that time, in response both to user demand and to technology developments. They are now mature products, and it is difficult to predict what other major facilities are likely to be added. What is happening instead is that the developers seem to be concentrating on other issues — deliverability, interfacing, extensions for particular types of application. Each of these toolkits is on the verge of producing a version 4 release, and the main improvement seems to be an X-windows interface to the toolkit. This will improve portability, and confirms the trend towards X-window support.

The graphics facilities are an important part of these toolkits. They reduce the concept distance between the user and the knowledge, allowing input and explanation to be carried out in a visual manner, as explored in chapter 3. The graphics facilities can also help the system developer with construction and debugging of the system.

6.5.1 ART

ART is a large knowledge-based toolkit with a large amount of syntax. The immediate consequences of these two factors are that it is potentially able to assist in the expression of a wide variety of complex algorithmic problems, whilst requiring a greater than average amount of training in order to use it effectively. Having said this, however, much of the top-level functionality of the toolkit is constructed in an orthogonal fashion. This, broadly, allows simple problems to use "simple" ART code.

Representation and reasoning

At its heart, ART is an agenda-based production rule system and therefore has many underlying concepts in common with other rule-based tools. Data is declared in the form of lists of atomic textual elements and a pattern-matching language is provided in which procedural knowledge may be expressed in a form easily identifiable with the inevitable *if <left-hand-side patterns> then <right-hand-side actions>* idiom. At the most basic level, then, we have a system which can express unstructured *facts*, together with *rules*. The rules are examined for the satisfaction of their left hand sides and those that meet the test are placed, in a non-deterministic fashion, upon a *first-in-first-out* stack called the *agenda*. After execution of one or more rules, the rulebase is again examined to determine whether any new candidates are to be placed at the top of the agenda and the cycle proceeds as before. The actions open to the programmer on the right-hand side of rules is largely unconstrained, as any valid LISP or ART expression may appear at this point in the rule. The range of types of action is vast, but any typical list of actions will include:

- modifying the fact-base
- performing I/O to a variety of stream-based devices, e.g. user input streams, window panels, concurrent foreign language processes, etc.
- modifying the rule-base

As will be seen later, modification can take place at a number of levels of abstraction, from the simple alteration of a single fact, to the deletion of an entire partitioned knowledge-base which contains that fact.

The way in which ART performs this most basic operation is the single most important factor in determining the overall cost-effectiveness of any application built using it. Without efficient pattern-matching such systems are effectively useless for large scale problems. Note, however, that this does *not* imply that an efficient pattern-matching substrate guarantees an efficient implementation. This is not expected to be the case in conventional programming methodologies and the implication is equally vacuous in the case of production systems! Optimization by the developer plays an important rôle in developing realistic-scale applications in ART and it requires a level of understanding of the operation of the system beyond that which is required simply to encode the problem in legal, functionally correct ART code. This may appear unusual to conventional programmers used to relegating the problems of compiler-level optimization to the compiler itself. A historical perspective may be useful here, and we might tentatively venture to suggest that in the early 1970s, few FORTRAN IV compilers performed optimization either.

ART is built upon a pattern-matching algorithm developed by Charles Forgy in the Computer Science Department at Carnegie Mellon University in the USA. His algorithm, RETE [Forgy], still appears to hold its own in the current literature.

Extra claims are made for the implementation of RETE in ART. These revolve principally around the fact that most of ART's extra functionality beyond basic production evaluation co-exists within the RETE framework, rather than being separate from it. These efficiency claims remain difficult to test because of their proprietary nature. Fundamental to the applicability of RETE, however, are a number of problem class constraints which are outlined by Forgy in his description of the algorithm. They include:

- "The objects (facts) must be constant. They cannot contain variables or other non-constants as patterns can."
- "The set of objects must change relatively slowly...."

These restrictions arise due to the mechanism that the RETE algorithm uses to avoid iteration over the base of declarative knowledge, often termed the *working memory*. Whilst these constraints are also applicable in ART, a recent version has added a feature called *procedural attachment* (active values) which uses a non-RETE method of relaxing the first constraint somewhat by allowing value generating procedures to be attached in an object-oriented fashion, to the objects themselves.

Having pointed out the restrictions on how knowledge base may change over time, it must be said that forward-chaining reasoning with ART works very efficiently. Backward-chaining, on the other hand, is implemented on top of the forward chaining, and happens very inefficiently compared with a good backward-chaining expert system shell.

A frame-based representation has been integrated with this forward-chaining rule language as a very natural extension. Frames in ART are known as *schemata*. In version 2 of ART, schemata were static representation entities — any manipulation of schema values was done via rules. Version 3 added object-oriented programming facilities, giving similar functionality to KEE's UNITS.

All that has been said so far about rules has had the implicit assumption that there exists only a single working memory. In many problems which rely on notions of alternative world state, such a restriction presents a significant problem. Some mechanism for scoping the applicability of procedures and the extent of facts is required in order to perform hypothetical reasoning for example. ART provides such a mechanism called *viewpoints*. The facilities provided by viewpoints are fairly easy to use and are similar to those provided by an ATMS.

Graphic interfaces

It is common to expect the interaction between a human and a computer in any realistically complex application to exploit the technology of the computer and its operating system to its limit, whilst still providing for some commonality across delivery platforms. ART's market is the mid to high end workstation and we therefore expect programmatic interaction to be via keyboard and mouse operating on multiple windows and active regions within those windows.

Like KEE, ART provides a range of powerful graphical facilities, both for the developer (rule / viewpoint tracers, debuggers, integration with the Emacs editor), and for constructing user interfaces.

Communicating with other languages and processes

There has to come a point where functions that are required by the sample application rely upon specific features of the delivery platform. ART implements a number of useful ways in which this can be performed:

C callin/callout It is possible to invoke a C routine from the right-hand side of a rule, or for a C routine to assert a fact in the database (which could cause new rules to fire).

Per cycle function A LISP function can be bound to the ART system in such a way that is invoked each time that any rule fires.

RHS LISP The developer can invoke an arbitrary LISP function in the right-hand side of an Art rule.

Advantages and disadvantages of ART

The different features of ART come together into a toolkit which is well fitted for applications which need quick focussing of attention on new facts in the knowledge base. It provides good frame-based abilities which allow it to attack more complex applications of this type than would be possible with a forward chaining shell that only allowed simple facts. The addition of viewpoints and good graphical facilities on top of these basic facilities make it a formidable toolkit, applicable in a wide range of situations.

On the other hand, there are drawbacks which might be relevant in some situations. Backward chaining is not done in a very efficient way, in order to make it fit in with the RETE system, and so in systems where it is wanted, other solutions might be better. In addition, the delivery system on small machines has not been the full ART system, but a cut-down version of it. This means that you should choose your use of ART facilities carefully if you wish to deliver on a small machine.

6.5.2 KEE

KEE, marketed by Intellicorp, is an example of a product that has evolved from being concept-based on earlier systems such as UNITS (see [Laurent 86]), to being market-based and market-driven. While the first commercial version of KEE mainly supported a sophisticated object-oriented environment based on LOOPS (see [Stefik and Bobrow]), the latest version (version 3) is much more comprehensive, and includes the following facilities:

Object-oriented programming. Objects can represent objects in the application as well as graphical objects for display purposes; this supports a direct manipulation style of interface. Objects are implemented as very flexible frames. Slots have attributes called slot facets.

Rule-based reasoning. There are three rule systems, each with its own syntax; these systems are as follows:

Action. Here the rules permanently modify a knowledge base of objects.

Deduction. In this system, an ATMS (Assumption-based Truth Maintenance System) is used to maintain dependencies between deductions.

Worlds. This system, again using the ATMS, allows hypothetical states of the knowledge base to be created and reasoned about.

Database query. This is a set of facilities, menu- or LISP-driven, for editing and inspecting knowledge bases.

The facilities listed are directly comparable to the representation and reasoning facilities provided by ART. However, both toolkits reveal their origins somewhat — KEE probably has the edge for applications that are object-oriented in nature (simulations for instance), and ART is probably better for rule-based programming.

The object-oriented graphics facilities of KEE, both menu-generated and programmable, are implemented using a portable underlying (LISP callable) substrate called Common Windows. This allows KEE applications to be hardware platform independent.

As with other LISP-based toolkits, KEE is implemented as a natural extension to LISP; this allows the developer to mix LISP with KEE and, most importantly, extend the functionality of KEE as necessary.

Booster kits

Intellicorp have implemented a number of reusable capabilities (mostly written using the facilities provided by KEE itself), These can be supplied at extra cost, and can be valuable if buying such capabilities saves the expenditure of a lot of money redeveloping the wheel.

Some of the booster kit extensions seem like features that one would expect to find bundled in the price of the toolkit if they were provided at all — interfaces to relational databases and to 'C' programs. Other extensions are potentially very useful, such as a simulation package.

One of the latest extensions, KLUE, produced by a KEE customer rather than Intellicorp themselves, is specifically for building diagnostic systems, and is mentioned in Appendix A.2.2.

Advantages and disadvantages of KEE

Like most products, software or otherwise, KEE has features that make it suitable for some tasks and less so for others. For example, KEE probably should not be used for critical real-time applications owing to the unpredictable nature of some LISP garbage collectors. However, KEE has many strengths:

- the development environment is very easy to use; a new developer can use the menu-based facilities while an experienced one can use LISP.
- there are high (functional objects), medium (primitive objects) and low (streams, bitmaps, hotspots, etc.) level graphics facilities, so that the sophistication of the interface can be adjusted as required for the application and the expertise of the developer.
- the range and accessibility of the inference facilities (rules, demons and LISP) supports experimentation (prototyping).
- there are additional packages to link KEE with conventional databases.
- the user manuals supplied with KEE are comprehensive.

The main drawbacks of KEE are:

- it is a large toolkit and therefore experience with LISP and proper training are needed to make full use of its facilities.
- the basic KEE product does not support facilities to define new semantic relationships between objects (or slots).
- the performance of KEE on some less capable hardware platforms (e.g. the 386) can be problematic for memory intensive applications.

Summary of KEE

In conclusion, KEE is an extensive and flexible toolkit that promotes highly productive KBS construction. KEE can be used for developing and delivering a range of AI and conventional (e.g. simulation software) applications. However, it is most effective when used as a prototyping tool for design and end-user requirement specification. This is due the combination of the LISP programming language, object-oriented representation facilities and the graphics tools.

6.6 Medium-priced integrated toolkits

As we observed in the introductory part of this chapter, these tools have lower prices and less features (at present) than the high-end toolkits. The main difference is the absence of any built-in hypothetical reasoning mechanism — this facility can be very useful for some applications.

These toolkits have been developed over a shorter time period than ART or KEE. To some extent, this has meant that the toolkit builders have been able to learn from developers' experience with the older toolkits — they seem to run more easily on smaller general-purpose workstations than the high-end toolkits. It also means that they are probably more likely to be significantly altered than the older toolkits — extra facilities have been added to both Nexpert-Object and Goldworks in the latest versions.

Goldworks has the edge over Nexpert in terms of representation and reasoning features. In part, this is due to being programmed in LISP — it is easier to keep a LISP system flexible than it is when implementing your toolkit in C. The penalty to pay when implementing in LISP is in terms of speed and deliverability — Nexpert is better for embedding in larger systems. Neuron Data have stressed this in their publicity, advertising Nexpert as "The AI library in C for Industrial Integration".

6.6.1 Nexpert-Object

Nexpert-Object version 1.1, usually referred to simply as Nexpert, is a medium-priced toolkit that supports forward and backward rule-based reasoning (with pattern matching), frame/object-based representation with multiple inheritance and demon (procedural attachment) based invocation. Unlike the larger toolkits, such as KEE and Knowledge Craft, Nexpert is written in 'C' and is available on a very large range of platforms (Apple Macintosh, IBM PC/AT, most UNIX workstations, VAXs, IBM mainframes, etc.).

Nexpert's development environment (including structured editors for rules and objects as well as dictionaries for objects, rules and properties), and the open architecture of the inference engine (Nexpert is designed to allow for embedding and linking with other software systems) has made it a very popular product.

Rules. Nexpert rules have the following format:

```
IF <conditions>
THEN <hypothesis>
DO  <action>
```

Generally, the condition part of a rule applies an operator to hypotheses, patterns (to be matched) and object states. The action part of the rule can be used to make modifications to the knowledge base, show pictures or retrieve data from a file or a database. Forward chaining is invoked when the conditions are true and backward chaining occurs when the hypothesis is to be proved (as a condition in another rule).

Objects. Nexpert objects are frames with slots. The slots can have single typed values. Objects can be structured into class hierarchies or as compositions (part-of links). The inheritance process and slot facets are defined using a structure called a meta-slot (see below).

Meta-slots. Each slot (which is referred to as a property) has an associated structure for describing the slot in more detail. The meta-slot allows one to define the sources for finding a value for the slot, the actions to perform when the slot value changes, the inheritance path to be used for inheriting a default value and the format for displaying the slot value.

The descriptions of the Nexpert facilities above is very brief, a complete description is given in the Nexpert manual and some examples are given in chapter 9, the case study using Nexpert.

Nexpert has been designed very much with the idea of integration into existing systems in mind. One particular topic worthy of specific mention is that of database interaction.

The Nexpert object/class system has a very natural mapping onto tables in a relational database, classes corresponding to (virtual) tables, objects to rows and properties to columns. When working with a file based database such as those found on PCs, Nexpert has easy access to information generated by such tools, and can easily generate information for them.

A multi-user relational database equipped with an SQL interfaced to Nexpert can be very beneficial for some developments. In most applications many rules in a knowledge base are concerned with selecting and filtering data. When interfacing with a relational database Nexpert can push most of this processing into the query language. Furthermore most simple constraint rules are easily expressed in terms of database relations. These too can be 'evaluated' using queries. The net result is a significant reduction in the number of rules, simplifying the knowledge base design, and increasing the speed with which the knowledge base can be developed.

The positive and negative features of Nexpert for developers are outlined below:

Positive features

- Nexpert's development environment makes it very easy to build and check expert systems.
- Nexpert's knowledge bases are portable across all the platforms on which it runs, so a system can be developed on one machine and delivered on another.
- Nexpert's open architecture makes it possible to interface to or embed in existing (conventional) software. It has built in interfaces and add on bridges to most major SQL databases.

- Nexpert has sold a large number of copies. This means that support is readily available, and an increasing number of third party products interfacing to or incorporating Nexpert are being marketed.
- Knowledge acquisition can be partially automated by using a product from Neuron Data (the developers of Nexpert) called Nextra that produces Nexpert rules and objects.

Negative features

- Although Nexpert's development environment is uniform over all platforms supporting it, the support for building user interfaces is much less consistent. Neuron Data are developing a toolkit for developing such interfaces on workstations, and this should be on the market in 1990.
- In principle, any algorithm can be implemented with Nexpert, but in practice there are some things easier done in a programming language. To do this with Nexpert involves programming separately (usually using 'C'), compiling and linking. Furthermore (on PCs and Macintoshes particularly) it may require the purchase of additional software. While effective, the interface is less flexible and friendly than, for example, the direct access to LISP possible from KEE.
- Nexpert does not allow for user defined data types, nor does it provide for any constructed data types like arrays, structures and lists. The general effect of these can be mimicked using the object–subobject (part-of) links, but this approach lacks the clarity, efficiency and security of a proper extensible type system. Objects themselves fail to correspond to types in that (new) operators cannot be defined on them.
- Objects in Nexpert have no encapsulation aspects — all slots are global. Compared to Smalltalk or KEE for example, objects in Nexpert are much less cohesive, and methods attach not to objects but to slots. The net result when combined with the lack of user-defined data types is to place Nexpert objects in a slightly uneasy position between an extensible type system as found in Ada and Pascal, and a truly object-oriented system such as Smalltalk. This hampers the development of 'libraries' of reusable knowledge-based components in Nexpert.

6.6.2 Goldworks

The main improvement in Goldworks II over the original Goldworks has been a much more graphical developer interface. Such an interface was a major selling point for Nexpert — seeing a VAXstation looking like a Symbolics that was running a high-end toolkit impressed a lot of potential customers. Goldworks II catches up on the lead that Nexpert had over the earlier version of Goldworks in this area.

Goldworks has a good rule and frame-based system — similar to KEE rather than ART, as the emphasis of the toolkit seems to be on the frame and object-oriented features rather than on efficiency of rule-based programming. Rules can be arranged in *rulesets* — clusters of rules that can be enabled or not, depending on the state of the knowledge base. This allows the developer to impose some degree of modularity on the knowledge base. The advantages of this are in terms of efficiency rather than true modularity — when rules in rulesets are active, they are still global in their effects.

User interface graphics are also similar to those of KEE. A graphical toolkit is provided of objects that can be used in building user interfaces. Like KEE, active images (called *dynamic images* here) are implemented, which can be attached to frame slots and updated as the slot is updated.

There is some difficulty in comparing Goldworks and Nexpert. They are both compromises on the high-end toolkit to some extent, but the choice of implementation language has put them at different points in the comparison. Neither contains all the features of ART or KEE, but they are cheaper and run on smaller machines. Nexpert is more efficient, but less flexible. Goldworks has a more powerful rule and frame syntax, but needs a more powerful version of a machine to produce the same sort of performance. It is also likely to be harder to embed Goldworks applications in a larger system.

6.7 Expert system shells

These were the first knowledge engineering tools to be generally available as commercial products. Typically, they are also the least expensive type of tool and the easiest to learn to use. This has meant that they have had a much wider range of users than any of the other types of tool. Most of them are perfectly adequate for building simple expert systems, and they are good tools for first experiments with expert systems technology. We have included them in the book, and as one of the case studies, for two reasons. The first is to inform those who have never used a simple shell of the possibilities and the limitations in such tools. The second reason is to allow those who have used such shells to compare the capabilities of a typical shell with the facilities available in the other types of tool.

We will consider three different shells (VP-Expert, LEVEL5, and Envisage) in order to illustrate the similarities and the differences that there are between products in the shell market. Each of these three shells has the features common to most commercial shells:

Common simple control and representation Each of these three shells is basically a backward-chaining rule-based system, and so only allows a limited control of reasoning. This simplicity and inflexibility is offset by different additions to control of reasoning in different shells. The most usual improvement is an imperative control structure above the backward chaining. Some shells also allow simple forward chaining.

The minimum representational capability of these shells is usually simple propositional facts and numeric values. Boolean and arithmetic operators are provided, and perhaps some sort of uncertainty operator.

Common hardware platform The IBM PC and compatible computers have become the standard delivery vehicle for simple expert systems. It is easy to see why — the hardware is freely available in most offices, removing the need to buy a computer specially to run the expert system shell. For VP-Expert, IBM PCs and compatibles are the only choice, but LEVEL5 and Envisage are also available on several other types of hardware.

Simple development environment We have described complex rule and frame building software for the more up-market tools. For the most part, they are not provided with expert system shells. The text of the knowledge base must be entered using a standard word processor or text editor. This text is either then interpreted directly by the shell, which can be slow, or the system includes a compiler which translates the knowledge base into some internal representation for faster execution. In either case, the process is usually not incremental — a change to the knowledge base means exiting from the shell and invoking the text editor again.

Given the limitations of most expert system shells, it must be repeated that people are building useful and profitable expert systems with these tools. Most shell vendors can point to a number of contented users of their tool who have constructed expert systems that are contributing to the viability of the user's company. If a particular shell has all the facilities that you need for a particular application, then don't waste your money on anything more powerful.

Each of the three shells mentioned is a mature product which has been developed and improved far beyond the common shell facilities outlined above. The rest of this section will look at the improvements made to each shell, and the sort of advantages that those improvements give.

6.7.1 VP-Expert

This is one of the most inexpensive expert system shells around, and has some facilities that you would only expect in a much more costly shell. The remarks in this section are based on VP-Expert version 2.0.

Reasoning

VP-Expert provides two control extensions to backward chaining which make it much more flexible. The first is a procedural level — a list of actions to perform. This is the top level of VP-Expert, and actions can be to DISPLAY advice or to FIND a value for a fact. As advice can include facts, either of these actions can cause backward chaining to happen. Rules can also have actions as consequences (IF condition THEN DISPLAY text), which makes it possible to give selective advice. The embedding of actions within rules also allows simple forward chaining — the system stops during its backward chaining and does something else because of the state of the system. This feature is also provided more generally and more explicitly by the WHENEVER command.

It is possible to write an expert system in VP-Expert which loops through all of the records in a VP-Info database performing analysis of each one — a very useful feature. It is also possible to add records to such a database, or to invoke an outside procedure or program.

Representation

VP-Expert has boolean and numeric facts. In addition, it has what might best be described as simple string facts. These are very useful when giving advice, allowing details like names of people and companies to be used.

There is a simple array feature, called *dimensioned variables*, which allows rules to be written about an array of facts (or linking items from several arrays of facts).

User interface

VP-Expert comes with a built in editor which can be used to build the knowledge base, or the developer can use his own favourite editor. More interesting is the graphical rule tracing tool. The developer can track all rules that are called during a consultation, and then turn them into a graphical tree annotated with all the values that were set during the consultation.

The run time explanation facilities are of two sorts. The first is "How", which explains how a value was arrived at for a variable. The second is the "Why" command, meaning "Why am I being asked this question". The default for each of these is a trace of which rules have fired. While this may be of interest to the developer, it is useless to the end user. If the developer attaches a "BECAUSE" text to each question when building the expert system, then it will be produced when the user asks "Why" or "How". Unfortunately, this dual use of the "BECAUSE" text means that it will either be irrelevant for one type of question or too bland to be of use in either case.

VP-Expert also provides a simple graphics interface to allow the developer to build pictures to make the user interface more friendly.

One of the features of VP-Expert that initially seems most remarkable, considering its low price, is the INDUCE command. It claims to induce rules from examples (see section 5.1 for an explanation of induction). Its performance, however, falls far short of an implementation of the ID3 algorithm. ID3 produces the minimal significant rules, merging rules with common characteristics and showing up which conditions are important. INDUCE produces a rule corresponding to each different example, and each rule contains all of the criteria in the example. This is much less useful than the work done by ID3. In fact, this induction claim for VP-Expert is a good example of a common problem when selecting a toolkit — words like "frames", "objects", and "induction" are used by different people to describe different levels of functionality. It is necessary to know what you want from each feature, and then find out whether the toolkit that you are considering actually provides that functionality.

6.7.2 LEVEL5

LEVEL5 Version 1 is a rule-based shell that evolved out of the INSIGHT shell (INSIGHT, INSIGHT 2, INSIGHT 2+ and now LEVEL5) produced by LEVEL5 Research, a company based in Florida, USA. LEVEL5 has been around since 1985, and has sold extensively in the United States (estimated in excess of 18,000 users). LEVEL5 is now marketed and supported by Information Builders, better known in the computing world for their 4GL/DBMS product FOCUS.

LEVEL5 runs across a range of hardware platforms (IBM PC, Apple Macintosh, DEC VAX and IBM mainframes) with development and run-time versions available for each of the platforms. It started life on the PC and VAX and is gradually being spread across the major hardware platforms.

In addition to the standard development and run only options, the PC version also has a 'Production Compiler' available, enabling the developer to deliver an unlimited number of copies of any applications built. This is worth mentioning, because the example application (discussed in chapter 8) used the PC Production Compiler for delivery.

LEVEL5 is currently a backward-chaining rule-based shell. Rules are described in a fairly standard *IF...THEN...ELSE...* type format, with multiple conclusions allowed in either the THEN or the ELSE part of the rule. Rules are also allowed to have a procedural component which will always be executed whenever the Inference Engine tries this rule in pursuit of a goal. Procedural actions or commands, such as to present a Display, or to assign to or instantiate a Fact are allowed anywhere in the rule (i.e. in the Procedural part, in the IF or in the THEN or the ELSE). This gives a very flexible rule representation. An example rule might be:

```
RULE to check if tie is stained by meal
DISPLAY Checking if Tie is stained
IF the person has a new tie
AND meal IS Spaghetti
OR meal IS Fettucini
THEN tie will be stained
AND DISPLAY sorry... tie is stained
AND cleaning needed
ELSE NOT tie will be stained
```

This will always put a message to say that the system is checking to see if the tie is stained (*DISPLAY Checking if Tie is stained*). If the premise (the IF side) evaluates to TRUE, then the rule will display a recommendation to say that the tie is stained and will then assert that the tie needs cleaning.

In this rule, there are two basic types of Fact used, SIMPLEFACTs (which are boolean True/False) and ATTRIBUTEs (which have a discrete set of values possible — the fact *meal* in the above example could have the value *Spaghetti* or *Fettucini*). There are a number of other basic types of Fact allowed in the system. These are:

- NUMERIC. Integers or Decimals.
- STRING. Character strings.
- TIME. An absolute time (e.g. 10.38 16/03/1989).
- INTERVAL. A relative time. (e.g. 300 seconds).

When running, the inference engine searches for Facts needed to evaluate a rule premise in the following order:

- Does the system already know the state/value?
- Can the system prove or assert the value using another rule (causing the system to backchain)?
- Finally, if no other option is available, ask the user for the value.

Most backward-chaining shells tend to search for facts in a similar way. If the fact is already known then use it, otherwise obtain it (either by inferring it or by asking for it). Prompting for the fact automatically if it cannot be determined any other way stops the rules getting cluttered by commands to ask for information. However, the questions generated in this way are not as 'user-friendly' as they are in systems where a question to be asked is a separately declared item.

The goals for the Inference Engine to pursue are described at the start of each knowledge base in a 'Goal Outline'. This is a structured series of successive and alternative goals. For example,

```
1.  Food IS Chinese
      1.1 Meal IS Sweet and Sour Pork
      1.2 Meal IS Crispy Fried Duck

2.  Food IS Italian
      2.1 Meal IS Spaghetti
      2.3 Meal IS Pizza

3.  Food IS French
```

and so on. In this case, the inference engine will first try and assert a value for the ATTRIBUTE *Food* (i.e. either *Chinese* or *Italian* or *French*). It may then move on to try and assert a value for *Meal*, but this will depend on what the value of *Food* is.

The combination of the flexible rule structure and the Goal Outline gives a reasonably powerful rule-based representation that is good for expressing procedural control statements as well as for the more declarative knowledge statements.

Other strengths of LEVEL5 lie in its interfaces with other programs and with databases. Any rule may ACTIVATE an external program or command file and pass it arguments and return results back to the rule. This is relatively painless for the developer and gives a straightforward way of running almost any other program (given the usual memory constraints of the hardware and operating system under which LEVEL5 is running).

LEVEL5 manipulates external databases via an extended rule syntax which defines commands such as OPEN, ADVANCE, DELETE, LOCATE and so on. A number of databases may be open at the same time, and the system maintains a current record reference for each open database. The fields of the current record are accessed by prefixing the field name with the table name, e.g. *client.name* would be the *name* field in the *client* database. Access and Update of the field is expressed using the same syntax as for a normal Fact in the system, for example:

```
client.salary := client.salary * 1.1
```

increases the value of the salary field in the current client record by 10%.

This form of database interface has two major advantages. Firstly, it is very easy to manipulate and access database records and fields. This makes the database code quite expressive. Secondly, because LEVEL5 syntax is used to manipulate the database (rather than external function calls), the code is generic and thus portable between different hardware platforms and databases.

Conclusions

LEVEL5 is described by the vendors as a rule-based shell for producing and delivering commercial applications. It uses a readable and expressive rule representation which, when coupled with the procedural level provided by the Goal Outline, gives a degree of control that is adequate for many expert systems applications. The way in which it interfaces with external programs and data is powerful and easy to use. The database interface is one of LEVEL5's strongest features. Because it is part of the rule syntax, and therefore platform-independent, it is handy for developing on one platform and delivering on another.

Significant upgrade of LEVEL5

Events happening as this description of LEVEL5 was being written illustrate the difficulty in categorizing particular products. Rather than bringing out successive versions of the current LEVEL5 with extra functionality, Information Builders have chosen to redesign and reimplement LEVEL5 from scratch. The first results of this, LEVEL5 Release 2.0 are intended to be available during 1990, and are supposed to move LEVEL5 from being a rule-based shell to an object-oriented toolkit.

"LEVEL5 Release 2.0 is a completely object-oriented architecture with both User Objects (e.g. House, Person etc.) and System Objects describing such things as the inference engines, window, menus etc. It uses an OODBMS to control access to internal objects and external datasources and databases. Release 2.0 also adds a forward chaining engine which can be used in conjunction or instead of the backward-chaining engine. The other major change is the use of an object-oriented WIMP user interface, both for the development environment and for developed applications. This combines high resolution multi-window text and graphics with hypertext facilities."

LEVEL5 Release 2.0 will be available on PCs (MS-Windows or OS/2 Presentation Manager), Macintosh, VAX, UNIX machines and IBM mainframes.

6.7.3 Envisage

This is a complete reimplementation and redesign based on SAGE, a much simpler shell that sold hundreds of copies in the UK and Europe in the early 1980s. The features that were added to Envisage during that rebuild phase illustrate areas where many of the simpler shells are lacking important capabilities:

Reasoning

While Envisage is basically a backward-chaining shell, control of inference is available at multiple levels:

- The top level control is procedural — there are a set of imperative actions, where each action is taken in order if its (optional) associated test was true.

Either the action or the test could cause the shell to perform backward chaining. The action taken could be to perform some backward chaining, to give some advice, or to interface with the outside world.

- The next level of control is backward-chaining inference. A goal is pursued until it is achieved or the third level of control causes an interruption of the backward chaining.
- The third level is forward chaining of a restricted sort. Whenever a fact is evaluated, then evaluation is attempted of all "demons" containing that fact (evaluation will fail if other facts in the demon have not be evaluated yet). If the precondition of the demon is true, then it triggers a set of actions (the same choice of actions that are available at the procedural top-level).

The knowledge base can be split up into areas, where each area has separate control knowledge (control can be passed from area to area) and reasoning between areas must be explicitly declared. This encourages modular (and often fairly hierarchical) knowledge bases, where changes to the knowledge base can often be limited to a single area.

Representation

Envisage has no pretensions to being frame-based. Instead, the implementors have chosen language extensions much more in line with standard programming languages. The Envisage language provides RECORDS — fact conglomerations consisting of several related facts of different types, and also ARRAYS — multiple facts of the same type. This is a much more traditional computing solution than frames, but has less power and flexibility. The designers decided this was a reasonable tradeoff against the ease with which programmers could learn the language. Being able to write rules which apply to a whole array of facts can make some applications much easier to build. Envisage provides dynamically sizeable arrays, operators to separate arrays of records on a particular field. So, for example, if you had an array of records with personal details of clients, then you could sort out all the over-65s and reason separately about them.

String variables and a range of operators that work on strings were an addition from the previous system, and one that allows a much greater degree of user-friendliness and relevance. String variables can be placed into question texts, explanation texts, advice texts. So, for example, it is possible to write questions for an array of records that rely heavily on previous answers. This facility can be used to produce an user interface which is easy to use and understand, able to produce questions like:

```
Please type in the ages of your children:
```

```
Mary:  12
John:  17
 etc...
```

(where the number and names of the children have been ascertained earlier in the consultation).

User interface

This is an area where some effort has been put into Envisage. Instead of interacting directly with the screen, Envisage interacts with a terminal handler program. This means that questions can be presented differently, depending on the abilities of the computer screen being used, and on the needs of the application. On different machines and for different applications, Envisage has been used with:

- a simple scrolling VDU interface.
- an interface which uses the screen segmenting and line-drawing abilities of a VT100 type terminal.
- a colour WIMP interface on IBM PCs.
- a form-filling interface which allows the user to answer a screenful of relevant questions at once.
- an interface which accesses a database of pictures and displays them, allowing the user to select the correct one.

The explanation and help facilities of Envisage are fairly novel. As well as an extendable help file facility, which regurgitates pieces of text from files (a fairly standard feature), it is possible to link the HELP facility to a special area of the application which tries to give "expert help". The user can also call on three different kinds of explanation text that can be attached to an application. MORE text is further explanation of what a question means. WHY text is an explanation of why a question is being asked. WHY text can be attached to facts and rules and actions as well as questions, and then produced to give progressively higher explanations as a user continues to ask "WHY". This can make the explanations seem much more sensible than is possible with a single level of WHY text.

One feature which makes life immeasurably easier for the naive user is the way in which the delivery system can be configured to a specific application to hide the mechanics of using the shell. Envisage can be attached to a startup file which contains commands to load knowledge bases and to configure the system. This means that the user does not need to know about arcane development commands

— indeed, all such commands can be masked from them, only allowing them to provide answers to questions.

If the user realizes he gave a wrong answer to a question, then answers can be retracted later on in a consultation — this is in sharp contrast to many other shells, where a wrong answer can mean starting all over again through a (possibly lengthy) question and answer session.

Conclusions

Envisage has several features which provide an expressiveness of representation and reasoning that is present in few other shells — extensive array and string handling facilities; a good mixture of imperative control with backward chaining and limited forward chaining; a large number of developer-definable interface features.

These features enable Envisage to be used on a wider range of applications than one would normally expect from an expert system shell.

6.8 The final word

We have looked at the surface features of tools in each of the categories. In the next four chapters, we will look in more detail at a selection of the different tools mentioned in this chapter. In each case study chapter, the case study is backed up with an examination of how that class of tool would tackle the representative set of problems outlined in chapter 7.

6.9 Further reading

AI languages. The following language textbooks are personal preferences — for each of LISP, Prolog and POP-11 there are several other reasonable choices. [Wilensky] is a good LISP textbook, as is [Bratko] for Prolog. [Anderson 89] shows the breadth of systems that have been implemented in POP-11 and includes some material on Flavours, while [Pountain 88] gives a brief introduction to the POP-11 language. [Brownston 85] gives details of using OPS5.

If a developer really insists on developing his own representation and reasoning systems, then [Charniak et al.] is an absolutely indispensable book, describing how to implement many useful types of representation and reasoning in COMMON LISP.

Toolkits. The book on toolkits edited by [Hawley] is somewhat variable in quality, but chapter 2 on POPLOG and chapter 10 on KEE are both very good.

[Pepper 86] gives details of the representation and reasoning facilities of Knowledge Craft.

[Laurent 86] is a comparative review of the "big three" knowledge engineering toolkits — ART, KEE and Knowledge Craft. It gives details of the facilities provided by each in such a way that it is easy to compare them.

Chapter 7

Typical KBS applications

Chris Price

But tasks in hours of insight willed,
Can be through hours of gloom fulfill'd.
Morality, Matthew Arnold.

This chapter considers the range of different types of application of knowledge-based systems (KBSs), and examines which tools are apt for particular classes of application.

The most important split between the different kinds of problems solved by knowledge-based systems is whether the problem can be solved by *classification* or by *construction*.

Classification tasks are ones which have a "reasonable" number of solutions. In practice, "reasonable" means that there are few enough different solutions that it would be possible to explicitly list them (although some refinement of the solution may be necessary for each of the different solutions listed). Examples of applications that can usually be performed by classification are: system monitoring; system prediction; diagnosis.

Construction tasks are ones where it is necessary to build up each solution from components, and the number of possible solutions is computationally very large. Many design problems, planning systems and system configuration applications fall into this category.

It is much harder to build applications for construction tasks than for classification tasks. However, some construction-type problems can be restricted in such a way that they can be solved by classification techniques. For example, if a computer company only sold ten different configurations of their machines, then the problem of configuring the machines for a particular customer could be solved by classification — each of the ten configurations is a possible solution. However, if the computer company can use 200 different components in different numbers for each customer, and must resolve conflicts between those different components when configuring each original machine configuration, then the problem is likely to be too large to solve by classification.

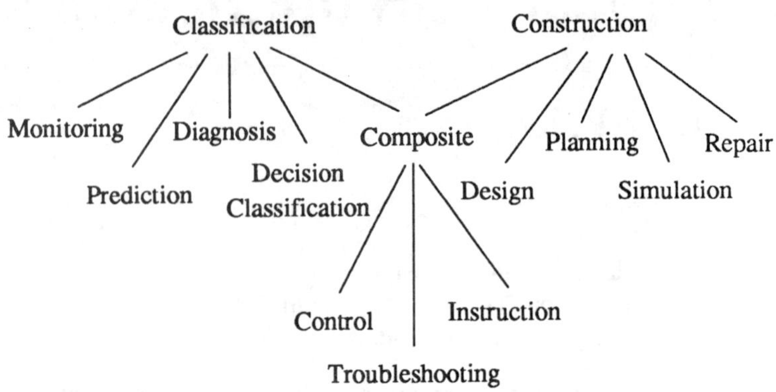

Figure 7.1: Relationship between different tasks

This means that it is impossible to make statements like: "simple expert system shells cannot deal with computer configuration problems" — it is necessary to decide whether the problem has been restated as a task which can be solved by classification, or whether it is in the unrestricted form that requires construction techniques. However, it does mean that if you are intending to build a KBS for a configuration task, you need to be aware of the greater difficulty of such tasks, and perhaps consciously restrict it to a subset of the task which can be solved by classification.

The way in which many knowledge-based systems are built can be looked on as achieving a compromise between the ideal system to be built, and the abilities of the toolkit being used. That means that it is often impossible to decide whether a particular toolkit can or cannot be used for a particular problem — what needs to be decided is the degree of compromise which will be necessary to use each tool on the problem.

As was the case when classifying KBS tools in chapter 6, choosing categories for applications can seem somewhat arbitrary whatever choices are made. The choice of categories in this chapter, like those in the works mentioned in the "Further reading" section at the end of this chapter, attempts to identify distinct types of problems that knowledge-based systems have been used to solve.

The first level of categorization is into three subgroups — classification, construction and composite tasks. Classification tasks and construction tasks have already been discussed in outline. The third category is made up of tasks that can be regarded as a combination of tasks from the first two groups. So, for example, troubleshooting can be viewed as the task of diagnosing a problem followed by the task of repairing the fault that has been diagnosed.

7.1 Types of classification problem

7.1.1 Monitoring

Monitoring classifies the state of a system against an expectation, using available observed values. For a chemical process plant, monitoring might involve combining the information from several sensors in order to decide whether the plant is working within its optimum capacity band or not. In order to implement such a monitoring application, the ability to interface the KBS to sensor readings is vital.

In the financial sector, a knowledge-based system which examined the indicators to a company's financial health and gave a verdict on the company's viability could also been seen as performing a monitoring task.

In many cases, monitoring can be a preliminary stage to diagnosis — deciding whether a problem exists with the system.

7.1.2 Prediction

Some types of monitoring have a characteristic which puts them into a slightly different category — the output classification is not just a verdict on the present state of the system, but predicts the future state of the system. At its simplest, this involves using the present state of the system and the current inputs to the system to predict what will happen.

The company health monitoring application mentioned above would become a prediction application if it could take the same inputs as the original monitoring application and combine the monitoring information with a chosen strategy for the coming year, producing as output the predicted state of the company's health in a year's time. Such prediction is usually a "more expert" task than simple monitoring, but is still amenable to solution by classification. It needs to be distinguished from genuine simulation (see section 7.3.3), which mirrors the system being simulated — prediction employs heuristics to reach its conclusions.

7.1.3 Diagnosis

This task is performed in the situation where a problem has already been identified (perhaps by a monitoring task). Ideally, diagnosis pinpoints the cause of the problem. Diagnosis can be performed at different levels of granularity. For example, diagnosing the same fault on a car could be carried out at the level of:

> There is an electrical fault.
> or
> There is a fault in the HT circuit.
> or
> The distributor cap is faulty.

These different levels of diagnosis can be represented within a diagnostic KBS as different levels of classification, where more specific tests of the system must be employed to perform the more specific classifications.

Diagnosis occurs in all sorts of domains where problems need to be identified in order to fix them — broken cars; faulty industrial machinery; business problems. While these domains are very different, and the emphasis of how diagnosis is performed will change from domain to domain, each of these types of application can be dealt with in a similar manner.

7.1.4 Decision classification

The first three types of classification occur in several different domains, with many features in common in the different domains.

However, there are many tasks which can be solved by classification that do not fit into those categories. For lack of a more precise set of categories, these other applications can be lumped together as *decision classification*.

Typically, the task to be performed is to make a choice from among several possibilities, with a number of criteria that need to be taken into consideration when making the choice.

Choosing a computer language to be used for a particular application is such a task — there are several possible choices, and the correct choice will depend on such criteria as:

- availability of a compiler for the target hardware;
- necessity of maintainability for the system;
- whether the system is for the DoD;

This is one example of a large subset of decision classification tasks, a subset that has been termed *catalogue selection*. The choice to be made is between a number of related products, and the classification criteria are the wants and needs of the particular customer. Both chapter 8 and chapter 9 contain case studies that fall into this category.

A different sort of example is deciding whether to grant a loan to a bank customer. Although there are only two possible choices for the classification in this case, it may be necessary to take many criteria into account when making the decision. This type of decision classification could be termed *checklist processing*. In such applications, there are a number of (possibly quite complex) conditions to be assessed, and the task is to examine them in an intelligent manner in order to make a decision about each case.

7.2 Solving classification problems

Many classification tasks can be solved using just an expert system shell, as long as it has reasonable capabilities. In a backward chaining shell, each possible classification can be represented as a goal which must be evaluated. If the shell also has some imperative control above the backward chaining, then it will be possible to focus on likely solutions before performing backward chaining.

The feature of a classification problem which would take it beyond the capabilities of most expert system shells is the need to reason simultaneously about many objects in the application domain, and about the relationships between them. A good example of this type of problem was explored at an early knowledge engineering workshop:

Given a chemical processing plant where many liquids (some hazardous) are stored, it is almost inevitable that some will eventually leak. When a leak occurs, the liquid will find its way into the drainage system, and eventually emerge, probably in a river. The task of the knowledge-based system is to identify the source of the spillage.

This is done by identifying the contents of the spillage, and tracing it backwards to its source, testing at manhole covers which drainage route has been followed by the leak. The problem could be treated as a simple classification task, listing the tests to be performed for every possible type of leak, but the number of possible routes from each source to each outfall make that a very impracticable way of investigating a leak. A much better solution is to build a structure in the computer which represents the structure of the drainage system and the positioning of sources and outfalls. Rules can then be written which act on this structure, examining drains upstream from the spill in order to progress towards the source of the leak. Once the contents of the spill have been established, it is also possible to work down from likely sources, examining for traces of a leak.

A quite neat solution to this problem is delivered as a demonstration with ART, but this type of application would prove impossible to implement in the same fashion using almost any expert system shell. The ART spill solution uses schemata to represent items like sources, drains and outfalls. These are linked into a structure using relations such as *is_upstream_of* and *nearby*. ART rules which match on these schemata are used to drive the investigation, along with the use of Viewpoints to hypothesize likely drainage routes.

This is a fairly complex example of a diagnosis system which is beyond implementation using an expert system shell, but long before such complexity is reached the need to make use of relationships between items in the problem area can mean that implementing an application fully in a shell would be difficult. With their greater ability to reason about this sort of complexity, any of the integrated toolkits should be able to tackle such applications. However, for the simpler classification applications, the use of an integrated toolkit may be too elaborate — if a shell is good enough, use it.

Because almost all classification tasks will be within reach either of an expert system shell or of an integrated toolkit, there seems little point to use either a loosely coupled toolkit or an AI language on such applications. Development using such tools takes longer, and the greater range of possibilities available with such toolkits will not be needed.

7.3 Construction problems

Construction tasks are more varied than classification tasks in the strategies that are useful in order to solve them. This means that it is much less sensible to consider them as a whole, as has just been done for classification tasks. Instead, the use of different types of toolkit will be discussed for each kind of construction task separately.

7.3.1 Design

One book on knowledge-based systems for design [Brown and Chandrasekaran] points out that there are two components that make up design problem solving. The first part is the construction of a design that might solve the problem. The second part is evaluation of a design. Evaluation of a design is really a decision classification task — *Is this design adequate or not?* The interestingly different part of performing design is the generation of likely designs. This design generation phase can be split into three classes of difficulty.

Class 1: Creative design. This activity is what could be called "invention" — the creation of radically new solutions to design problems. It is beyond present technology to build class 1 knowledge-based design systems, which makes it unnecessary to worry about the type of knowledge representation needed to build such systems. For the interested, some relevant exploration has been done into the nature of such design [Dyer et al.].

Class 2: Complex design. In this class, the design problem can be structured from experience and decomposed into likely sub-designs. However, in class 2 design there are too many possible cases for the decomposition to be represented as a classification problem. This means that the resolution of all the constraints on the design must be done explicitly whenever an actual problem is being solved.

Class 3: Routine design. This could be termed *variant* design. There is one basic design, which varies depending on the particular needs of the customer. These variations may be at different levels of details, and can be represented in a tree of design decisions. This is essentially a classification hierarchy, with the choice nodes corresponding to the different variations on the design. Therefore, if a design problem can be solved with a class 3 approach, then it really belongs in the classification task category, not the construction task category.

The identification of design tasks that can be solved by classification means that many class 3 design problems can be tackled with expert system shells, with the same sort of limitations that were discussed for other kinds of classification tasks.

Class 2 design is a different matter. The resolution of many constraints on the design, and the need to explore many possibilities means that some sort of frame-based reasoning is vital. The consequence of this is that at least a medium-priced integrated toolkit is needed for class 2 design. In some cases, the availability of facilities for hypothetical reasoning might cut down the search space considerably, which would tip the balance in favour of a high-end toolkit.

Other class 2 design problems would benefit from the ability to construct a descriptive language specific to the domain (such design tools are now appearing as commercial propositions, such as the engineering design tool ICAD). If it is intended to build such a tool for a new domain, then a loosely coupled toolkit is the best choice.

7.3.2 Planning

Planning has a number of features in common with design (in fact, Clancey terms it "designing actions"). In event planning, the planner must choose sequences of activities which enable the system to reach the required goal — the steps to be taken in constructing a new factory; the breakdown of work on a software project. In location planning, the planner must decide where to place things in relation to one another — how best to fill a freight container with irregularly shaped objects (it is a matter of personal preference whether you class this example as planning or design). Chapter 11 contains a case study which tackles a location planning problem.

Both planning and design problems are generally difficult to solve, though planning problems are somewhat better understood (because they are less varied). Simple planning problems can be solved by the same sort of methods as class 3 design, but many planning problems require the search for a solution in a large space of possible plans, with the application of constraints and heuristics. This makes them as complex as class 2 design.

The comments made previously concerning what tools to use for design problems are also applicable to planning problems. For planning problems, the developer is even more likely to want to employ a loosely coupled toolkit, because the ability to develop a special language in which to express plans and their consequences will make the application developer's knowledge representation task much easier.

7.3.3 Simulation

The attempt to model a system symbolically and predict what will happen to it over time can be very challenging. It is discussed in greater detail in Appendix A.4. Simulation differs from prediction, mentioned in section 7.1.2 in degree rather than in purpose. Instead of classifying the future state of the system by applying heuristics to the present state of the system (what usually happens in prediction), simulation involves constructing a model of the system that is to be simulated. This model must be able to mirror the ongoing behaviour of the system to some level.

It is impossible to build a system capable of this type of simulation with an expert system shell. KEE has proven popular for certain kinds of simulation which naturally suit its object-oriented features. In other cases, a loosely coupled toolkit might be best, using both the object-oriented features of such toolkits, and perhaps the more specific language building features provided in POPLOG, or the powerful user definable relationships built into Knowledge Craft.

7.3.4 Repair

Repair is the activity that takes place once a fault has been diagnosed in a system. In general, this will involve forming a plan for performing the repair. The precise nature of the plan needed will depend on both the system and the fault. The simplest form of repair is often replacement.

Even replacing a faulty component in a device can involve the generation of a correct sequence of actions (possibly demanding precautions against side-effects) in order to obtain access to the faulty part and to reassemble the system afterwards.

An example of this is the detailed instructions in car repair manuals for replacing parts that are difficult to reach.

Some sorts of faults can not be solved by replacement, but only by treatment. In medical circles, replacement is looked on as a very last resort. For performing treatment too, it is necessary to form a plan for how the treatment must be carried out, for what monitoring of the problem must be done during treatment, and for what further action should be taken if the treatment proves ineffective.

For complex repair activities, the type of tool needed to build a KBS for repair will be similar to that needed to build a complex planning or design system — unsurprising, as the activity that is performed will be very similar to planning.

Repair is often built into a KBS in combination with diagnosis, and this combined activity, known as troubleshooting, is considered in section 7.4.2.

7.4 Composite problems

This section considers process control, troubleshooting, and intelligent computer-aided instruction. Many other combinations of classification and construction tasks are possible apart from the ones outlined here. These combinations have been chosen because of the frequency with which they occur as applications for knowledge-based systems. This means that they can be characterized in a way that is not possible for many of the other combinations of tasks that are less popular.

7.4.1 Process control

Process control combines the monitoring of a process with a reaction when the state of the process is outside desired working conditions. The reaction is intended to bring the state of the process back within acceptable boundaries. This might be done in order to keep the process within safety criteria, or within the correct environment for fault-free production, or in order to optimize the performance of the process.

The type of tool needed to build a solution to this problem will depend on the level of solution chosen. A simple process control solution might perform a classification of the state of the process, associating each possible state with an action that must be taken. This simple solution could be implemented using an expert system shell. Medium hard solutions might perform simulation of the process in order to calculate what would happen if a particular reaction to the present state was carried out. The medium solution would need an integrated toolkit of some sort.

Chapter 10 contains an example of a difficult process control KBS (except that the feedback is not directly to the process — the system makes recommendations to plant operators). That system needs to reason about time and has a very sophisticated task control structure. Consequently, the implementors chose to design, construct and use their own representation language in a loosely coupled toolkit.

There is a further examination of some facets of process control in chapter 12.3.4.

7.4.2 Troubleshooting

Troubleshooting an identified fault combines the task diagnosing the fault with that of repairing it. Many attempts at building troubleshooting system concentrate on diagnosis and gloss over the repair phase. This is particularly true of man-made systems such as a car, where many faults can be repaired by replacement. The repair part of this process is often simplified to "replace the component", relying on the abilities of the engineer using the system. This simplification of the repair stage can cause confusion, because troubleshooting then becomes very like diagnosis (in fact, when people talk about diagnosis, they actually often mean the compound task of diagnosis and repair).

One benefit from combining diagnosis and repair is that attempts at repair can be used to further the diagnostic task, because the result of the replacement can constitute a further level of test for the diagnosis — if that repair did not cure it, then there must be something else wrong.

Troubleshooting applications where the repair activity is kept to a minimum can be solved with the same tools as the equivalent diagnostic task alone. Where it is necessary to construct complex repair plans, then an integrated or loosely coupled toolkit will be necessary.

7.4.3 Instruction

In theory, instructing a student in a subject could be regarded as troubleshooting that student's understanding of the subject — diagnosing missing knowledge and repairing it. In practice, there are several problems with this view if one is attempting to build practical knowledge-based systems for intelligent computer-aided instruction.

Representing the student's understanding. The student's model of what is happening in a domain may not be the one that the teacher expects, without it being necessarily wrong. Good human teachers can adapt to this — *"Yes, you could look at it like that, in which case..."*.

Natural language understanding. In order to diagnose what the student understands in detail, it might be necessary to analyse free form explanations supplied by the student.

Complex repairs. Even if a correct model of the subject matter can be represented, and an accurate diagnosis of the student's present understanding made, then the process of repairing the student's understanding of the subject matter is likely to involve a complex treatment plan with many tests to detect further deviations from the correct understanding.

These problems mean that comprehensive tutoring systems are an AI research topic. However, some parts of the problem can be built into realistic systems.

The EDUC case study in chapter 8 is an example of a system which attempts to gauge both the level of experience that a student has in a subject (implementing database systems in this case), and the level of experience which the student wishes to attain. Such a system would be useful as an intelligent front end to a series of computer-based training aids, and can be built using an expert system shell (as EDUC shows).

Intelligent instruction systems that help with a particular task rather than a whole subject area are also feasible. It has been claimed that this is a benefit of expert systems in general — build a KBS for troubleshooting a complex machine, and human trainees will be able to try it out and gradually understand how to troubleshoot the machine. In order for this to be useful, the expert system will need to be embellished with a level of explanation which is appropriate for such trainees (this is not normally provided by default), and their training will need to be directed, at least to the level of providing a set of typical cases to work through and understand. This level of training system can usually be constructed using the same level of KBS toolkit as would be needed for the expert system without the training element.

7.5 Conclusions

This chapter has illustrated a number of standard types of problem to which knowledge-based systems can provide a reasonable solution. For each type of problem, there has been some discussion of what sort of KBS tools should be used to construct the solution. In each of the next four chapters, a case studies will examine the detailed construction of a solution to one of these standard problems. Each case study will use a different type of toolkit, also exploring more fully the range of toolkits available.

7.6 Further reading

[Hayes-Roth et al.] contains one of the first attempts to identify different types of application that frequently occur. The list of applications in that book was reordered and categorized by [Clancey 85], who talks about analysis (classification) and synthesis (construction) tasks.

Other reasonable attempts at categorizing types of KBS applications have been made by [Reichgelt and van Harmelen], and for applications in manufacturing industry by [Lee]. The interpretation models in KADS (see Appendix A.3) also have a very similar categorization.

Chapter 8

First case study: Expert system shell

David Wilson

The first case study describes a system that was implemented using an expert system shell. Expert system shells tend to be tools designed for producing applications around a single knowledge representation paradigm, usually a rule-based paradigm. The shell used for this case study was LEVEL5 (version 1), whose features are outlined in section 6.7.2.

8.1 The case study problem

This case study provides an example of a problem which fits the classification style of problem-solving — the most common (and fruitful) area of use for expert system shells. Information Builders (IB) offers a large number of different training courses for its 4GL/DBMS product FOCUS. There are currently approximately 25 different courses on offer, which cater for different levels of FOCUS experience and teach various aspects of the FOCUS system. The task which this case study addresses is the correct selection of a training course from the range of courses offered. However, courses are described in terms of their contents, whereas the prospective attenders know only what their experience is, and what they wish to do, not what they need to know about. Selecting which course is the 'correct' course to attend is not an easy task, unless you are familiar with the contents of the courses, the level of ability and experience of the students, and of course, what they wish to be able to do.

In general, there is no guarantee that the person wishing to attend a course will be booked on the 'correct' course. It is not unknown to find someone with a reasonable amount of data processing (DP) experience on the same course as other people who have little experience. Alternatively, people who are basically End-Users (who just want to learn how to get information and reports out of FOCUS) can find themselves on courses with experience DP Professionals. Whichever way round it is, some of these people have been on a course with the wrong content or going at the wrong pace.

The basic problem is that, in a significant number of cases, a course is booked without recourse to the experience of the attenders and without looking at what the desired result of the course should be. This often occurs because it is not the attenders who are booking the course. Although Information Builders' Training Manager would know what the correct course should be, the person who actually phones up and books the course does not.

In order to try and solve this problem, and thus reduce the number of incorrectly booked courses, an Expert Training Adviser system, EDUC, was developed, which would make a recommendation on which course would be right for a given set of circumstances. It is sent out with the Customer Education Guides, which describe details of the courses that are offered. The constraint that the training system needed to run on a computer that was available to all customers meant that the chosen delivery vehicle for the system was a standard IBM PC or compatible.

8.2 Features of the solution

The course recommendation is based on two main factors — the experience, both of FOCUS and in DP in general, of the attender, and also the competence desired by the attender. The level of competence required is defined in terms of the type of knowledge required (for example, just reporting of information, or building new databases and applications) as well as the level of knowledge.

EDUC evaluates these two factors and recommends one (or more) course(s) to take the attender to the desired level of competence and knowledge. Because courses are frequently reviewed and upgraded, the representation of the courses needed to be flexible and easy to maintain. Therefore it was decided that this information should be held in an external database. In fact, this was represented by holding the standard course paths (i.e. series of courses) in a database with each course path having one record for each comprising course. When extra courses were added, new records could be inserted to hold the new course information as appropriate.

The experience of the attender is judged using questions about the level of FOCUS knowledge, previous experience using FOCUS, and more general DP experience. This experience effectively defined the equivalent course experience that the attender already had, and also defined some overall facts about the attender (for example, whether the user was an end user or a DP professional).

EDUC then asks questions that are intended to determine the level of experience/knowledge of FOCUS that is desired. This is principally split between knowledge of how to generate reports and experience of developing applications, with some specialist areas. This, coupled with whether the attender is an End User or a DP Professional, defines the course path which the attender should follow. The system then reads the database to find which course should be attended, and recommends those relevant courses that are not covered by their existing experience.

Under the appropriate circumstances, the system will state that the attender seems to have sufficient experience already. In this case, it recommends calling the Information Builders Training Manager either to check whether any new relevant courses have been added since the system was last updated, or in order to discuss the user's training requirement in more detail. Here are some example rules from the system:

```
RULE main end user objectives selection
IF end user objective IS systems
OR end user objective IS reporting and systems
AND assigned end user systems search name
THEN worked out end user high level objectives

RULE simple departmental systems
IF  end user systems IS Simple departmental systems
AND NOT end user systems IS Complex systems
THEN assigned end user systems search name
AND search name := "simple departmental systems"
```

These two rules cover part of the course path selection process. There are a number of standard course paths which can be selected (currently seven). Once a path has been selected, a search name is assigned. The courses in each course path are actually held in a database which is keyed using the search name.

```
RULE determining level of reporting knowledge
IF reporting covered IS Basic Reporting
THEN got IB reporting equivalent
AND experience IS E01
AND experience IS E02
```

This rule is one of series of rules comparing the user's stated knowledge of FOCUS with the content of IB FOCUS courses. This means that the courses listed

(E01, E02) would not be recommended as the user is now assumed to already know the content of these,

The application was put through the Production Compiler, which created a run-time version complete with installation program and customized on-line help, all on one 360K diskette. This was then copied and sent to over 1000 FOCUS customers.

One interesting aspect of EDUC is that it is able to make better recommendations than could be easily gleaned from the Training Brochure. This is especially true when someone needs to take a number of courses, as the system can recommend 'fast-track' courses designed to get people up to speed quickly and covering a number of smaller courses in one go.

8.3 Using LEVEL5 for EDUC

EDUC was initially prototyped in a period of about three man-weeks by a trainee working under supervision. This person had no expert systems or LEVEL5 experience but did have some experience with FOCUS. In total, about four to five man weeks was spent on producing EDUC. In addition to the knowledge about how to select courses, this involved adding most of the course information from the training brochure into the system. This information includes dates of courses, contents, cost etc., and is made available to the user on a selective basis (e.g. *tell me about course E02*). It is a common experience with this type of advisory system that, as well as providing new functionality, such systems need to provide information which is already available only in a more accessible form.

EDUC was developed on a IBM PC/AT. The LEVEL5 PC development system has a Wordstar-like editor through which a knowledge base is written. This proved easy to use, with standard function key commands. In addition, the knowledge base is compiled by hitting a function key in the editor. If an error occurs, you have the option of going back to the file or continuing compilation. This process is simple and fairly quick to use.

Although not incrementally compiled, the compiler is quick enough not to cause much of a delay. This does depend on the size of knowledge base written, of course (about 2000 lines of code/text in the EDUC system was fine). Compilation time may conceivably become a problem if dealing with massive single knowledge bases (e.g. 20,000 lines). However, the complexity of the knowledge tends to demand subdivision into multiple knowledge bases before that size is reached. A typical large LEVEL5 application will comprise of a number of linked knowledge bases. In fact, the production EDUC system contains four knowledge bases:

- EDUC. High level control and selection.

- EDUGUIDE. The training selector.
- COURSE. Information on FOCUS courses.
- EXSYS. Information on expert systems.

The first EDUC prototype demonstrated almost the full functionality required for the final system. The main shortcoming of the prototype was that it did not fully handle cases where the customer desired experience of both FOCUS Reporting and Application Development. It was very easy to start writing LEVEL5 code, expressing the outline structure of the solution (using the Goal Outline) and also the basic rules governing relationships between different levels and types of experience and which FOCUS courses were applicable.

As the prototype developed, the rules were amended in order to reflect the structure of the knowledge better, and also to guide the sequence of the desired consultation between user and system.

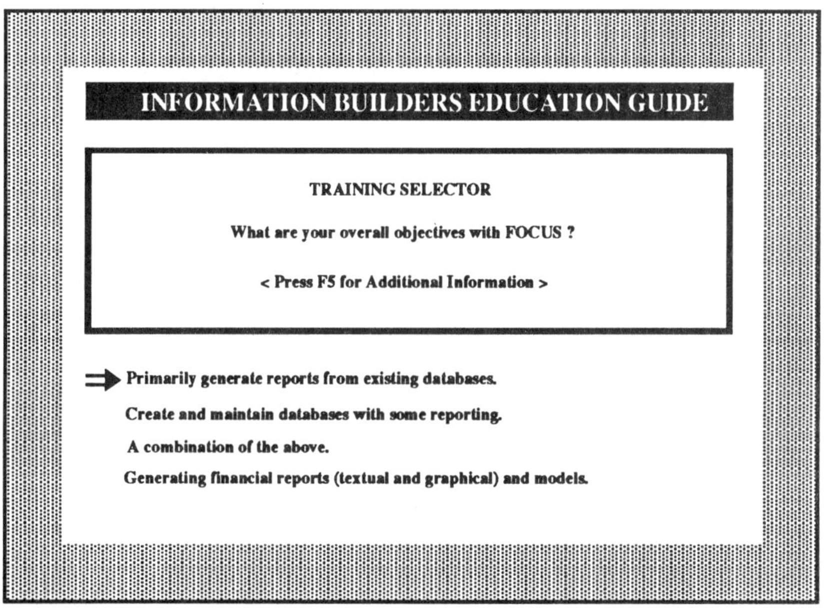

Figure 8.1: Example of EDUC screen

A database interface was added so that when the course path had been selected, the database was searched sequentially and all courses on the course path were considered for recommendation. This proved straightforward, and was accomplished using a LEVEL5 LOCATE command to match all courses on the course path. In fact, the database search and comparison is controlled by only a couple of rules:

```
RULE search for next course on path
LOCATE search name = path.name IN path
IF NOT EOF path
AND course added to list
THEN got next course in path
AND FORGET course added to list
AND LOOP
```

This rule will cause LEVEL5 to scan through the 'path' database, adding the course to the list of required courses. The FORGET command causes LEVEL5 to search again (i.e. to re-prove) the fact *course added to list*.

The LEVEL5 interface to EDUC is screen-based, showing each question as a separate screen (as shown in figure 8.1). The following exchange of questions and answers is a summary of a fairly typical session with EDUC.

```
Which option best describes your level of experience?

    1. End User
    2. DP Professional

Please reply: 1

Have you had any FOCUS training from Information Builders?

Please reply: No

Have you had any prior FOCUS experience?

Please reply: Yes

Which of the following areas have you worked in?

    1. Primarily generating reports from existing databases.
    2. Creating and maintaining databases with some reporting.
    3. A combination of the above.

Please reply: <Asked for clarification for question>

 (SIMPLE REPORTING
   You must be able to create ad hoc TABLE requests against
   existing databases and format the reports with headings,
   footings and new and defined fields.
```

```
 BASIC REPORTING
   All the above plus COMPUTEs, JOINs, HOLD Files and
   summarisation.

 ADVANCED REPORTING
   All the above plus Dialogue Manager, Match file,
   File Views, Sub-Matrix Reports.
)

Please reply: 2


PHASE 1 COMPLETE - we have now completed the information
gathering phase of this system. Next are series of questions
which ask about your objectives with FOCUS.

What are your overall objectives with FOCUS?

     1. Primarily generate reports from existing databases.
     2. Create and maintain databases with some reporting.
     3. A combination of the above.
     4. Generating financial reports (textual and graphical) and models.

Please reply: 3

What are your objectives with FOCUS reporting?

     1. Simple Menu Based Reporting.
     2. Simple Ad Hoc Reporting.
     3. Complex Reporting.

Please reply: 1

What type of systems are you going to be using FOCUS for?

     1. Small Personal Systems.
     2. Simple Departmental Systems.
     3. Complex Departmental or Company Systems.

Please reply: 2


PHASE 2 COMPLETE - we have ascertained your objectives with FOCUS. The
next phase of the system will pick up the course path that is tailored
```

```
to these objectives.

Based on the information supplied, you need to attend the following
courses:

    Course code              Course description
    -----------              ------------------

    E04        -        2 Day File Description and Maintenance

    E12        -        3 Day Application Development with FOCUS

To achieve your objective of - simple departmental systems.
```

As a final note, the EDUC system was subsequently ported to the VAX and IBM mainframe to run against a FOCUS database rather than dBase 3. The porting took about 2 hours in total, showing the portability both of LEVEL5 and of the database interface.

Chapter 9

Second case study: Medium-priced integrated toolkit

Baggy Shah and Bob Moore

9.1 WAMPAS: a WAshing Machine Purchase Advice System

This case study demonstrates how a problem can be structured for symbolic programming using the medium-priced integrated toolkit Nexpert-Object. The case study problem is to build a rule-based system to give advice on the purchase of a washing machine. This relatively simple problem is used to illustrate:

- how a problem can be analysed so that an appropriate AI solution can be chosen.
- how the solution can be structured to make use of the features of Nexpert-Object.
- how the implementation can support incremental growth and change.

Section 9.2 briefly describes the washing machine purchase problem, and section 9.3 describes the development of a solution and the approach taken for its implementation.

9.2 The case study problem

A high-street retailer requires a computer-based system for advising customers on the purchase of washing machines. The system has to support the following functions:

- Ask the customers a set of questions concerning their garment washing habits, budgetary constraints and other requirements.
- Ask the retailer about which washing machines are on special offer or the lines that need to be cleared.
- Match the customer and retailer requirements to recommend a washing machine(s) from those currently stocked.

The requirements above are typical of those stated by the users of software systems. However, there are many requirements that are not stated until initial versions of a system are delivered. The late requirements that emerged for this system are fairly typical of the sort of needs that can be overlooked:

- Password protection on the modification of knowledge.
- Explanation, what-if and re-answer facilities.
- The integration of the advice system with existing software (spreadsheets and databases) and hardware.

9.3 Features of the solution

There are three aspects of the solution that have to be developed:

1. The identification of the generic nature of the problem, irrespective of its final software manifestation.
2. The choice of appropriate AI techniques to allow the problem to be solved.
3. The design for implementation, that is, the choice of the appropriate toolkit (Nexpert) facilities to allow the chosen AI techniques to be implemented.

Each of the above aspects of the overall solution are covered in the following subsections.

9.3.1 Generic nature of the problem

As AI systems have been developed, a pattern has emerged in the choice of application areas. The popularity of some application areas can be traced to historic associations between AI and domain practitioners. There are a set of labels that are used to characterize application areas. These labels reflect, in some cases, the types of AI techniques (reasoning and representation) that have been used or the nature of the problem, or the consultation style of implemented systems. One authority [Reichgelt and van Harmelen] has identified these application areas: design, monitoring, simulation, planning, classification and diagnosis. The washing machine purchase problem is a classification task. The problem to be solved is one of finding a washing machine (a goal node in the solution space) that meets the requirements of the customer and retailer.

9.3.2 Choice of AI techniques

The choice of AI techniques depends on how the classification problem is conceptualized. For example, if the solution is seen as one of search where goals and sub-goals are generated to establish if particular washing machines meet the requirements ("does the customer want a ZANSI XYZ?") , then one approach would be to use a backward-chaining type inference mechanism. In the WAMPAS case study, the problem has been conceptualized as one of applying a set of constraints to eliminate the washing machines that do not meet the requirements, that is, the requirements of the customer and the retailer are seen as a set of constraints on the possible choices. If by applying the constraints no solution is found, then we have an over-constrained problem. Some constraints may need to be relaxed, as would happen in discussions between the customer and retailer.

9.3.3 Nexpert implementation

Figure 9.1 shows how a constraint-based classification system can be implemented for the washing machine purchase problem. From the control diagram we can see that the following modules have to be built:

Customer requirements. This module asks the customer a set of questions about the kind of factors that influence the choice of a washing machine from the customer's perspective.

Retailer requirements. This module asks the retailer a set of questions concerning machines on special offer, etc.

Mapping. This is a rule-base that applies, directly or via some further inference, the customer and retailer requirements as a set of constraints on the choice of washing machines.

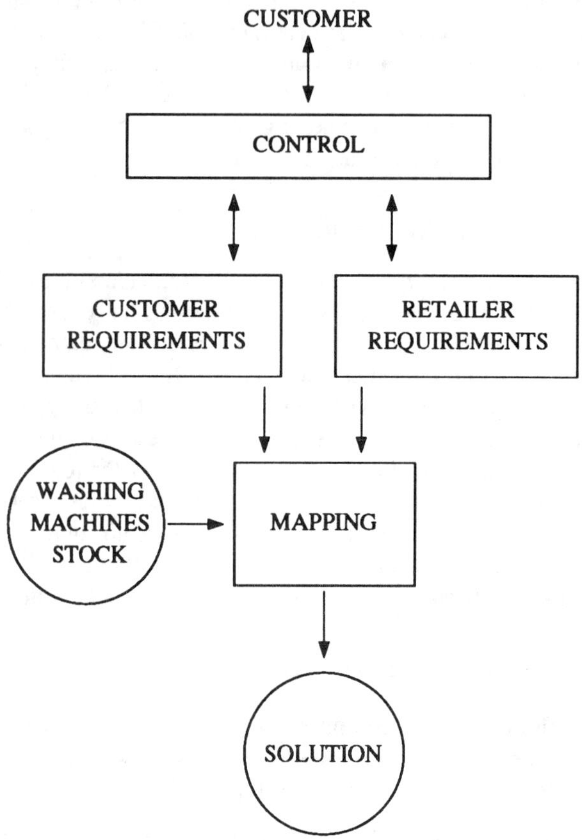

Figure 9.1: Control diagram

Control. This module controls the overall functioning of the system. It initiates an interaction and presents a solution to a customer. If there is no solution, the control module may request that the customer relax some constraints (e.g. preference for a make, or price range) or, as an extension to the above system, a rule-base could be executed to analyse the constraints to find methods for relaxing them (e.g. suggest credit and long-term loan facilities to the customer if the constraint is budgetary).

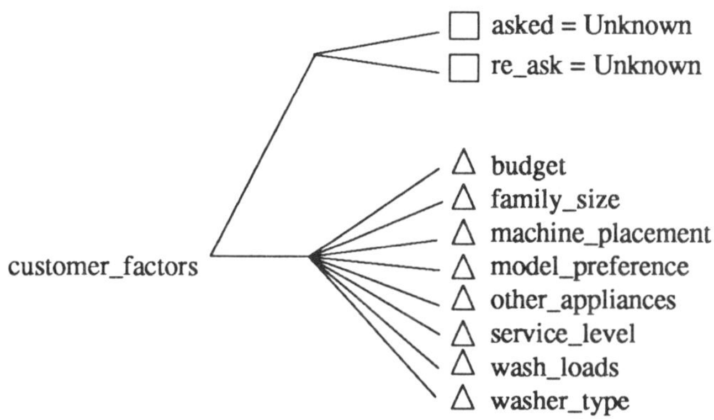

Figure 9.2: Customer requirements

The aim of a good design is to allow changes to one module without affecting other modules. For example, it should be possible to add new requirements (questions) without having to modify an existing mapping rule-base.

The following sections describe how each of these four modules was implemented using Nexpert facilities.

Customer requirements

The requirements are as follows: budget, size of family, placement of washing machine, preferences for make, make of other appliances in the household, level of after-sales service required, number of wash loads a week and the product type (washer or washer-dryer). Each requirement is implemented as an object which was an instance of a class object **customer_factors**. This is shown in figure 9.2.

Each object has three slots, two (**asked** and **re_ask**) that are inherited from the class object and one which refers to the requirement. An example of the budget object is:

```
NAME :  budget
CLASSES :
      customer_factors
PROPERTIES :
    asked = (B) Unknown
NAME :  budget.asked

    budget = (I) Unknown
NAME :  budget.budget

    re_ask = (B) Unknown
NAME :  budget.re_ask
```

with **I** referring to integer and **B** to boolean. The notation **budget.asked** means the **asked** slot of the **budget** object.

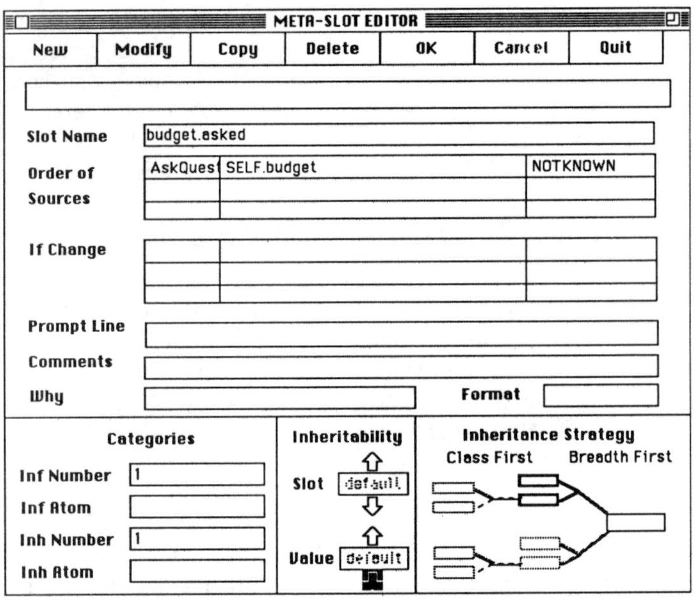

Figure 9.3: Meta-slot

The question concerning a requirement is asked by the side-effect of a rule attempting to establish a value for the **asked** slot. When the inference engine attempts to find a value for the **asked** slot, the meta-slot associated with it has a definition for the potential source of the value. An example meta-slot is shown in figure 9.3.

The **order of sources** field, of the meta-slot, states that to find a value for the **asked** slot one has to ask the value for the **budget** slot. This is stated as an operator (**Askquestion**) with the argument **self.budget**. In a meta-slot, **self** is an identifier that is bound to the name of the meta-slot's object. The meta-slot for the **budget** slot also has a description of the prompt line that should be displayed to a user when asking for a value for the slot. Once a value has been given by a user, the **if changed** demon in the **budget** meta-slot (see figure 9.4) sets the value of the **asked** slot as **true**.

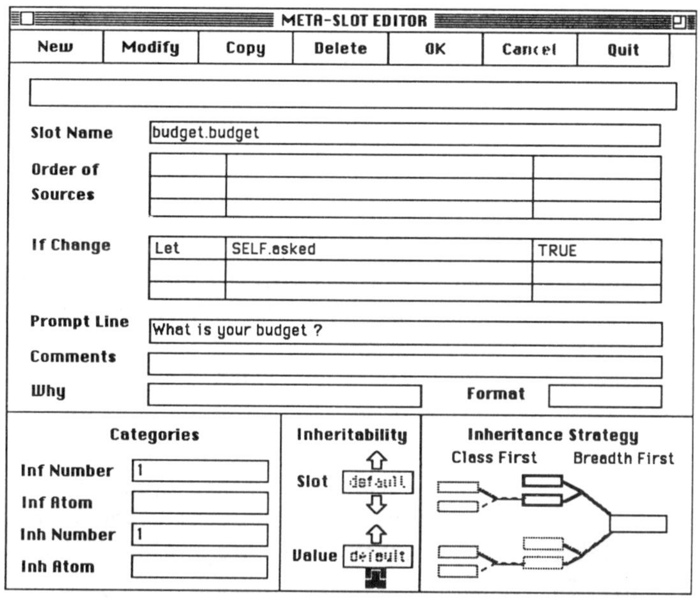

Figure 9.4: Budget meta-slot

This chain of actions is repeated for all the requirement objects. The reason the **order of sources** and the **if changed** demons are used rather then rules is that generally objects can be added and removed from the knowledge base much quicker then rules. The rule that causes the search for values for all the asked slots for all objects is:

```
CONDITIONS :
    Yes          <|customer_factors|>.asked
HYPOTHESIS :     next_question
ACTIONS :
```

```
    Reset        <|customer_factors|>.asked
        INFERENCE CATEGORY :    1

NAME :  ask_all_questions_rule
        Why : You are being asked a question to establish
              your requirements for a washing machine
```

In the rule above, the condition **Yes <|customer_factors|>.asked** means make a list of all the objects whose slot value for **asked** is true. It is the search process that triggers the **order of sources** demon (see figure 9.3). The **Yes** operator is applied to check slot values and hypotheses.

Retailer requirements

The set of requirements for the retailer are: high profit lines and special offers. The method of establishing the values for these requirements will use the same approach as that for the customer requirements.

Mapping rules and washing machines

The aim of the mapping rules is first to use the answers given by the customer to eliminate those washing machines that do not match the requirements, then the rules apply the retailer requirements to those remaining. An example of a rule that eliminates washing machines that are not of the type required (that is, either a washer or washer-dryer) is:

```
CONDITIONS :
    Name         washer_type.washer_type type
    NotEqual     <|washing_machines|>.type type
HYPOTHESIS :     customer_factors_eval
ACTIONS :
    Let          <|washing_machines|>.recommended FALSE
        INFERENCE CATEGORY :    1

NAME :  eliminate_wrong_type_machines
```

This rule states that all washing machines not of the type required are not recommendable. The first condition of the rule **Name washer_type.washer_type type** means let **type** (a local variable in the rule defined by the **Name** operator) have the value of the slot **washer_type** of the object **washer_type**. The second condition **Notequal <|washing_machines|>.type type** means let **<|washing_machines|>** be a list of washing machines that are not of the type **type**. The action part of the rule sets the slot **recommended** for each washing machine in the list **<|washing_machines|>** to **false** (not recommendable machines).

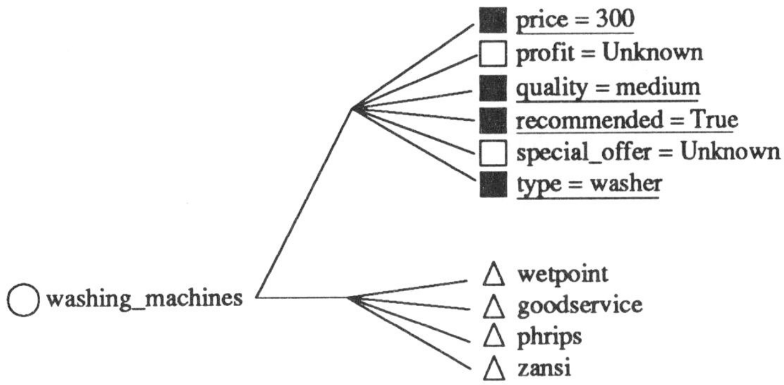

Figure 9.5: Washing machines

The mythical washing machines of which the system has knowledge are shown in figure 9.5. The object/frame representation in Nexpert is used, in this example, both for structuring the domain and as a working memory. For a practical system, this information would probably be retrieved from a database during an enquiry rather than being *hard coded* into the knowledge base.

Control

As explained earlier, the complexity of the control depends on the application. For the system described here, a simple set of rules are implemented to control such things as allowing the customer to re-answer questions. Control rules are best implemented in Nexpert in a backward-chaining manner. That is, the top level control goal (hypothesis **top_goal**) has a set of sub-goals, such as **ask customer all the questions** (hypothesis **next_question**) and **apply mapping rules** (hypothesis **customer_factors_eval**); these sub-goals are in the condition part of a top-level rule. An example of such a rule is:

```
CONDITIONS :
    Yes          next_question
    Yes          customer_factors_eval
HYPOTHESIS :     top_goal
        INFERENCE CATEGORY :    1

NAME :  top_level_rule
```

The control rule states that in order to achieve the top-level goal, you should ask the customer a set of questions and then evaluate the requirements (apply the mapping rules). The advantage of organizing the control in this manner is that it is possible to insert other sub-goals (e.g. to display diagrams) or rearrange the order of the satisfaction of sub-goals and thus the nature of the interaction with the user.

The washing machine example was intended to demonstrate how a problem can be defined with respect to well-understood and practised AI techniques with implementation in Nexpert. A partial implementation of the software described above took a few hours. This speed is a function of the approach taken and toolkit used, and gives some indication of how easily Nexpert can be applied to this kind of problem.

Chapter 10

The third case study: Loosely coupled toolkit

Ryllan Kraft

This case study describes a system that was implemented using a loosely coupled toolkit. The toolkit used was POPLOG, described in detail in section 6.4.1. The application that is described involves the implementation of a specialized knowledge representation language, and so illustrates excellently the advantages of this type of toolkit.

10.1 The case study problem

10.1.1 RESCU

In 1984, as part of the UK Government's Alvey Initiative [Wheldon 87], the RESCU KBS Awareness Collaborative Club in the area of process control engineering was formed on the initiative of SPL International, later Systems Designers.

The aims of the RESCU (Real-Time Expert System Club of Users) club were to seek to demonstrate the validity and effectiveness of expert systems in real-time industrial applications, and to promote awareness of the technology involved amongst the club members. The members were 23 industrial companies and 3 academic institutions.

The club membership selected a chairman, and a steering committee was formed. The business of the club was run by regular full club meetings. Systems

Designers (SD), as the prime contractor to the club, was charged with fulfilling the requirements of the club.

The club decided to achieve its objectives by contracting SD to develop a demonstration expert system application (despite the fact that it was not an ALVEY large demonstrator project). The club established a number of criteria to evaluate proposed applications, covering:

- the characteristics of the application;
- the applicability of the technology elsewhere;
- the feasibility of the application;
- the demonstrability of the results;
- development issues.

The development of the application would test whether expert systems technology could be applied in this type of system.

The awareness objective would be fulfilled by extensive reports from the contractor during all stages of the development process, and the system would then be shown to club members, and seminars, seminar packs, and education sessions would be available to the club.

10.1.2 The problem

The criteria established by the club for judging proposed applications included:

- the plant to be used for the application must be operating successfully;
- there must be experts available;
- the application should be an advisory system;
- it should be implemented on a widely used or reasonably priced computer;
- the application should be representative of a problem of general interest to club members, preferably fault diagnosis, change of plant state, or quality control;
- the plant must have a computer-based control or monitoring system;
- there must be a well-defined, quantifiable target against which the system may be assessed;
- the plant and site must be open to visitors;

- reasonable access to experts must be available throughout the project.

Two sites were proposed by club members as available for the demonstrator, a chemical plant and a power house, and a study was made of the sites and possible applications. The study concluded that the site should be the chemical plant, and that the application should be quality control. The chemical plant was an ICI batch plant for the manufacture of general-purpose liquid detergents at ICI's Wilton site in the north of England. The basic structure of the plant is as shown in figure 10.1.

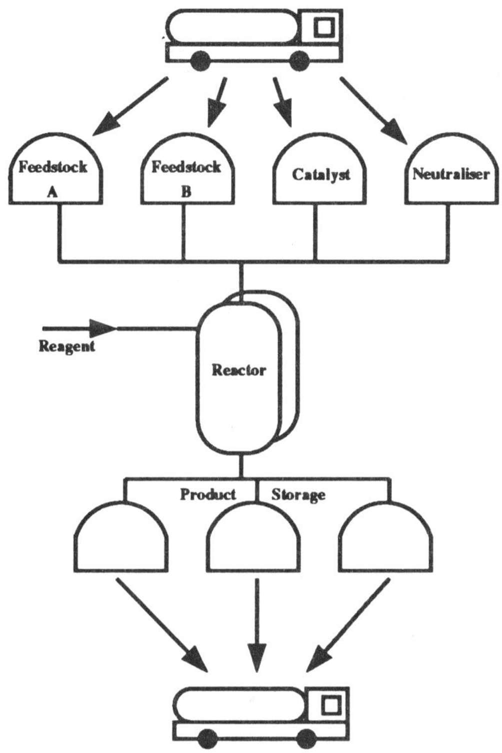

Figure 10.1: Plant schematic

It is a modern plant, which is frequently shown to visitors by ICI. The plant has two batch reactors, and is controlled by a Foxborough Fox 1/A process sequence control computer. For a given product a set amount of feedstock is charged into the reactor. The reaction conditions are then established and reagent is charged until either a set amount has been added or a set density, continuously monitored by the Fox computer, has been reached. There is then a cookdown phase in which the reaction is taken to completion. At this point there is the potential for more reagent to be added (an *adjustment*). The batch is then pumped out to a storage tank.

The plant operators have, for the most part, been working at the plant since it was commissioned and these are the experts in getting the best from the plant. Their task is to set the *recipe* on the Fox to make products at the required quality and to initiate and monitor the process sequence. When a batch has been produced, they test the quality of the batch and can take a sample for laboratory analysis. If they judge it necessary, they make an adjustment or take other remedial action. A cost penalty is incurred if the desired product quality is exceeded, or if insufficient reagent has been reacted and an adjustment has to be made.

The quality control task for the expert system was to help the operator by making recommendations to assist his decisions. To do this it must:

- monitor the plant and chemical process, and form judgements on the state of the plant, its instrumentation, and the raw materials affecting product quality;
- identify the decision points in the process and advise on the initial recipe, whether to modify a recipe (after charging feedstock), whether an addition (of extra reagent) should be done, what the estimated batch quality is, and whether an analysis of the batch should be done;
- provide justifications for its recommendations.

In addition, the application had to provide facilities to demonstrate the expert system techniques to the club members.

10.1.3 Overview of development

The development project for the demonstrator had the following major stages:

- the design of the Knowledge Representation Language (KRL) used for the RESCU system;
- the development of the system software — the *development system* and the *run-time system*;
- the knowledge acquisition, the design and refinement of the application.

A fundamental design choice was whether to use an existing expert system environment or shell, or to develop one specifically for this class of application. Prior to the development phase, the requirements on a knowledge representation language were established, and the available commercial systems reviewed. No such system met the requirements and it was decided to develop a RESCU KRL.

The KRL was developed based on the contractor's experience with other systems (SAGE, MXA), and as the results of studies of the plant and application. It was during this stage that some preliminary knowledge acquisition was done, and the tasks and basic architecture for the application knowledge base determined. A naïve knowledge base was developed on a similar style of application to investigate the power and expressiveness of the KRL.

The system software *development system* was designed to provide the environment for developing and refining a knowledge base in RESCU KRL. The system software *run-time system* was designed to run a knowledge base on the RESCU computer system, which was linked to the chemical plant. It was essential that the part concerned with running the knowledge base should be as independent of the precise nature of the application as possible, to permit changes to be made in the knowledge base without any changes in the system software.

The final stage was a continuous prototype and refinement cycle involving the detailed knowledge acquisition and development of the knowledge base. There were a number of prototype versions of the knowledge base which were released and installed on the running system incorporating specific refinements.

10.1.4 Features of KRL

The RESCU KRL is based on the blackboard model of KBS architecture (fully explored in [Engelmore and Morgan 88]). The blackboard architecture is characterized by having a number of different knowledge-based system activities, which can operate on shared data (the blackboard), and which cooperate to perform the desired tasks.

The RESCU KRL allows the explicit representation of two programming styles (see [Leitch and Kraft 88]): the procedural (or imperative) style represented by active knowledge sources, and the declarative style represented by passive knowledge sources.

The initiation of a knowledge-based activity is performed by invoking an active knowledge source, which then executes the actions specified in it in the given sequence. These actions will generally require values to be inferred, and the system will then automatically draw on the declarative knowledge to try to obtain these values.

The knowledge representation is entirely rule-based. This was a consciously conservative decision to adopt established KBS technology rather than the then still-emerging techniques of frame-based representation, constraints or predicate logic.

The basic representation in an active knowledge source is an active-rule with a component of the form:

```
ON <condition> DO <action>;
```

Possible actions include:

- invoking or chaining to another active knowledge source;
- explicitly using one of the inference mechanisms, for instance a form of forward chaining;
- input and output, including requesting data from the plant, reading plant data or messages from the operator, and outputting reports to the operator;
- asserting a value for an entity on the blackboard. This is equivalent to making a hypothesis, or retracting a previous assertion.

The basic form of representation in a passive knowledge source, is a rule with a component:

```
IF <antecedent> THEN <conclusion>;
```

Conclusions are used to declare how the system may infer a value for an entity. These may be drawn upon when an active knowledge source initiates one of the inference mechanisms. The two basic forms of inference, goal-driven (backward chaining) and data-driven (forward chaining) use the same form of rules. There are additional inference mechanisms that do automatic consistency checking. The default form of inference is goal-driven.

A special feature of the declarative representation is the ability to explicitly represent algebraic relationships as a constraint. For instance, the constraint:

$mass\_feedstock = density\_feedstock * volume\_feedstock$

would be represented as a conclusion (possibly contingent on some condition) of the form:

```
REVERSIBLE
mass_feedstock IS
        density_feedstock * volume_feedstock;
```

The system would automatically translate this into the three conclusions (all with the same condition if any):

```
mass_feedstock IS
        density_feedstock * volume_feedstock;
density_feedstock IS
        mass_feedstock / volume_feedstock;
volume_feedstock IS
        mass_feedstock / density_feedstock;
```

The system incorporates an explicit representation of time and can handle time-dependent situations. Blocks of data can be requested and received from the plant and held as scans, and the data, and any time-dependent entity inferred from this data, is qualified by a scan-number with an associated timestamp (its time-relevance). An example of a conclusion using time-dependent reasoning to infer a value at one scan based on data obtained from a previous scan is:

```
Net_vol_into_Tank AT Scan IS
               Vol_in AT (Scan - 1)
               - Calc_Vol_out(tank_level AT Scan);
```

The KRL permits an active knowledge source to assert values for entities on the blackboard. Inferences may be made in which the ends of an inference chain (actually the terminating leaves of the inference tree) may be these asserted values rather than values read from outside (i.e. measured values received from the plant). Using this facility, a knowledge base can employ an hypothesis and test reasoning strategy, in which hypotheses are represented by asserting one or more values. Inferences can be made, founded on the assertions, and the knowledge base can test to see if the conclusions it can draw based on the hypotheses are all consistent. If not, it may retract the invalid assertions and try alternatives. The system incorporates a truth maintenance system, so that all inferences made that depend on a value belonging to some assertion are linked to that value. If the assertion is retracted, the values that were set in the assertion, together with all that were inferred from any of them, are cleared from the blackboard.

The RESCU KRL also maintains a "degree of confidence" or likelihood associated with every value on the blackboard. When a value is inferred its likelihood is also determined from the likelihoods of the entities needed for the inference (unless explicitly specified in the knowledge base).

A special feature of the RESCU KRL, due to the nature of the implementation, is the ability to embed blocks of POP-11 code in actions as well as interfacing external functions into the KRL. This feature allows algorithmic knowledge to be represented, and also proved an invaluable debugging and prototyping facility.

A fundamental aim in developing the KRL was to achieve an expressive, easily understood language, appropriate to the class of applications. This approach means that the knowledge base source code can easily be read and understood by plant experts which aids the development and validation of the knowledge base.

10.1.5 Development system

The RESCU development system consists of two basic facilities which run on the same VAX as for the run-time system (see section 10.1.6). The two facilities are the Translator, and the Statistics Analysis. Figure 10.2 shows these facilities.

A knowledge base is formed from a set of modules, which are text files containing the source code of the knowledge base in KRL. These files must be prepared (i.e. created and edited), the syntax checked, each module compiled into a KRL intermediate stage file, and a knowledge base (KB) executable file produced by linking together the intermediate stage files from a number of modules. It is the KB file which forms the knowledge base which is later operated on by the inference engine of RESCU run-time system.

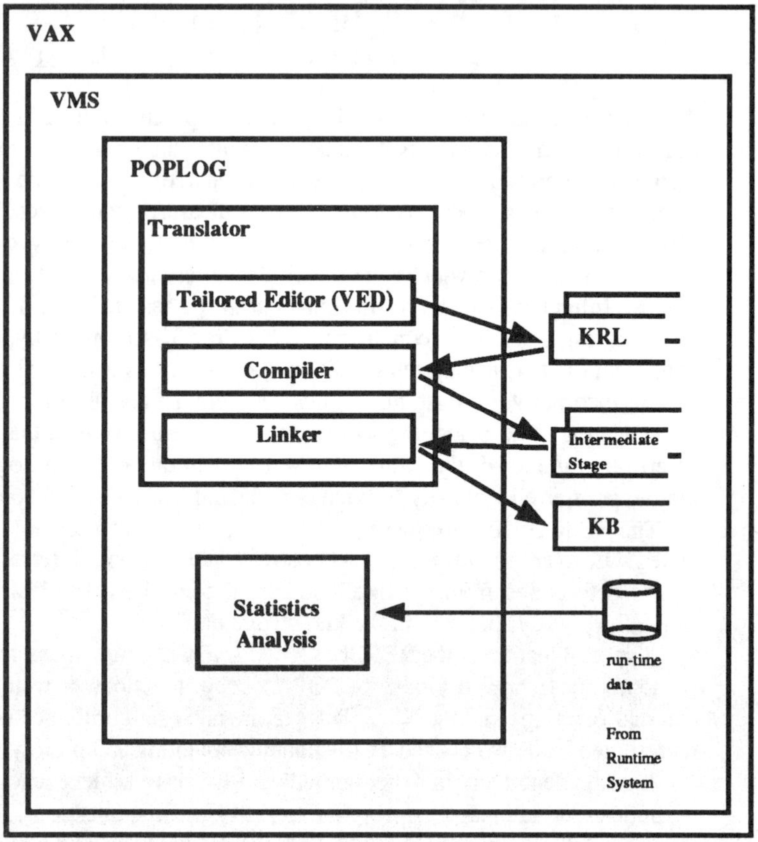

Figure 10.2: Development system

The Translator provides the facilities mentioned above and makes full use of the facilities of POPLOG (e.g. by customizing the full screen editor — VED) to help the developer to incrementally build up the knowledge base.

Moreover the Translator's compiler and linker can do a certain amount of checking (e.g. type checking, referencing things not explicitly declared in scope).

The Translator converts the KRL into an internal representation which is loaded into the inference engine, and runs faster there than would a directly interpretable representation. The Translator allows for separate compilation of modules to help speed up knowledge base development (since changes are generally restricted to one or two modules at any one time).

The Statistics Analysis facility is used in connection with raw statistics data, which has been gathered during the running of the system (when instigated by the appropriate command). This data is analysed independently (off-line) from the run-time system. There are facilities to present the behaviour of the system as it tracks through the active parts of the knowledge base, or to see how and when it is making inferences. These real-time events are displayed in the form of gantt charts.

10.1.6 Run-time system

The RESCU application ran on a DEC VAX 11/730 minicomputer and, in addition to two VT102 terminals for development work, it was equipped with a Gresham-Lion colour graphics terminal and controller which provided the operators' interface to the system. The RESCU system communicated via an RS232 link to the Foxborough Fox 1/A process control computer.

The software infrastructure, that is software not developed by the RESCU team but on which the system was built, consisted of:

- VMS from DEC — the operating system used on RESCU's VAX 11/730;
- POPLOG from SD (and Sussex University) — the artificial intelligence (AI) development environment (which includes the AI language POP-11 in which the RESCU system software is written);
- Gresham-Lion kit — the graphics controller driver and library routines to use the graphics terminal.

In addition, ICI provided software to run on the Fox process control computer to handle communications with the RESCU system and provide the required information.

The RESCU run-time system consists of a number of VMS processes which run on the VAX. The KBS process contains the AI component in the RESCU run-time system. There are four other conventional processes, COMMS, LOGS, OPER, and MON, which, with other system software, form the run-time system conventional component. Figure 10.3 shows the processes in the run-time system.

The KBS process is the part of the RESCU run-time system which contains the knowledge base in the internal representation produced by the Translator (see the next section). The system software component contains the inference engine to execute the knowledge base. The system software component of the KBS process contains a mechanism for tracking through the active parts of the knowledge base when a KBS activity is invoked, and carrying out the actions described there when the conditions specified for them are satisfied. It has the task of performing the different inference mechanisms, maintaining the current set of values and likelihoods (together with their dependencies for truth maintenance) and assertions.

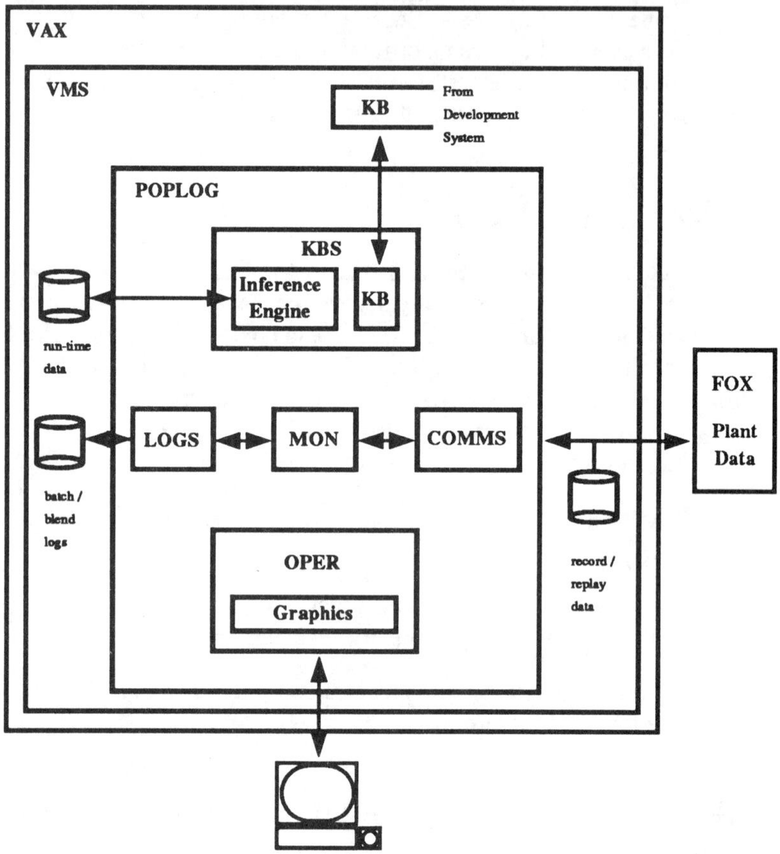

Figure 10.3: Run-time System

It also provides facilities to aid debugging and refining the knowledge base, including facilities for explaining how items were inferred (or otherwise got their values); for tracing the flow through the active parts of the knowledge base; and for gathering statistics on the behaviour of the running system in terms of the knowledge base which may be analysed independently from the run-time system.

The KBS process treats each KBS activity (i.e. a sequence of actions for a given task) as something which, once started, must go through to completion. This commonly used approach avoids the problem of developing inconsistencies in the data on the blackboard, without requiring a full transaction maintenance system for concurrent KBS activities.

The external communications (COMMS) process is responsible for communications with the Fox 1/A process control computer. It receives a command to request information from the Fox (i.e. scan data readings, or recipe data) and handles the protocol with the Fox to get hold of the data which is then transmitted to the process that requested it. This process also contains the facility for recording raw Fox data which can later be replayed via this process. This process has the highest (VMS) priority in the run-time system to ensure data is transferred as rapidly as possible.

The batch and blend logging (LOGS) process is used to store and retrieve significant information about a batch or a blend.

The operator (OPER) process is the interface between the operator and the system, primarily the KBS process. It employs the graphics software to present information on the graphics terminal, and the operator can use the tracker-ball associated with the terminal as well as the key board to provide input to the system. The operator process embodies a lot of knowledge about the plant, process, and knowledge base. The process is normally in tracker-ball mode waiting for the operator to select some option from the menu, and if necessary supplement it by typing in information needed for the particular function (e.g. when he requests a recipe recommendation he must say what product it is for). If he selects an option this process responds, which may involve sending a command to another run-time process. When a message is received from another process the tracker-ball is interrupted (if necessary), and the message handled appropriately (i.e. text messages printed, reports printed and stored for later recall, alerted graphics objects made to flash, etc.).

The graphics software, which is incorporated in the OPER process, handles the Gresham-Lion graphics terminal and provides facilities for the operator process. The display consists of a window for a *mimic* diagram which shows one of a number of schematic diagrams of the plant, a menu option window which displays the options available to the operator, and a third window for text (which is opened up from the bottom of the screen when required). When the operator process is in tracker-ball mode a cursor is displayed. The operator may move this to a menu box to select that option, to a control point on the current mimic diagram to change to a neighbouring one, or to any object on the diagram to get information about that object from the graphics database.

The monitor (MON) process acts as a clearing house for messages. It receives messages from all the other run-time processes and forwards them to the appropriate destination process if it can, otherwise it holds on to it until the other process is ready to receive it. It also takes care of interrupting the operator interface when a message is to be forwarded to it and that process is waiting in tracker-ball mode for input from the operator. This process has a higher (VMS) priority than the other processes in the run-time system, except for the COMMS process.

The internal communications software, incorporated in all the run-time processes, provides for the communication between the competing asynchronous processes running in the VMS environment. The communications code uses the VMS mailbox facility and uses VMS common event flags for synchronization.

10.1.7 Knowledge acquisition

The knowledge acquisition for the application was carried out in two main stages.

The first stage, the preliminary knowledge acquisition, followed the framing of the requirements for the RESCU KRL. It consisted of a number of visits to the site designed to familiarize the team with the plant and the process and come to a fuller understanding of the task for the expert system. It was also intended to see if the KRL was reasonable and powerful enough for the application, and a trial model for the knowledge base was developed to test this. Further visits were used to established the basics of the operators task, to interview a number of specialists in addition to the operators, to observe the operators on the job in the control room, and to gather all the necessary documents.

At the end of that stage the task for the expert system was refined and the limits on the prototype system specified, and the appropriate knowledge acquired was summarized.

The next stage in the knowledge acquisition process, which began after the computer was installed on site and the bulk of the system software was developed, took place during the construction of the various versions of the expert system.

During this phase the fact that the team were on site made it easy to question whichever operator was on duty whenever an ambiguity or dilemma appeared during the coding or testing of the knowledge base, or to get information directly from the Fox computer.

The first prototype version was installed and set running on the plant as soon as possible and development continued to enhance it for the next version. This allowed the operators to gain experience of using the system in earnest, and to get feedback in particular about the accuracy of the knowledge base and their confidence in the system to highlight where the prototype was failing (as well as the acceptability of the human–computer interface). When a new version of the knowledge base, containing refinements on the previous one, was ready it was installed to gain experience and feedback to help refine that one.

It was during this period that ICI made a plant supervisor and former operator responsible for liaison with the knowledge engineering team.

The types of knowledge that were looked for, having determined the basic concepts involved in the task, were mainly procedural and declarative. The procedural knowledge is concerned with what to do in a particular situation, how it is assessed and dealt with and what sequences of actions must be taken, and what decisions made. This includes:

- recognizing particular situations in the course of the process, and the actions to take when these occur;
- strategies for recipe recommendation;
- strategies for assessing the quality of the product, and combining different methods;
- strategies for assessing the results of analyses so that the system can improve its performance.

The declarative knowledge consists of the passive rules which the system may use as and when required, which express relationships between concepts, or define facts valid under certain conditions. These include:

- straightforward facts about the chemicals (such as the densities);
- a model of the chemistry of the reaction with regard to determining the quality of the desired product;
- models of the state of the plant and of the quality of the raw materials insofar as these effect product quality;

There is also some straightforward algorithmic knowledge in the system including the sorting of more likely hypotheses, and interpolating tables of calibration data.

The main source of knowledge was from people, in particular the plant operators. Most have been on the plant since it started, and are extremely knowledgeable about it and confident of their expertise. They provided knowledge about the how the plant operated, what decisions were made and how they were made. Another important source of knowledge was the plant supervisor. Also the plant manager provided a lot of knowledge on how and why the plant was run, and the causes of changes in batch quality.

Other people consulted were the process engineer who was involved in the plant design; the present project instrumentation and electrical manager who was involved in the design and commissioning of the plant; the traffic coordinator, who is also a former control operator; a specialist in the chemistry involved; and the person responsible for computing on the plant and wrote the software for the Fox 1/A for the project.

Other information came from studying and analysing the various plant documentation. This included the Process Engineering Data Book (which was particularly useful for explaining the chemistry of the process in the early phases of knowledge acquisition), the batch processing record sheets (as recorded by the operators as they produce the batches); the product manufacturing process sheets (that is the specifications for each product); the plant fault log; and the Fox computer process control data (e.g. the process sequence descriptions, flow charts, etc.).

The plant itself provided information, in particular when some value was required. This information could be obtained by consulting the Fox data recorded in the Fox computer directly, or by using the backup control mechanism which can display trends and show how values having changed with time. Also the raw data received from the Fox could be recorded by the RESCU system and analysed.

One major technique for knowledge acquisition that was used was structured interviewing, in which a person is asked questions about some specific topics. This was most applicable in the early days for finding out about such things as the chemical reaction, what can and cannot be assumed, and reliability of measurements. This was also useful later for refining and validating existing knowledge represented in KRL or an intermediate representation, when the expert would read and have this explained to him and his comments immediately registered.

Another major technique of knowledge acquisition was observation of the operators at work coupled with interviewing them. This was the main source of experiential knowledge, such as strategies for recipe recommendation, or the diagnosis of problems with the parameters of the plant or raw materials which effect the product quality. Even an ordinary situation on plant, when being described and explained, often elicited examples of special cases. In both this technique and the structured interview the two members of the knowledge engineering team were present. This double act proved very useful since it kept the interview going, giving one person a chance to think and take notes on what has been said while the other continues talking to the expert. The experts were not put off by having to deal with two people. This was especially good in that it allowed the team to discuss what was said afterwards and to compare understandings.

These techniques were aimed at getting the team taught the basics of task, that is so they should learn enough to be able to reason about it for themselves. This is possible since the task is not too hard, demanding no great academic background, and much of the reasoning processes involved are of the common sense variety.

In the early phases of knowledge acquisition most of the interviews were recorded on an ordinary cassette player. It was hoped that to have transcripts prepared to allow the actual words spoken in the interviews to be analysed. However, there were problems with this due to the noisy work environment in the plant building, and especially in the control room, so only a small proportion was actually transcribed. This could have been rectified by interviewing elsewhere in an office, or by using better recording equipment. The tapes were used in some cases by listening to them, as a supplement to the interview notes.

Another knowledge acquisition technique is the analysis of the failures of the expert system as it is in the process of development, done in conjunction with the operators (or anyone else who can help). This has been useful in refining and elaborating, in particular, the experiential knowledge.

Also raw data logged from the plant was useful in clarifying what data was being received, and for providing a number of past runs for off-line testing and for calibration purposes. Examination of this data exposed areas for further questioning, and in one case revealed a badly working control loop on the plant.

Note, however, it was not within the scope of the RESCU project to attempt to induce rules from data, moreover it was considered likely that, since the knowledge is highly structured, the rules to be induced would be too complex for the usual kind of induction algorithm.

It was not considered that other techniques for knowledge structuring (such as repertory grid analysis) or high level descriptions (such as systemic grammar networks) would be applicable for knowledge acquisition for the RESCU project and there was very little difficulty in eliciting the concepts involved from the experts by interviews and observation.

With all the techniques, and especially the interview/observation types, it is important to consolidate the knowledge that has been acquired (at least in note form) and if possible to refer it back to an authoritative expert to be reviewed.

There are a few facilities in the system to test the knowledge base for consistency and completeness and help a developer validate it. These include run-time commands to display all the rules for deriving a particular entity, and show how values have been obtained, and for tracing the different features in the knowledge base.

The development techniques employed to ensure quality were to use small well-structured modules, such that no individual knowledge source becomes so large that it is hard to understand.

Wherever possible, the plant supervisor reviewed the KRL for changed modules before a new version of the knowledge base was installed.

10.1.8 Knowledge base

The knowledge base contains models of the plant and of the chemicals involved which together with a set of hypotheses relating to these models, termed the system parameters, represent the system's understanding of the current state of the plant and raw materials used in the process. These are used to prepare reports to the operator including recipe recommendations and batch quality assessments.

When the system has enough information it assesses whether any of the system parameters should be changed, and if so modifies them accordingly. The new set

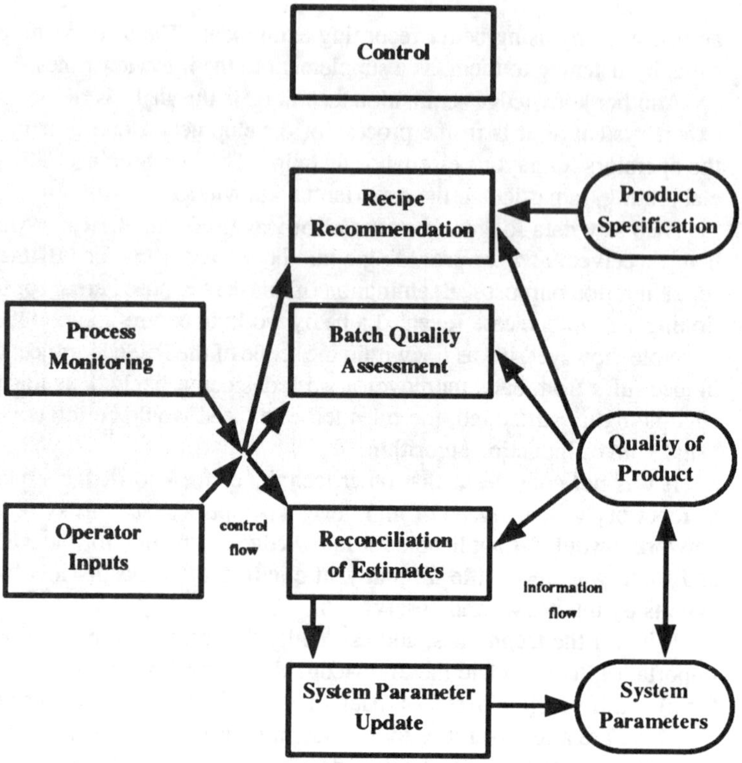

Figure 10.4: Structure of knowledge base

of system parameters will be used for subsequent reports. This constitutes the adaptive learning of the system.

Figure 10.4 shows the structure of the knowledge base, and indicates the main control and information flows. There are the following types of knowledge in the RESCU knowledge base:

Control. This comprises such features as scheduling knowledge base activities, handling communications with the Fox process control computer, and various other utility functions.

Passive knowledge. This is used when needed by the system, and consists of:

- the specification of products, i.e. rules defining the attributes required for each product known to the system;

- estimating of the quality of the product, i.e. rules which relate the quality of a batch to analysis results, the quantities of materials used, and the density;
- models of the plant and chemicals, with states determines by a set of hypotheses, the system parameters.

Active knowledge. This governs the behaviour of the system in response (primarily) to changes on the plant. Generally, the active facilities give information to the operator. They consists of:

- Process monitoring and other monitoring;
- Operator input handling;
- Recipe recommendation;
- Batch quality assessment;
- Reconciliation of estimates;
- Update of system parameters.

The monitoring facilities keep a watch on the processes in the reactors, and the feedstock and product storage tanks, maintaining information about them and scheduling any knowledge base activities that may be required.

The operator (or developer) may communicate with the RESCU system to give it specific information that it would not otherwise have, or to ask for specific information from the system. The system responds to these inputs in a similar way to the monitoring facilities. Examples of these inputs are:

- directly entered analysis results;
- special information, such as that a previously inaccurate meter as been adjusted;
- and requests for reports, e.g. recipe requests, explanations and justifications, and status reports.

The recipe recommendation facility provides spontaneous or requested recommendations to the operator as to how to set the recipe in the Fox to produce the desired product.

The batch quality assessment facility generates reports on the quality of a batch to the operator and advises on any action that may be required to change its quality.

The reconciliation of estimates facility tries to reconcile the various estimates of the batch quality to decide what it can rely on (e.g. whether to trust the analysis result), and whether to update any system parameters.

The update of system parameters facility is used to determine which system parameters need to be changed and by how much, that is to understand the reason for any discrepancy in different quality estimates, to allow adaptive learning in the system.

The states of the plant and chemicals are represented as a current set of hypotheses, the system parameters, each of which has a degree of confidence associated with it (see [Bailey, Kraft and Leitch 87]). The active functions, other than the update of system parameters facility, operate on the basis of the values and degrees of confidence for the hypotheses for recipe recommendation and quality estimates.

Various events detected on the plant and process (such as a new supply of feedstock) or in the operation of the system (such as no quality discrepancy being detected), cause changes in the degrees of confidence associated with values for the parameters. On detection of a significant discrepancy between the various quality estimates by the reconciliation process, the update system parameter process generates plausible hypotheses of the cause of the discrepancy. For each of these, it changes system parameter values to resolve the discrepancy, and tests them against various specific cross-checks to revise the degree of confidence associated with them. It can then update the system state accordingly by selecting resolution of the most likely cause.

10.1.9 Growth of knowledge base

The knowledge base was developed in a number of versions, each of which was able to run on the plant. This method of development is a hybrid between the conventional development life-cycle, in which a system is fully designed and then implemented according to the design, and the prototype and refine life-cycle, in which a tentative design is prototyped and this system is refined during the development.

The initial expert system framework was built in order to support this style of incremental construction. The different versions were installed on the plant and run for sustained periods, so that problems with it would have time to emerge.

The fact that a version could be readily refined, typical of most expert systems development, permitted the developers to respond to the problems in one version, in addition to developing the enhanced features for the next version. While the development team was on site, the new versions were developed on the same machine that was running the latest version.

Table 10.1 lists the different versions of the RESCU system, with the dates that they were installed and set running, and with a measure of the size of the knowledge base (the number of internal data structures produced by the Translator for the knowledge base). Figure 10.5 shows this information graphically.

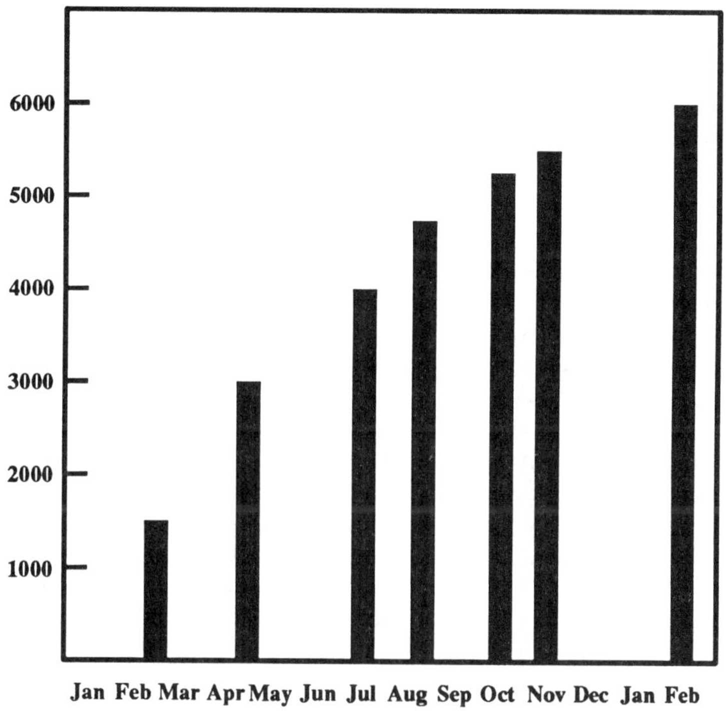

Figure 10.5: Graph of knowledge base growth

Version	Installation	Size
Demonstration version	26th February 1986	1451
Handover version	2nd May 1986	3174
Extended handover	11th July 1986	4033
Enhanced extended handover	22nd August 1986	4752
Preliminary full version	24th October 1986	5275
Full version	18th November 1986	5658
Improved full version	11th February 1987	5966

Table 10.1: Details of knowledge base growth

10.1.10 Validation

The RESCU project was subject to an unusually large number of appraisals of various kinds.

The contractor carried out validation of the software, both the system software and knowledge base. The knowledge base was reviewed in conjunction with the plant supervisor to seek to achieve correctness.

ICI carried out an internal evaluation of the expert system (primarily on the enhanced extended handover version), from the viewpoint of the benefits to themselves. This included a statistical analysis of the performance of the plant with respect to quality when the system's advice was followed, compared to when the plant operators rejected it. The application logged certain information specially to facilitate this analysis. On the whole the evaluation found much the same dispersion in quality for the system as for the plant operators. The appraisal highlighted areas in which the application could be improved.

A review of the reactions of all the main participants in the RESCU project was commissioned by the club from Patricia Rees of the Manchester Business School. This involved an evaluation of the expert system by the operators, an evaluation of the RESCU club by the members, and an evaluation by the contractor of working for the club. Most operators considered the expert system had little to offer them, however, the plant supervisor considered that the system had almost reached full development and was disappointed that no further development would take place. The review found drawbacks with the way the club (because of its nature) had to run. The long gaps between club meetings and the widely differing types of people led to changes in emphasis, though the steering committee generally guided the membership and ensured continuity in direction. It advocated the use of more frequent meetings of involved members in sub-committees. On the whole the club membership found their awareness in expert systems had been raised by the club, and that expert systems technology could be applied in these types of applications. They considered the club experience to be good value for money. The people on the contractors team, who had had most involvement with the club, expressed the view that most problems arose from the disparate nature of the club. Each member has a different need and aspiration, which is manifested to the contractor as an inconsistent set of requirements, liable to change at the next club meeting to a new inconsistent set. The contractors felt the original objectives of the club had been more than met, but that some of the club members had not appreciated this, as their expectation had changed as the project progressed.

The club also commissioned a retrospective review on the technology from Roy Leitch of Heriot-Watt University (see [Leitch and Dulieu 88]). In addition to reviewing the expert systems approach in process control and analysing the RESCU technology, this review described a number of other prototype expert systems in related areas. The review expressed the view that the technology transfer aspect of the club had been extremely successful, and that RESCU, which had pioneered the development of collaborative clubs in the UK, had been one of the most successful of the ALVEY community clubs, and advocated a continuance or successor club. On the technical level, it made recommendations for extending the application, in particular with regard to the control of the dynamics of the adaptive loop.

In addition to those formal appraisals, the expert system was the subject of a number of club visits, and both formal and informal demonstrations of the system. Furthermore, formal education sessions were organized to explain the application and the underlying knowledge base and system software.

In response to a special requirement of the club (towards the end of the project), the system software was modified to form a generally runnable version, and made available to club members.

10.2 Experience with POPLOG on RESCU

10.2.1 The choice of POPLOG

The club required that development should be based on a readily available package with a large well supported user base. Given the decision that the RESCU project should implement its own KRL and system software (as there were no suitable shells), this boiled down to a decision as to which AI toolkit would be most appropriate for the project. The toolkit had to embody a good development environment, supporting appropriate rapid prototyping, and it must be robust and able to be made fast enough for continuous real-time operation.

There were a number of pragmatic reasons for the choice of POPLOG over similar rapid prototyping AI development environments. They included:

- the contractor's experience with POPLOG on other projects;
- the project team would have convenient access to the POPLOG development team (at SD);
- the fact that SD had good contacts with Sussex, which were used for advice with the use of POPLOG in the initial stages of the project, and when the project included a team member on assignment from Sussex during the development of the system software.

Another aspect considered by the club was the support that the ALVEY Directorate was giving to POPLOG. Within the POPLOG system, the project team decided to adopt the POP-11 language. The main reasons for that choice were:

- POP-11 is the base language of the POPLOG system, and provides the most flexibility and power;

- it was also the language with the fastest execution;
- being a procedural (imperative) language meant it would be the most appropriate choice for the conventional components (i.e. not the KBS process);
- furthermore, it would be easy for team members without previous experience of applicative languages to pick up;
- its extensive list processing and other AI facilities provided ample power and expressiveness for developing the KBS process system software and the Translator;
- it was considered an advantage for the project development to be done in a single language.

The development was begun in version 9 of POPLOG (on VMS 3.7) and later moved over to version 11 (on VMS 4.2).

10.2.2 Prototyping during development

Extensive use of prototyping was made during the development of the system software. This was a natural result of using POPLOG and use of the environment's editor (VED), which permits rapid informal testing of procedures during the coding process, and of the ability to save the state of a POPLOG image. These, and other, features, help a developer to avoid spending too long going down false tracks in coding by exposing them at the earliest opportunity.

Prototyping was also used in the combined process of framing and refining the KRL, and trying it out on a naïve trial model, while work went ahead on the development of the Translator, particularly the compiler. The basic structure of the compiler was designed to make it easy to make changes to the parsing routines, so this was exploited during prototyping to test the consequences of changes in the KRL grammar. This was amplified by the use of a semi-interactive KRL generation utility (written in Prolog), which guaranteed correct KRL syntax.

In a similar way, refining took place across two sub-systems during the development, in the back-end of the Translator (in the development system), which produces an internal representation of the knowledge base, and in the KBS process inference mechanisms (in the run-time system) which operate on this representation to perform the functions specified for as expressed in the KRL. This parallel development ensured that the internal representation produced by the Translator contained the features necessary for the use of the KBS process at run-time.

This refinement capability was also exploited in areas where it was not so essential, in the conventional processes, notably in the creation of the graphics screens and mimic diagrams.

As the architecture of the final expert system stablised, advantage was taken of a POPLOG facility that permits the evaluation of an arbitrary input as though it were POP-11 code being invoked in the POPLOG process. Two commands to the expert system (for use by developers only) were provided, one (**popval**) to execute any POP-11 expression in the operator (OPER) process, and another (**popexport**) to pass the POP-11 expression to the KBS process and execute it there.

This proved immensely valuable, permitting the developer to dynamically replace procedures that needed debugging, particularly in the KBS process, while the whole system was running, by editing and downloading from the OPER process. This facility was used both for the system software and for the POP-11 code and procedures that were incorporated in the knowledge base.

10.2.3 External functions

The system software made use of external routines linked into the POPLOG system for the different processes. These included VMS system services routines, other routines written by the development team in assembler and FORTRAN, and supplied object code that was originally FORTRAN routines.

The code written for the interprocess communication and synchronization made extensive use of the VMS system services (notably for VMS common event flags used as semaphores to ensure mutual exclusion by the different processes of shared resources). The special assembler and FORTRAN routines developed for the project were for such aspects as rapidly accessing the system clock and converting the form of it (a procedure that is done frequently in the KBS process and that must therefore be as fast as possible), and for other data type conversion. The control of the Gresham-Lion graphics terminal was done via the object library routines provided.

10.2.4 Performance

Initially, development concentrated on getting the system to function correctly, rather than paying too much attention to optimizing the code for speed. However, when the first (demonstration) version of the knowledge base was installed it became clear that the run-time system would not have the speed that would be needed for the final version.

The main reason for the lack of required speed was due to the choice of the VAX 11/730, the least powerful of the VAX range, with, at that time, 2 Megabytes of memory. Later this was extended to the maximum for the RESCU VAX configuration of 4 Megabytes which cut down the amount of process swapping, but it was still considered that the system would be too slow to operate satisfactorily when the final version was installed (particularly as much of these gains were to be lost when the move to VMS 4.2 from the smaller VMS 3.7 was made).

A major reason for the comparative slowness of the software was the fact that many of the basic procedures in POP-11 embody a number of checks on the type of the data that is passed to them. This is necessary in an AI system which does not have strong typing, and where the same procedure is used for a given function on a wide variety of data types. The first approach to speeding up the system, therefore, was obvious, namely to exploit the fast versions of these procedures (called *fastprocs*), that lacked this type checking where this was appropriate, and make use of the other facilities for improving efficiency that are described in the POPLOG documentation.

In order to achieve still better performance, special trace facilities were created to monitor not only the time spent in particular procedures, but also how much garbage they created. If a procedure can be optimized to produce less garbage then the system as a whole will be faster as it will not need to do garbage collection as often, something that is particularly important in a system that must run continuously for long periods.

While most of this optimization was required in the system software for the KBS process (since this runs practically all the time), this monitoring did expose inefficiencies in the COMMS process handling the communications between the VAX and the Fox computer (including the regular scanning of the plant data), so this code was optimized for speed and to reduce garbage.

This monitoring demonstrated that certain POP-11 standard procedures were inordinately slow or garbage creating, and so these were replaced with versions exploiting the fast procedures and the internal representation of lists, and (knowing how the procedures were used) avoiding unnecessary checking. This had a striking impact in increasing the speed of the system.

10.2.5 Flexibility

The main aim of the development, throughout the project, was to keep flexibility and ensure that it would be easy to makes changes where necessary. This was considered necessary, taking into account the investigative and concept proving nature of the project, and of the educational or awareness aspect requirement of the club. Thus, in the development of the knowledge base, the approach of installing different versions (once the overall architecture had been framed to permit this), was used. Also, in the system software development, a prototyping approach was made an integrated aspect of the detailed design (again after the basic design had been framed), exploiting POPLOG's facilities for this.

In addition, the ease of change approach came into its own, as the club requirements themselves got refined. Thus certain aspects, in particular pertaining to the operator (OPER) process arose out of the club revising its views as to what was needed to demonstrate the expert system satisfactory. The human–computer interface (HCI) of a system is particularly prone to being changed as a result of the users, and others, seeing it. This is because, to a large extent, the way an interface should operate is a matter of personal preference.

10.2.6 Lessons from RESCU

The RESCU project aimed to demonstrate the validity of the expert system techniques in real-time industrial applications, and as such the project had an experimental nature making much use of the prototyping and refining approach to development.

The choice of POPLOG for the project (a Club policy decision) worked extremely well on the whole, as it provides a very good development environment. The use of the POP-11 language also proved very successful. However, some components, particularly the time critical aspects such as the COMMS process and parts of the OPER process (the graphics), could have been rewritten in a conventional language (e.g. C) to improve run-time performance.

One drawback with POPLOG for a real-time continuously operating system is its stop/go garbage collection method. It would have been nice to have been able to select a continuous garbage collection facility in place of the standard one.

At the end of the RESCU project the lessons learned were considered from the viewpoint of developing real-time expert systems in a much more controlled, well engineered style of development. This considered the requirements on the sort of shell or construction kit that would be needed, by considering the deficiencies of the RESCU system.

The main problem with the RESCU system was that, although it was fast enough for the application that was developed, it would not be sufficiently fast for a wide number of real-time process control and other industrial expert system applications.

Moreover, the RESCU KRL needed extending in a number of areas, particularly to support frame-based knowledge representations and inheritance. An important feature for advanced real-time blackboard systems is the ability to handle concurrent KBS activities (requiring a transaction maintenance system to avoid inconsistencies of data on the blackboard). Another requirement is a general purpose interface that can be used to describe the configuration of the links to the expert system from the external world, that can be easily tailored to suit particular applications.

These features have been incorporated in the design of the successor to RESCU, a construction kit for developing real-time expert system applications, COGSYS [Morgan 88]. The COGSYS product is being developed for an independent club of some 35 industrial companies, the successor of the RESCU club [Shaw 88], and which includes the majority of the RESCU members. The run-time system is written in C, but the development system has been built using the POPLOG toolkit. The club has set up two test-sites which are developing independent applications in the COGSYS product [Williams and Kraft 89], [Davison and Kraft 90]. These will be used to evaluate the product initially and to enable improvements to be incorporated in the first full release (late 1990).

Chapter 11

The fourth case study: High-end integrated toolkit

Chris Orgill

11.1 The case study problem

The problem presented here is one of constraint-based search. The constraints are simple algebraic ones and the overall problem has a straightforward geometric structure. The programming of the problem in ART is developed after evolving a design which can easily be specified in terms of ART's data manipulation operators.

We have a board, comprising a large equilateral triangles subdivided into 9 smaller equilateral triangles, as shown in figure 11.1. Each small triangle is labelled from a to i. Quite separately, we have nine tiles of the same size as the nine board triangles; these are labelled from 1 to 9. On each of the latter there are between 0 and 3 hemispheres placed with their diameter along the edges of the triangles, as shown in figure 11.2.

The problem is to find an assignment of the tiles $\{1 \ldots 9\}$ such that all the hemispheres match, i.e. form a circle, where they meet an internal edge.

The first thing to note is that the board does not form a part of the solution. It exists merely as a convenient means of noting part of the current assignment, i.e. which tile from $\{1 \ldots 9\}$ is assigned to which place from $\{a \ldots i\}$. It is only a *partial* description of assignment because we also need to know the rotation of each triangle, which can be any one of $\{0°, 60°, 120°\}$.

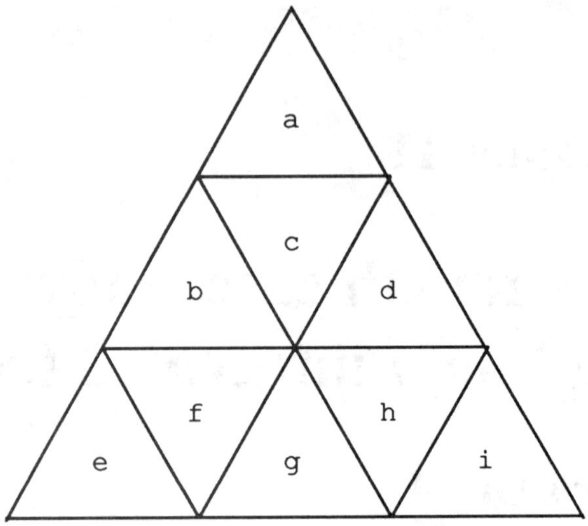

Figure 11.1: The problem board

We can see that the number of assignments that has to be tested with the most unconstrained search procedure is quite large[1] and hence it is important to try to discover some structure to the problem that will allow us to reduce this to a tractable level.

The approach to a solution algorithm can best be described in the spirit of *one-step deductions* [Stallman and Sussman]. Here we essentially describe what the rules are required to do at the specification stage, rather than formulate pseudo-code in a procedural language. This approach has the advantage that the programmer starts to "think in rules" all the earlier. The traditional pseudo-code approach may well be redundant, as it captures the solution knowledge in a formulation that requires another level of transformation before it can be used as the basis of an implementation.

Before we present the deductions it is necessary to describe the way in which the solution will be searched for. The strategy will be to create a tree in which each node represents an assignment of a tile in a particular rotation to a triangle on the board. All the ancestral nodes in the tree (which must not merge at any point, so a node has more than one immediate ancestor) inherit the assignments from above.

[1] The number of unique assignments is actually $3^9 \times 9! = 7,142,567,040$.

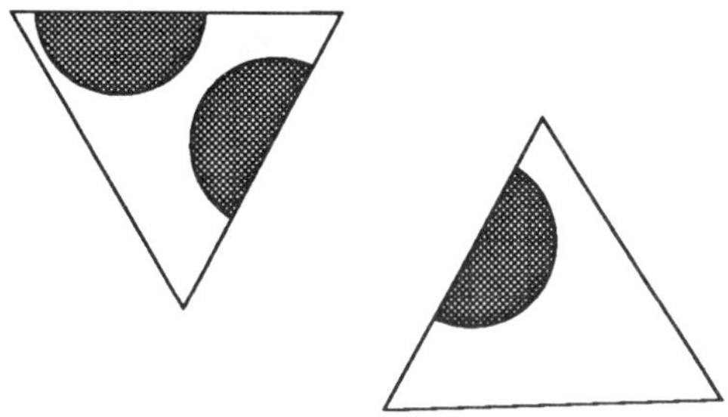

Figure 11.2: A pair of tiles

The deductions simply:

- manage the selection of valid assignments, based on static and dynamic problem constraints;
- create nodes in the tree;
- destroy insoluble sub-trees;

The program should terminate with a tree with branches of varying depth. If one or more solutions are found, there will be a sub-tree, rooted at the top-level, in which each tile has a valid assignment. The form of the solution sub-tree depends upon the approach we adopt for generating new assignment nodes when a tile already placed has two or three boundaries. At the expense of generating placement order variants we can construct a tree like that on the right of figure 11.3.

The only advantage here is that a solution can be found simply by recording the traversal[2] of the tree from root to leaf for all traversals of depth equal to the number of tiles. It is inefficient because the same solution, except with different order of tile placement, may be generated more than once, thus increasing working memory unnecessarily.

Instead, we choose the approach which results in a structure of the form shown on the left of figure 11.3. Here the solution is found in a *sub-tree* which has the same number of nodes as tiles, rather than a simple traversal. The problem has an important piece of structure which we have not mentioned. The board has the fortunate property that, if any place has two or more neighbours, no pair of its neighbours are themselves neighbours. This simplifies the match testing

[2]That is, a tree of unit width.

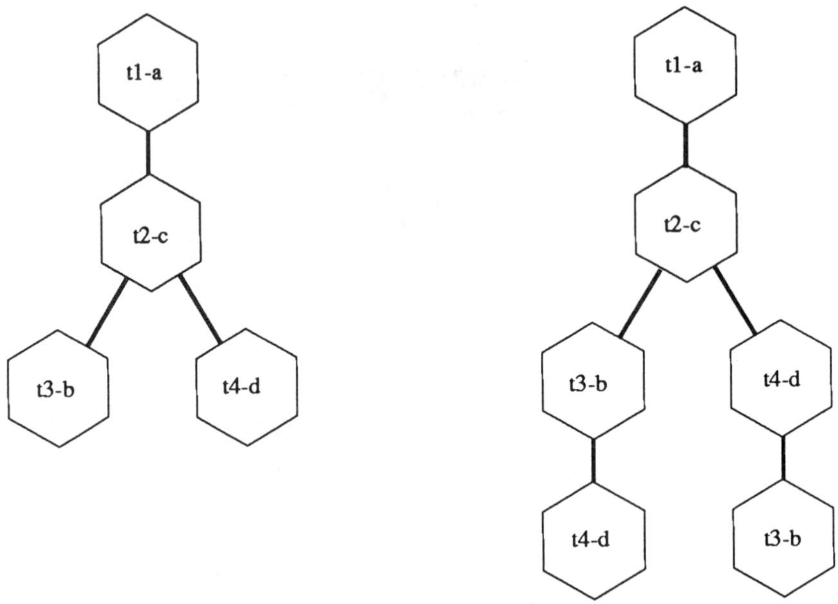

Figure 11.3: Placement order variants are a costly redundancy

enormously, as well as making the extraction of solutions from the final viewpoint tree easier than it might have been with similar problems with different board geometries.

Some extra pieces of pseudo-code syntax are used below. The node-matching operator '`at` *keyword*' is used, where *keyword* is one of `here` or `here-and-above` or `root`. This selects a node, which contains state information about the problem, and constrains that state information to have been asserted either in this node and its descendants *only*, or in this node and its ancestors, or to have been asserted in the root node, i.e. it is a search constraint.

We also use the phrase 'shadowing-assert' to mean that state information is introduced into a node such that it *shadows* old values for the same state, i.e. the old information, implicit via inheritance is no longer visible and the new information is visible in the node in which it is asserted and in its children. We also use the function #() to mean the cardinality of the set object to which it is applied.

So, the deductions, or *rule specifications*, are:

Rule 1 *Do any first assignment of a tile that puts a hemisphere onto each internal boundary*
`salience:` *very low*[3]

```
at here
        if | there is a tile, t with default rotation r, without an assignment and
           | there is an unassigned place, p and
           | there is no restriction on the assignment t ↔ p
          then
              if p has more internal boundaries than t has hemispheres.
                then
                    at root assert a global restriction on the assignment t ↔ p
                    end em at
                else
                    foreach rotation of t at p that puts a hemisphere onto
                    each boundary
                               create a child node, c
                               at c
                                  shadowing-assert the new assignment t, r' ↔ p
                    end foreach
              end if
        end if
```

Rule 2 *Do all subsequent tile assignments which bound upon at least one successful assignment that meet the constraint of having a hemisphere on each internal boundary without necessarily matching any neighbours. Prepare the state information necessary to perform the neighbour-matching operation.*
`salience:` *low*

```
at here
        if | there is a tile t_b which is assigned to a place p_b and
           | there is another tile t_a which is unassigned and
           | there is an unassigned place p_a which bounds on p_b and
           | there is no restriction on the assignment t_a ↔ p_a and
           | there is not already a match computed for this assignment.
```

[3] In contrast with *Algol*-like pseudo-codes, the flow of control in this type of agenda-based system is intimately bound up with the salience (or priority) of the rules. In many cases incorrect behaviour will result if a rule falls into the wrong salience class. In this rule, the only effect of reducing the salience is to ensure that search proceeds depth-first, rather than breadth-first.

then
    if p_a has more internal boundaries than t_a has hemispheres.
        then
            at root assert a global restriction on the assignment $t_a \leftrightarrow p_a$
            end *at*
        else
            assert a control fact for this assignment to test for all the neighbour places of p_a
        end *if*
end *if*

Rule 3 *Check, via a previously asserted control fact, that an assignment matches an assigned neighbour.*
salience: *normal*

at here
    if | there is a control fact asserting all neighbours, $\mathbf{n}$, required to be tested for hemisphere-match against a tile, t with default rotation r at place p, and there is a neighbour, $n \in \mathbf{n}$, assigned to place p_n with rotation r_n
    then
        add the result of the hemisphere-match test on $n, r_n \Leftrightarrow t$ into the control fact
end *if*

Rule 4 *Check, via a previously asserted control fact, that the intersection of all pairwise match constraints still leaves a feasible rotation for assignment of the candidate tile.*
salience: *not-so-low*

at here
    if | there is a complete set of hemisphere-match tests available as a set of feasible rotations $\mathbf{r}_i$ for an unassigned tile, t, with neighbours $n_i \in \mathbf{n}$ tested for assignment in the empty place p.
    then
        if the intersection over the $\mathbf{r}_i$ is not equal to the empty set
            then
                foreach $r \in \bigcap_{i=1}^{\#n} \mathbf{r}_i$
                        create a child node, c
                        at c
                            shadowing-assert the new assignment $t, r \leftrightarrow p$
                            foreach $n_i \in \mathbf{n}$

```
                                      shadowing-assert the match t, r ⇔ n_i
                              end foreach
                           end at
           else
               at here
                           shadowing-assert a local constraint on
                           the assignment t, r ↔ p
               end at
       end if
end if
```

Rule 5 *If all the unassigned tiles at a leaf node have assignment constraints, remove the leaf, as it can never have any descendants.*
`salience:` *normal*

```
at here
        |  there is a node with an unassigned place p and forall
      if|  unassigned tiles t ∈ t there is a constraint on
        |  the assignment t ↔ p
      then delete the sub-tree rooted here
      end if
```

This completes the specification of how the solution may efficiently be produced. We shall now see how this can be programmed in ART.

11.2 The main features of the solution

The case study problem of the previous section is now considered as a task in ART programming. We shall find that the solution involves the following ART features:

- viewpoints–creation, matching within, and destruction
- relations– trivial and assertion consequences
- ab initio facts and LISP data within them
- salience search control
- negation and choice
- pattern net tests and join net tests

- the COMMON LISP/ART and ART/COMMON LISP interfaces
- establishing rule clusters by intermediary control facts
- iteration over rules and right-hand side iteration

We begin by defining the declarative knowledge available to us, i.e. the structure of the tiles and the board. We adopt an ordering convention for a triangle on the board, saying that the edge which is uppermost or rightward is said to be edge 1 and edges 2 and 3 follow in clockwise fashion when the entire board is oriented apex upward, as in figure 11.4. Then we express which edge touches another edge by defining a 4-ary relation with an *assertion consequence*:

```
(defrelation touches (?a ?b ?c ?d)
  (touches ?b ?a ?d ?c))
```

which says that edge `?c` of tile `?a` touches edge `?d` of tile `?b` and that, if a fact exists that matches this pattern, then *also* assert the inverse of the relation as a consequence.

We then define the boundaries of the board in the following form:

```
(deffacts boundaries
;;
;; read as (boundary <place>
;;                   <internal-boundary-cardinality>
;;                   <internal-boundary-edges>*
;;                   <internal-boundary-places>*)
;;
  (boundaries a 1 2 called c)
  (boundaries b 2 1 2 called c f)
  (boundaries c 3 1 2 3 called a d b)
  (boundaries d 2 2 3 called h c)
  (boundaries e 1 1 called f)
  (boundaries f 3 1 2 3 called b g e)
  (boundaries g 2 1 3 called h f)
  (boundaries h 3 1 2 3 called d i g)
  (boundaries i 1 3 called h))
```

As the *boundary* relation is not of fixed arity we cannot define it beforehand. We read the fact as:

triangle `<place>`has

> `<internal boundary cardinality>` *internal boundaries*, designated by the *numbers* `<internal-boundary-edges>*` and has *neighbouring board triangles*, designated by the *letters* `<internal-boundary-places>*`.

So `(boundaries d 2 2 3 called h c)` means that triangle *d* shares internal boundaries with 2 other triangles, on edges 2 and 3. On edge 2 it abuts triangle *h*, and on edge 3 it abuts triangle *c*.

This completes the definition of the board, so we now proceed to the tiles. Define a 4-ary relation called `spots`:

```
(deffacts tile-structure
  (tiles tile-1 tile-2 tile-3 tile-4 tile-5 tile-6 tile-7 tile-8 tile-9 )
  (spots tile-1 7 18 none)
  (spots tile-2 7 10 15)
  (spots tile-3 #L25/2 none 10)
  (spots tile-4 7 #L25/2 7)
  (spots tile-5 #L25/2 18 none)
  (spots tile-6 none 7 10)
  (spots tile-7 15 #L25/2 7)
  (spots tile-8 15 none 18)
  (spots tile-9 10 10 18))
```

which is read as:

tile `?a` has

3 possible *spots* whose *centres* are located at:

`?1`, `?2` and `?3` units from the start of an edge in a clockwise sense

So `(spots tile-4 7 #L25/2 7)` means that `tile-4` has spots that start 7 units from the start of the first edge, 12.5 units from the start of the second edge, and 7 units from the start of the third edge. This is similar to the tile shown in figure 11.4.

These facts will exist in different forms throughout the solution tree subject to the constraint that any change in places `?1`, `?2`, `?3` are equivalent to an order-preserving rotation, corresponding to a new orientation for a tile at that point in the solution tree. We find it convenient to use a data type from LISP here, the *ratio*, and do so simply by prefacing it with an ART reader macro, `#L`, which indicates that the object parsed from the following non-whitespace characters is to evaluated as LISP and not as ART code. We shall meet it again later, when we wish to use some user-defined LISP functions to perform tests which are not straightforward within ART itself.

All that remains is to intialize the problem by defining six more relations, all of which will change as the rulebase executes. Four of these are control facts used for holding partial results and synchronizing execution of particular clusters of rules. The last two will ultimately represent the solutions. They are:

- `matches-to-go` *<neighbours>* `for` *<tile>* `with` *<rotation>* `at` *<place>*
- `match-rotations for` *<tile>* `at` *<place>* `with` *<rotation>** `touching` *<other-tiles>**
- `matches` *<tile-1>* *<tile-2>*
- `never-at` *<tile>* *<place>*
- `assigned-to` *<tile>* *<place>*

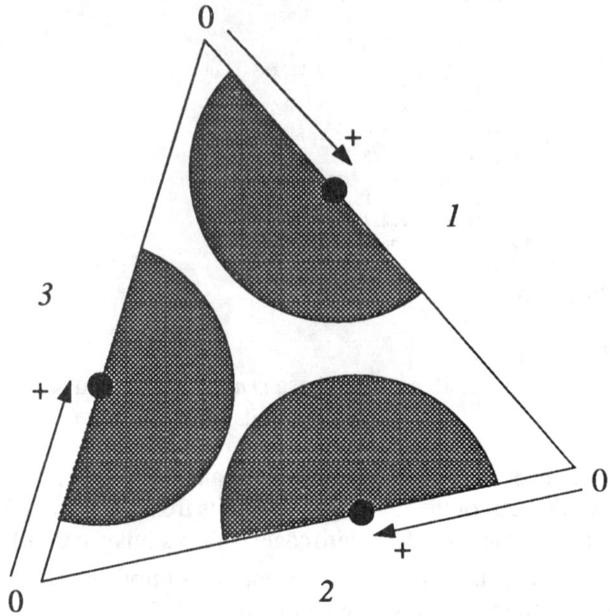

Figure 11.4: Sign conventions for describing hemispheres

- has-tile *<place>* *<tile>*

where *<rotation>* is a triple of hemisphere lengths. The control facts `matches-to-go` and `match-rotations` determine the flow of control for placement hypothesis testing, as we shall now show.

```
(defrule do-primary-placements
  "any first placement that puts a sphere onto each internal boundary of the triangle"
  (declare (salience (- *default-salience* 50)))

;;
;; by lowering the salience of the root asserting rule we ensure that the
;; search proceeds depth-first
;;
;; ART is a good example of how control of flow differs in production systems
;; from conventional imperative style programming.
;;

  (viewpoint @?v
              ?x<-(assigned-to ?tile none)
              ?y<-(has-tile ?place none)
              ?z<-(spots ?tile $?s-a)
              (not (never-at ?tile ?place)))
```

The first action is to set the *salience* of the rule. By setting it to fifty below default we ensure that all subsequent rules which are activated by the action of this top-level placement rule are fired first. The variable `*default-salience*` is predefined in ART. The tree structure specified in the pseudo-code maps to ART's viewpoint mechanism. The `viewpoint @?v` syntax allows us to constrain subsequent pattern searches to a particular node within the solution tree. Next, we *bind* some *pattern instantiations* to ART variables by use of the ?<*var*> <- <*pattern*> syntax. The first two patterns contain atomic wildcards, i.e. only patterns consisting of a sequence of a literal; (`assigned-to` or `has-tile`), followed by any single item and followed by the literal `none` can match the pattern. Each unique fact can generate an instance of a match, so this rule may be *instantiated*, or selected for execution, more than once. The fourth pattern uses a negation form, which selects a rule for instantiation, all other patterns being satisfied, only if there is *no* pattern that matches the enclosing `(not (...` specification. The third pattern uses ART's *sequence* wildcard `$?`<*var*> which matches with zero or more items. This must be used with caution to avoid a combinatorial problem with multiple instantiations. The effect of the first two patterns without further constraint would be to instantiate 9^2 rules corresponding to selecting all possible tile↔triangle pairs. However, since the best philosophy is to write the most constraining patterns we add both further restrictive patterns and also *tests*. The `(not (...` pattern ensures we never make the same bad assignment twice. It will match both global restrictions on assignment, such as those asserted in Rule 1 and also the local ones which may be asserted in Rule 4. Patterns are implicitly read in conjunctive normal form; $p_1 \wedge p_2 \wedge \ldots \wedge p_n$, i.e. `and`-connected without any extra syntax. However, there are occasions where we wish to give terse lexical expression to two or more rules which share a common pattern sequence. When this situation arises it is advantageous to ensure that pattern ordering is maintained across such a rule group. ART provides syntax to achieve *case* and *or*-like constructs within the rule-based paradigm. The effect of these selection functions is actually to create more than one rule out of the single textual definition. The user must be aware of this when attempting to understand what is happening whilst developing programs. This is shown for the rule under consideration in figure 11.5.

We have need of an ART `case` statement next, to allow us to select between two different courses of action depending upon whether the assignment instantiated so far with the simple patterns meets our heuristic of ensuring that there are at least the same number of spots, `$?s-a`, on the selected tile, `?tile`, as internal edges on the triangle, `?place`.

```
(case
   ((boundaries ?place
                ?card&:#L( > ?card
                             (length
                              (user::all-positions (list$ ?s-a)
                                                   'none
```

```
COMMAND WINDOW
WARNING:  Failure to match the argument pattern of SPOTS:
  (SPOTS ?TILE-A $ ?S-A)
WARNING:  MATCHES-TO-GO defined as an implicit 7-ary relation.
WARNING:  Failure to match the argument pattern of SPOTS:
  (SPOTS ?TILE-A $ ?S-A)
Compiling rule DO-SECONDARY-PLACEMENTS-disjunct-1... +P=P+J=P+J+P+J=P+J=P+J=P+J
Compiling rule DO-SECONDARY-PLACEMENTS-disjunct-2... =P=P=J=P=J=P=J=P=J=P=J=P+J
  (SPOTS ?TILE $ ?S-A)
Compiling rule DO-PRIMARY-PLACEMENTS-disjunct-1... +P+P+J+P+J+P+J+P+J
Compiling rule DO-PRIMARY-PLACEMENTS-disjunct-2... =P=P=J=P=J=P=J=P+J=P+J
WARNING:  Failure to match the argument pattern of SPOTS:
  (SPOTS ?TILE-A $ ?S-A)
```

Figure 11.5: Some rule definitions are compiled as more than one rule

```
                                                    #'(lambda(edge item)
                                                        (not
                                                         (equal edge item))))))
                        $?boundaries called $?)
        =>
  ;;
  ;; there are more internal boundaries than occurrences of spots,
  ;;  so this is an invalid placement
  ;;
        (root
         (assert
          (never-at ?tile ?place))))
```

This involves a simple arithmetic comparison. What follows shows how we integrate arbitrary predicate tests *within* a declarative pattern syntax. Our previous usage of patterns could be classified as *data selection.* We sometimes want to perform *data collection* at the same time. Here, the `(boundaries...` pattern is being used to collect a value for the number of boundaries, so that a conjunctive predicate test can be attached to the instance of the variable `?card`. The syntax is `&:`*<test>*, and is read as *and such that...*

The test itself is performed as COMMON LISP, hence the `#L` syntax, already explained, and also references some LISP functions defined on the ART objects. In the test, functions from three different *packages*[4] are used. Function `list$` from the ART package is used to convert from an ART sequence to a LISP list, function `user::all-positions` is used from the COMMON LISP User package and is actually defined by the programmer as part of his application, hence the `user::` introducer to the function name, and the remaining functions are all part of COMMON LISP. The actual definition of *all-positions* is:

```
(defun all-positions (edge-list edge evaluator-function
                      &optional (index-list nil) (start 0))
  "return 1-based positions of all occurrences of edge in edge-list"
  (cond
```

[4] A package is a collection of symbols that share the same package attribute.

```
((> (length edge-list) start)
 (funcall
  #'(lambda (index)
        (cond
         (index
          (all-positions edge-list
                         edge
                         evaluator-function
                         (cons (1+ index)
                               index-list)
                         (1+ index)))
        (t (values index-list))))

  (position-if #'(lambda (item)
                     (funcall evaluator-function edge item))
                 edge-list
                 :start start)))
(t (values index-list))))
```

Its function is to apply a comparison test, supplied by the caller, to the list of edges and the second argument, here `none`. So, as the test succeeds if the items are not equal, the overall result is to return the number of valid spots found on tile `?tile`. If the outer inequality succeeds *and* the enclosing pattern also gets instantiated, then this case limb is satisfied, and the right-hand side action is asserted, namely a global constraint on the assignment `?tile`↔`?place`. Note that as the `otherwise` limb contains exactly the same pattern, `(boundaries...`, we have achieved selection solely on the basis of the predicate test. There is another mechanism for achieving an arbitrary predicate test, namely `(test (`*<predicate test>*`))`, illustrated in the next rule. It is good programming practice, however, to write pattern specifications that achieve the greatest possible constraint as early as possible in the left-hand side. Had we used an unconstrained `(boundaries...` pattern and subsequently tested the number of valid spots using a `test` construct, then the resulting RETE net would have been larger, due to a greater number of instantiations of the `(boundaries...` pattern.

```
(otherwise
 (boundaries ?place ?card $?boundaries called $?)
 =>
 (bind ?rotations #L(remove-duplicates
                      (for boundary in$ ?boundaries join
                           (user::constrained-rotate (list$ ?s-a)
                                                     boundary
                                                     'none
                                                     #'(lambda (edge item)
                                                         (not (equal edge item)))))
                      :test #'equal))

 (at ?v
     (for rotation in ?rotations do
          (sprout
           (retract ?x ?y)
           (if (not (equal rotation (list$ ?s-a)))
             then
             (retract ?z)
             (assert
```

```
          (spots ?tile $=(seq$ rotation))))
        (assert
         (partial-solution =#L(gentemp "solution") ?current) ;an INTERNED symbol
         (has-tile ?place ?tile)
         (assigned-to ?tile ?place))))))))
```

The second limb has a trivial left-hand side, but the actions are somewhat more complex, involving both ***right-hand side*** ART and COMMON LISP. We begin by binding the result of some computation to an ART variable. The computation actually performs a test upon the selected tile, `?tile`, to see which rotations do not leave an edge without a hemisphere on an internal boundary. The test uses a user-defined function, `user::constrained-rotate`, to test each boundary, collected as an ART sequence, `$?boundaries`, in the left-hand side, by use of the ART right-hand side iterator construct `for` used with the per-cycle action `join` to accumulate results into a LISP list.

```
(defun constrained-rotate (edge-list-a touches-a edge-b evaluator-function)
  "determine whether there is any rotation of edge-list-a relative to edge-b
that results in a coincident hemisphere. return a list of rotated edge-lists or nil"
  (values
   (funcall #'(lambda (index-list)
                (cond
                 ((null index-list) index-list)
                 (t (values
                     (mapcar #'(lambda (index)
                                 (list-rotate edge-list-a (- touches-a  index)))
                             index-list)))))
            (all-positions edge-list-a edge-b evaluator-function))))
```

This function also calls upon the function `user::list-rotate` and the function `user::all-positions`. The former is defined as:

```
(defun list-rotate (spots index)
  "rotate the cw ordered spots  by <index> steps. cw if <index> >0, ccw if <index> < 0,
   no rotation if <index> = 0"
  (cond
   ((zerop index) (values spots))
   ((plusp index) (list-rotate (cons (car (reverse spots)) (butlast spots)) (1- index)))
   (t (list-rotate (append (cdr spots) (list (car spots))) (1+ index)))))
```

Duplicate rotations are then removed using the function `remove-duplicates`, implemented in COMMON LISP. Once the valid rotations have been established for the tile, the solution tree can be expanded to reflect this new assignment. To do this we make use of the ART *viewpoint* mechanism. The original left-hand side pattern established a viewpoint ?v in which all enclosing patterns were to match. Having performed tests upon the working memory which is partitioned in viewpoint ?v, we now wish actually to modify that portion of working memory. We do this using the `at` construct, which selects a region of viewpoint space[5] for the scope of the construct. We then make use of the iterator `for` in its simplest form, with the `do` qualifier, to perform iteration purely for its side-effects. For

[5]Or, more accurately, a set of facts in working memory that match the specified viewpoint against their additional viewpoint qualifiers.

each valid rotation, now represented as a LISP variable `rotation`, we create a child viewpoint, by use of the `(sprout...` construct. The remainder of the rule shadows the old problem state information, by use of the `(retract...` construct, and asserts the new assignment, by using the ART `(assert...` statement. The LISP variable `rotation` is converted back to an ART sequence by use of the functions `$=` and `seq$`.

The second rule is substantially similar to the first, in that it also tries to prune candidate tile assignments by the same test as above. As it is testing the n-th assignment, $n > 1$, however, it asserts extra solution state information pertinent to performing the actual neighbour match tests absent in the previous rule.

```
(defrule do-secondary-placements ""
;;
;; this rule must ensure that placement order variants are suppressed
;;
;; i.e. we would increase the pattern search space unnecessarily if we
;; allowed two viewpoint structures separately to assert the placings a-1 b-2 as
;; v1 = (a-1 then b-2), v2 = (b-2 then a-1)
;;
;;

  (declare (salience (- *default-salience* 20)))
  (viewpoint @?v
             (assigned-to ?tile-b ?b&~none) ;trigger fact

             ?x<-(assigned-to ?tile-a&~?tile-b none)
             ?y<-(has-tile ?place none)
             (not (matches ?tile-a ?tile-b))
             (not (never-at ?tile-a ?place))
             ?z<-(spots ?tile-a $?s-a))

  (boundaries ?place ?card $?boundaries called $?names)
  (test #L(plusp (member$ ?b ?names)))
```

The first pattern serves to trigger the rule whenever a new assignment is made. Once again we use a form of the pattern qualifier syntax `&`. Here the usage is `?b&~ none`, which is read as "the variable `b`, such that it is not the value `none`". Similarly the second pattern also ensures that it does not match on the same fact as the first by constraining the `?tile-`*?* variable to be different to that matched above. This may the point at which to make the binding rules of ART a little clearer. A pattern may rely on a variable being bound if it is referred to higher up the pattern body. Certain constructs, such as `or` and `case`, have special binding rules to reflect the fact that they are actually macros which author two or more rules, where bindings established inside them would not have useful value. This rule also illustrates the use of a `(test...` construct. It could equally well have been implemented as a test inside the `(boundaries...` pattern.

```
  (case
;;
;; are there more boundaries than spots ?
;;
     ((test #L( > ?card (length
```

```
                                 (user::all-positions (list$ ?s-a)
                                                      'none
                                                      #'(lambda (edge item)
                                                          (not (equal edge item)))))))
;;
;; assert at the root the strong constraint 'never-at
;;
        =>
        (root
         (assert
          (never-at ?tile-a ?place))))

;;
;; if the tile passes the test for having enough spots, then see if, for each
;; assigned neighbouring tile, a rotation exists that matches all neighbours
;;
;; this cannot be done within a single rule and is a good example of the use
;; of a transient control fact , 'match-rotations in ART, establishing a RULE CLUSTER
;;
     (otherwise
      =>
      (at ?v
       (assert
        (matches-to-go $?names for ?tile-a with $?s-a at ?place)))))
;;
;; this control fact structure illustrates an interesting point about ITERATION
;; in ART. ART provides two distinct types of iteration, namely Left Hand Side
;; and Right Hand Side. Here, although Left Hand Side iteration looks to solve
;; the problem about how to make the rule match for all neighbouring tiles that have
;; been assigned, in fact it DOESN'T. LHS iteration in ART is only useful for
;; testing that ALL members of the set of patterns being iterated over exist in
;; the database. If ONE is missing, which may be the case here, then the rule will
;; not fire at all. To get one rule firing per match we need a control fact
;;
```

The `(case...` statement is similar to that used in the previous rule. The hemisphere counting test is used, as before, and its failure causes a global constraint, `(never-at...`, to be written.

Success, however, causes a control fact, `(matches-to-go...`, to be asserted at the point of the putative assignment, to serve as a control iterator for the next rule...

```
(defrule check-assigned-neighbours-for-pairwise-match
  ""

  (match-rotations for ?
                        at ?
                        with  $?rotations
                        touching $?other-tiles)

  (viewpoint @?v
             ?mtg<-(matches-to-go $?names for ?tile with $?spots at ?place)
             (assigned-to ?other-tile ?name)
             (spots ?other-tile $?other-spots)
             (touches ?place ?name ?c ?d))

  (test
   #L(plusp (member$ ?name ?names)))

  =>
```

The control fact is used by successive firings of this rule to iterate over the neighbours which bound upon the tile under test. We make best use of the available static problem knowledge by use of the `(touches...` relation base.

```
    =>

    (bind ?initial-rotation (create$ '(none)))
    (bind ?pair-matches
  ;;
  ;; the following test will return nil if the tile doesn't match a SINGLE neighbour
  ;; in any rotation
  ;;
            #L(user::constrained-rotate (list$ ?spots)
                                         ?c
                                         (nth$ ?other-spots ?d)
                                         'user::sphere-match))

  ;; then add this list of pairwise-valid orientations to the others
  ;;
    (at ?v
        (retract ?mtg)
        (assert
         (matches-to-go $=#L(seq$
                                (remove ?name (list$ ?names) :test #'art-equal))
                          for ?tile
                          with $?spots
                          at ?place)))

    (if (art-equal ?rotations ?initial-rotation)
      then
      (root
       (assert
        (match-rotations for ?tile
                           at ?place
                           with  =(seq$ ?pair-matches)
                           touching ?other-tile)))
      else

      (root
       (assert
        (match-rotations for ?tile
                           at ?place
                           with  ?rotations =(seq$ ?pair-matches)
                           touching ?other-tiles ?other-tile)))))


  ; the rule could be smart enough to terminate the iteration prematurely
  ; if 'pair-match was ever nil, as subsequent match list intersection
  ; testing in rule 'do-secondary-placement-assertions would always be nil.
  ; this would, in fact, complicate the control fact handling and lose
  ; clarity
```

The right-hand side is conventional, with the usual flexible mix of ART and COMMON LISP code. The actual hemisphere test is performed in the user-defined generic function `user::constrained-rotate`. This is supplied with the test function `user::sphere-match`, defined as:

```
(defun sphere-match (centre opposing-centre)
  "deal with no spheres too !"
  (cond
   ((or
```

```
    (equal centre 'art-user::none)
    (equal opposing-centre 'art-user::none)) nil) ;can't have no spheres as a match
  ((= centre (- *triangle-side* opposing-centre)) t)
  (t nil)))
```

where `*triangle-side*` is defined as `(defconstant *triangle-side* 25)`. We bind the result, which is a list of feasible rotations of the tile such that it matches a single assigned neighbour, and assert these in the accumulating control fact `(match-rotations...`, while simultaneously deleting each test from the control fact `(matches-to-go...`

```
(defrule do-secondary-placement-assertions
  "perform the intersection of all neighbour constraints to see if there IS a
match"
  (declare (salience (- *default-salience* 10)))
;;
;; this salience makes sure that all the matches have been performed before
;; the placement is asserted
;;
  ?m<-(match-rotations for ?tile
                       at ?place
                       with $?rotations
                       touching $?other-tiles)

  (viewpoint @?v
             ?mtg<-(matches-to-go $? for ?tile with $?spots at ?place)
             ?x<-(assigned-to ?tile none)
             ?y<-(has-tile ?place none)
             ?z<-(spots ?tile $?s-a))

  =>
```

The penultimate rule, which is triggered when all pairwise tests have been assembled, finds the feasible intersection of the previous tests. To preserve this behaviour we ensure that its salience is less than the previous rule. It can be seen that an entirely spurious solution tree would be generated if this salience ordering was not preserved. The left-hand side is straightforward, serving only to select the appropriate control fact for the unproven assignment.

```
  =>
  (bind ?all-matches #L(user::list-intersect (list*$ ?rotations)))

  (at ?v
      (retract ?mtg))
  (root
   (retract ?m)
   (assert
    (match-rotations for none at none with none touching none)))

  (if ?all-matches
    then

    (for valid-rotation in ?all-matches do
         (at ?v
             (sprout
              (retract ?x ?y)
              (for other-tile in$ ?other-tiles do
                   (assert
```

```
                    (matches ?tile =other-tile)))
             (if (not (equal valid-rotation (list$ ?s-a)))
                  then
                  (retract ?z)
                  (assert
                   (spots ?tile $=(seq$ valid-rotation))))
             (assert
              (assigned-to ?tile ?place)
              (has-tile ?place ?tile)))))
    else
;;
;; this part cannot be fitted here because it fails to match all neighbours
;; for all rotations ...
;;
    (at ?v
           (assert
            (never-at ?tile ?place)))))
```

The right-hand side performs the test here, as opposed to previously, where selection was performed on the left-hand side, as quite a few pieces of problem state information need to be shadowed or modified regardless of the existence of a feasible assignment. Again, the bulk of the work is done in a user-defined function, `user::list-intersect`, defined as:

```
(defun list-intersect (arg-list &optional (int-list (car arg-list)))
  "intersect every list in the arg-list"
  (cond
   ((null arg-list) (values int-list))
   (t (funcall
       #'(lambda (a rest)
             (list-intersect rest (intersection a
                                                   int-list
                                                   :test #'equal)))
       (pop arg-list)
       arg-list))))
```

with appropriate datastructure conversion across the ART/COMMON LISP interface provided by the ART function `(list*$`.... We use a right-hand side conditional, the ART `if`[6] to determine which state information we process, either creating new nodes in our solution tree for the valid assignments, or asserting a local constraint on the unmatched tile...

```
(defrule prune-stale-leaves
  "if all the free, unmatched, tiles at a leaf have never-at
constraints, then poison this leaf, as it can never have any descendants"
  (viewpoint ?v
             (has-tile ?place none))

;; there is an assignment

  (forall
   (viewpoint @?v
              (assigned-to ?tile none))
   (viewpoint @?v
              (never-at ?tile ?place)))
```

[6] A potential source of confusion, as COMMON LISP also provides an `if` function, but with different syntax. That function could have been used by the idiom `cl:if`.

```
;;
;; but there are unallocated tiles that cannot match,
;; so we cannot solve this subtree
;;

  =>

  (at ?v
      (poison "insoluble sub-tree")))
```

The final rule is the shortest, but not the simplest. Its job is to determine if a node can have no further valid assignments, and hence cannot form part of a solution tree. The first pattern establishes that there is a place, `?place`, without a tile and therefore there is a viewpoint in which the board is incomplete. If *in that viewpoint*, and not its children, all unassigned tiles have constraints upon being placed on `?place`, then this node can never have children and it should be excised from the solution tree. This is accomplished using the ART right-hand side viewpoint action `(poison...`

11.2.1 Running the code

Now we have the ART facts, rules and COMMON LISP support functions, we want to run it all inside ART. The first step is to create a load file, so that in future months we can remember the components of the solution. For our problem it looks like:

```
;;;
;;; load the  problem
;;;
;;;
(in-package 'art-user)

(change-memory-management
 :growth-limit 1024                    ; this is 32Mbytes per semi-space
 :expand 512
 :growth-rate 64                       ; grow by 4 Mbytes when needed
 :expand-p t)

(load "~/pubs/toolkit_book/functions")        ;load in the Common Lisp binaries...
(art-load "~/pubs/toolkit_book/runner9.art") ;...and the ART code...
(reset)                                              ;...and let it do its mungeing
(gc)

(unwatch 'justifiers)                 ;turn off unwanted data collection
(unwatch 'justifications)             ;and again...
```

This will load our COMMON LISP function definitions, loading compiled versions preferentially for speed. Then ART will compile the fact and rule definitions and will reset itself, ready for the problem run. At this stage we may choose to watch the agenda, if we are developing, as in figure 11.6, or we may be content to let it run to completion, and then to inspect the viewpoint structure generated by the code, as shown in figure 11.7. We have not specified rules to print the solutions.

Some results of running the problem, first on a 4-tile board, and then the full 9-tiles, are shown in Table 11.1.

No. of tiles	Size of unconstrained search space	No. of nodes examined	Time to complete (min)
4	1 944	115	3.56
9	7 142 567 040	???	> 24 hours

Table 11.1: Some problem details

```
                        AGENDA
0 TOUCHES-assertion-consequence-1 (f-18,) in HYP-1
0 TOUCHES-assertion-consequence-1 (f-17,) in HYP-1
0 TOUCHES-assertion-consequence-1 (f-16,) in HYP-1
-50 DO-PRIMARY-PLACEMENTS-disjunct-2 (f-3,f-10,f-12,,
-50 DO-PRIMARY-PLACEMENTS-disjunct-2 (f-4,f-10,f-13,,
-50 DO-PRIMARY-PLACEMENTS-disjunct-2 (f-5,f-10,f-14,,
-50 DO-PRIMARY-PLACEMENTS-disjunct-2 (f-6,f-10,f-15,,
-50 DO-PRIMARY-PLACEMENTS-disjunct-2 (f-4,f-9,f-13,,,
-50 DO-PRIMARY-PLACEMENTS-disjunct-1 (f-3,f-9,f-12,,f
-50 DO-PRIMARY-PLACEMENTS-disjunct-1 (f-5,f-9,f-14,,f
-50 DO-PRIMARY-PLACEMENTS-disjunct-1 (f-6,f-9,f-15,,f
-50 DO-PRIMARY-PLACEMENTS-disjunct-2 (f-3,f-8,f-12,,,
-50 DO-PRIMARY-PLACEMENTS-disjunct-2 (f-4,f-8,f-13,,,
-50 DO-PRIMARY-PLACEMENTS-disjunct-2 (f-5,f-8,f-14,,,
-50 DO-PRIMARY-PLACEMENTS-disjunct-2 (f-6,f-8,f-15,,,
-50 DO-PRIMARY-PLACEMENTS-disjunct-2 (f-3,f-7,f-12,,,
-50 DO-PRIMARY-PLACEMENTS-disjunct-2 (f-4,f-7,f-13,,,
-50 DO-PRIMARY-PLACEMENTS-disjunct-2 (f-5,f-7,f-14,,,
-50 DO-PRIMARY-PLACEMENTS-disjunct-2 (f-6,f-7,f-15,,,
```

Figure 11.6: The agenda can be watched as the program runs, if you have the time...

The details of the 4-tile problem are:

tile:

3 with spots `(25/2 none 10)`
4 with spots `(7 25/2 7)`
5 with spots `(25/2 18 none)`
8 with spots `(15 none 18)`

to be placed on the top section a, b, c, d of the 9-tile board. The code finds the

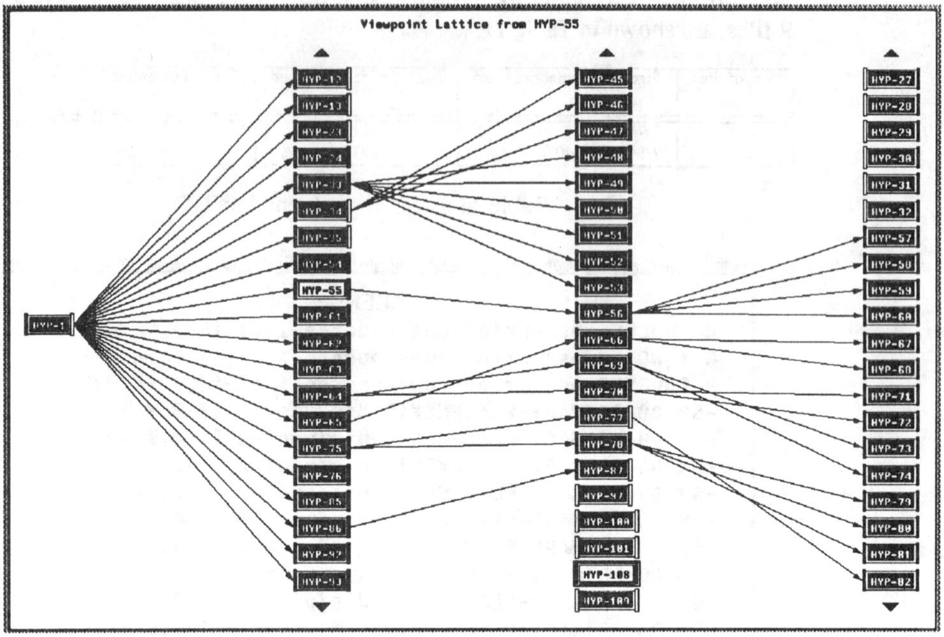

Figure 11.7: Some of the viewpoint tree created. The solutions are in there somewhere...

following solutions:

#	a	b	c	d
1	{5,0°}	{3,0°}	{4,60°}	{8,0°}
2	{8,120°}	{3,0°}	{4,60°}	{5,60°}
3	{3,120°}	{5,120°}	{4,120°}	{8,0°}
4	{8,120°}	{5,120°}	{4,0°}	{3,120°}
5	{3,60°}	{8,60°}	{4,120°}	{5,60°}
6	{5,0°}	{8,60°}	{4,0°}	{3,120°}
7	{5,0°}	{3,0°}	{4,60°}	{8,0°}
8	{8,120°}	{3,0°}	{4,60°}	{5,60°}

This example should not be taken as the optimal way of solving the problem, merely as an illustrative exercise in flexing a number of ART's facilities. In particular, extra rules could be defined to prune more unwanted solution nodes.

11.3 How it felt to use the toolkit

The following section contains personal opinions regarding features and performance levels of Inference ART versions 2.0 (*Symbolics Genera 6.1*), 3.0 (*Symbol-*

ics Genera 7.1, Sun UNIX v3.4) and 3.1.1 (Sun UNIX v3.4). Some preferences are for/against the toolkit, *per se*, whilst others merely provide suggestive evidence for the efficacy of the toolkit on a particular hardware platform.

Conventional benchmarking of the application developed has been included, but the reader should note that the two platforms discussed are very different in architecture and no strong interpretation of comparative metrics such as swap space or physical memory size should be attempted. ART is also available on a number of other platforms not reviewed here.[7]

11.3.1 Commissioning the software

The commissioning process is straightforward on both the platforms with the exception that, due to the security provisions taken by Inference Corporation, the software must be recommissioned at certain major host system events such as change of CPU or Ethernet address. The former is quite possible after a hardware repair visit. The commissioning process must be be carried out in liaison with Inference Corporation or their appointed distributors.

11.3.2 Editors

Certain assumptions are tacitly made about ART. One of which, is that the potential user has a level of computer literacy adequate to deal with the concept of an editor. It is a reasonable assumption and most users will find that ART is well integrated with their favourite editor if they have used other software on the hardware platform. Using either ZMACS under Genera or a choice of VI or GnuEmacs+Emacstool[8] under Sun UNIX, functions are provided to operate on ART and LISP code fragments within the editor window, the most useful being the incremental compilation or evaluation of:

- the innermost expression around the cursor
- the outermost expression enclosed by a region
- the entire buffer contents

It must be noted that ZMACS and its SUN equivalent, GnuEmacs, are of greater sophistication and have a number of facilities not present in the VI editor. These include:

- the concept of a 'syntax mode', permitting a language-specific set of key bindings and 'intelligent tabbing'.

[7] Also, at the time of completion of this article, ART 4.x had just been released. This version can run the graphics studio under the M.I.T. X windowing system.

[8] GnuEmacs and Emacstool are programs made available by the Free Software Foundation.

- robust indication of matching parentheses, unlike VI which often gets it wrong.
- easy extension through a self-contained LISP
- mouse support
- extensive, hierarchical, on-line help systems
- access to a large body of public domain editor extensions for GnuEmacs, such as: template editor modes to automate input of common ART idioms, integration with network communication facilities for multi-site ART development via e-mail; with version control software such as RCCS and with high-quality typesetting products such as LaTeX.

11.3.3 Debugging

The debugging process in ART is more complex than in a lower-level language. This is partly due to the way problems are implemented on agenda-based production rule systems in general and partly due to the fact that ART statements simply cause more changes to the *system state* than in, say, LISP, so the grain-size, when we talk of "incremental development" is necessarily coarser.

It should have been evident in the section that described the case-study that the salience of rules is a vital part of determining the flow of control. This is not always conveyed by the received wisdom on production systems, where a common introduction describes rules as self-contained, non-interacting entities, where salience is not an issue. There *are* problems where the causality of change in the working memory is unimportant, but in general, salience will play a part in the construction of any medium to large scale ART application.

The mechanics of debugging centres around a more or less conventional *think, edit, compile* cycle. The ART environment provides breakpointing, stepping, agenda display, RETE statistics collection, dribble files and, most importantly, incremental compilation. This latter feature becomes very powerful once the user has learned the exceptional cases where employing an incremental compilation would be invalid.

11.3.4 Delivering the software

We now come to the question of the utility of ART as a delivery language. Having developed an ART application we want to deliver it, either as a saleable product or as a tool to other departments within our organisation. If the product is going outside the concern it is usually important to ensure that the proprietary knowledge that makes the application effective is hidden from ART-literate programmers in similar concerns. The mechanism put forward for achieving this is the save-d ruleset,[9] which causes a LISP-binary file to be created. This speeds up the process of launching an application from cold. Unfortunately, the file still contains the documentation fields for ART statements as plain ASCII and does not make any attempt to encode symbols. In consequence, a potential vendor may consider it necessary to have to develop some form of preprocessor to strip out the documentation strings and modify symbol names depending upon the sensitivity of the application.

Even with the speed-up achieved by restore-ing a save-d ruleset, there may still be a potential launch problem with applications which either:

- have a long reset time
- require a significant amount of computation to be performed by the running rulebase before the end-user can interact with the application.

The problem may be alleviated for some applications by use of the ART disksave function. This allows the entire LISP image, which contains the current state of the application and all of ART, to be stored as an executable file.[10] Unfortunately, this only works with applications which do not use either the graphics or scrolling studios in the pre-disksave running phase, as the Sun version implements these as separate UNIX processes. Even with modifications, the size of the resulting image must be carefully budgeted for as can be seen from the directory listing for a major application [Orgill] when disksave-d:

```
total 25682
drwxrwxr-x  2 cho          512 Jan 23 14:34 ./
drwxr-xr-x  8 root         512 Mar 17 15:57 ../
-rwx------  1 cho     26271744 Oct 15 21:25 old.working.critic*
```

The listing shows that the executable is 25Mbytes! A knowledge of the memory management techniques of the LISP substrate is required to use disksave effectively.

Inference Corp. supply, at reduced cost, a delivery-only version of ART in an attempt to keep multiple machine installations cost-effective. This product does not offer the development functions, but retains the ability to launch applications developed at other sites.[11]

---

[9] Version 3.1 additionally allows ALL top-level statements to be save-d.

[10] Sun only tested.

[11] Inspecting the BNF for ART, however, reveals that, since it is quite possible for an ART application to write rules at run-time, the rule-compiler must be present in the delivery version also.

Chapter 12

Selecting a tool for an application

Chris Price

> Use a shell if you can,
> an environment where you should,
> and an AI language when you must.
> *Expert Systems in Business* [Barrett and Beerel].

One of the problems with choosing the right tool for implementing a particular application is that there almost never will be one 'right' choice. Any selection will be a matter of compromise, a case of weighing advantages against limitations. Several tools with quite different characteristics can appear to be equally reasonable as solution vehicles for a given project. This is especially true when the requirements phase of the project has not established in detail the level of knowledge representation and reasoning that is necessary to solve the problem.

Assuming the representation and reasoning needs of a project have been established, then the most important question needing to be addressed when selecting a tool to build a particular system is:

How well does this tool enable you to build the system you designed?

There are two levels of analysis that need to be done in order to answer that question adequately. The first problem that needs to be addressed is the identification of which of the categories of tool outlined in chapter 6 will be most suitable for this type of problem.

Once a class of tool (for example, a high-end toolkit) has been identified as being suitable for the job, more detailed questions will need to be examined in order to select a particular tool within that class. Not all of these detailed questions are concerned with the technical abilities of the tool. Many of them embrace wider issues concerning the demands of the particular application.

12.1 Identifying the correct class of tool

In the quote at the start of this chapter, Mike Barrett puts his finger on an important rule of knowledge engineering: when you are selecting a tool to use in building a particular application, it makes sense to choose the simplest tool that is powerful enough to perform the task.

If an application is suitable for being performed by an expert system shell, then the correct decision is likely to be the use of shell technology. For example, if what is required is a simple classification task, with a question/answer session between the application and a user or with a form-filling type of interface, then it is often actually easier to build systems with such interfaces using a shell than it is using more complex tools.

The first question to be considered in order to decide whether shell technology is adequate for building the application is:

> *Can the application be represented in terms of a classification task?*

The main feature of a classification task is that it is possible to identify a number of separate categories of solution, and to use available criteria to decide how to classify each case (see chapter 7 for more details of classification tasks).

The first question is a useful guide to whether a shell can be used, but it is not enough to decide for certain. The next question is:

> *Do the relationships between many different items in the application area need to be reasoned about at the same time?*

For instance, if one was constructing a KBS to reason about military movements, it might be necessary to reason about the positions of all single enemy tanks, clustering them into likely divisions, and relating the positions of enemy divisions to the position of friendly divisions.

This sort of reasoning is quite difficult to do by using the mechanisms provided in expert system shells. There is a simpler type of reasoning about multiple items where only one item needs to be reasoned about at one time — for example, an analysis of how each one of many loan applications should be dealt with. In that example, each loan application can be dealt with in isolation. Expert system shells can often deal with this simpler type of application. The database access routines of a shell such as LEVEL5 would allow it to step through a database of such loan application records, examining each one separately.

If a shell is not powerful enough to build the solution, then the best choice is likely to be some sort of integrated toolkit. The decision between high-end or medium-priced toolkit needs to be based on the more detailed criteria in section 12.2, unless specific representation and reasoning criteria (such as the need to employ an ATMS) can be identified at this stage.

Finally, there is a more arcane type of application, where a special representation style or reasoning mechanism is required which does not match what is provided by any of the shells or integrated toolkit systems. Loosely coupled toolkits are usually the best sort to use for this type of application. If you are constructing your own representation or performing complex reasoning, or if you are building experimental state-of-art systems, then loosely-coupled toolkits will be the best choice. The case study in chapter 10 is an example of such a system.

Applications which have significant real-time requirements are a specialised area. They are probably better carried out with a toolkit such as G2 or MUSE, which is designed specifically for that type of application. However, simple monitoring tasks where a fairly slow response time is needed could probably be accomplished by most types of tool. What must be done in order to ensure that the tool meets the requirements of the application is careful calculation of the performance of the knowledge-based system.

For most applications, the outcome of analysing which class of tool best fits the application will be the selection of a single type of tool (shell or integrated toolkit or loosely coupled toolkit). Occasionally, the correct selection will be less obvious, and it will be necessary to keep the option of a couple of types of tool. In that case, it is worth compiling a list of the representational advantages or drawbacks of each choice. This list can be expanded when considering the lesser issues given in the next section. The best actual tool can then be picked in the same way as if it had been possible to identify a single class of tool as correct for the application.

12.2 Selecting a tool within a class

Having examined the representation and reasoning needs of an application, and narrowed the choice of possible tools by identifying the likely best class of tool to handle the application, then the next task is to sort out which tool in that class (or those classes) best suits the particular application.

There are several other important criteria apart from representation and reasoning that might affect the suitability of a tool for an application. In fact, the most important lesson to be learned from the following list of criteria is that many factors need to be taken into account when choosing a tool. In some cases, these lesser issues can outweigh the representation and reasoning criteria that were applied to decide on the right class of tool for the application. Certainly these issues must be given serious consideration when making a decision between several tools within the same tool class.

Developer interface

The advantages of a good interface for the developer were extolled in chapter 3, along with an examination of the main interface features that were available in the best toolkits. Questions to bear in mind are:

- When the knowledge-based system is being developed, what sort of debugging tools are provided to help that development (intelligent syntax directed editors, inspectors, rule execution tracers, etc.)?
- What sort of development turnaround is there? When you make a small change to a large KBS, how long is it before you can test the system again (i.e does the edit-compile-debug cycle get in the way of development)?
- Is there a knowledge acquisition system that produces output which can be executed by the tool?
- Is there rule validation software provided which will check the contents of the KBS and highlight any likely problems?

User interface

It is easier to build some sort of reasonable user interface with the facilities provided by a shell than with those in most integrated toolkits, but harder to construct a complex graphical user interface. However, interface requirements will change from project to project, and so it is important to ask the following questions in the context of a particular set of user interface requirements:

- Does the system have a ready-made user interface? If so, is it appropriate for the application? If the answer to either of those questions is "No" , then is it possible to build such an interface, and how easy would it be?
- What sort of explanations will be available to the user when the system has been completed? Are such explanations sufficient? How much extra work is needed to construct the explanations?
- If the application requires the user to provide a great deal of information, is there any built-in mechanism to help the user to retract answers after they have been given (users are notorious for making mistakes).

Delivery considerations

The requirements for deliverability vary between applications. Three delivery requirements that are possible in different situations are:

Portability. Even when constructing an exploratory system, there are advantages to being able to demonstrate it on a portable machine or on one that is commonly available around the company. If the KBS has to be available for use by field service personnel, then the need for portability is even greater.

Cost per unit delivered. Alternatively, if the application is to be delivered to many sites, then the cost of the machine that must be purchased at each site in order to run the application becomes a significant factor (another possibility is that it might run on a type of machine already available at each of the sites).

Central control. A third possibility is that the application will need to run on a central machine that is accessible from many sites. Central control of the KBS can alleviate some of the problems of maintaining it — only one copy of the application needs to be kept up to date.

Depending on which of these possibilities is chosen, some of the following questions will be relevant:

- Does the tool run on a particular type of machine (mainframe, PC or whatever is required for this application)?
- If the KBS is to be delivered on a PC, can the development work be carried out on a more powerful machine? This calls for a toolkit to be available compatibly on different computers.
- Delivery costs? If the application is to be delivered to many sites, is there a charge by the supplier for each copy of the application? — Some suppliers make a charge for what they call a *delivery licence*. Basically, you have to pay them a fee for each copy of your KBS that you deliver.

Limitations

When delivered on smaller machines, many of the available tools have some limitations compared to the way in which they run on larger machines. The most obvious one is speed, but in some cases, there is also a limitation on the size of the KBS. If delivery does need to be on some sort of PC, then the following questions are worth asking:

- Is there a limit on the size of the knowledge base that can be built with this tool? If so, is it so small that it may be a problem for this application?
- What happens to the speed of execution of the application as the size of the knowledge base increases? (This question can often be of relevance on larger machines too.)
- Assuming that it is possible for the knowledge base to be bigger than the available memory on a PC, what happens to speed of execution when the knowledge base has to be paged?

Cost of the toolkit

Value for money is difficult to judge, and it can often be hard to justify to the management the cost of a more expensive toolkit even when it can be shown to be in a more powerful class. Reasonable comparisons of price can only be made between tools in the same class.

- How does this tool's price compare to similar products?
- What are the justifications for any significant differences (more expensive *or* cheaper)?
- If it will be necessary to deliver lots of copies of the KBS being built, will that cost extra money (see delivery considerations section above).

Interaction with the outside world

For most applications, whatever knowledge engineering tool is used, it will probably be necessary to write some parts of the system in a conventional language (e.g. any file access routines or innovative screen handling software). This means that some of the following issues may be of importance:

- Does the tool provide an interface for calling routines written in other languages and for importing information from them? Can such outside routines be written in a language with which the developers feel comfortable?
- Are database access routines provided, or do they need to be written? If they are provided, are they flexible enough for the requirements of the application? (If they are provided at extra cost, then that cost should be taken into account when considering the price of different tools).
- Can the tool be embedded within another program? (Only relevant if needed for the application.)

Training and support

Some of the suppliers of the more complex toolkits suggest that it takes three to six months of exposure to become competent at using their toolkits. Effective training courses can provide a short-cut to much of the experience that must be assimilated. The easy availability of consultancy can also be invaluable on the occasions when in-house expertise has proved insufficient.

- Does in-house expertise with the toolkit already exist? When personnel are already trained in using a particular toolkit, and the toolkit is good enough for the intended application, it makes no sense to change to another toolkit.
- Does training exist? How much training is needed in order to be able to use the toolkit efficiently? How much does that training cost? How good are the training courses?
- Are other skills necessary apart from using the toolkit itself. For example, some of the integrated toolkits require the knowledge engineer to be able to write a great deal of LISP.
- Is the training course adaptable to your needs? — Some courses encourage you to take details of a relevant application problem along with you, so that you can begin working on that rather than on some hypothetical example. This can be invaluable, as you will have access to a consultant when you need it most, and this can give you a head start on developing your application.
- Can the suppliers demonstrate that they themselves have proven experience using the tool? This is especially relevant when you are buying the tool from a distributor rather than the original builders of the tool.
- Do the supplier's staff seem capable, knowledgeable and eager to please?
- Has the supplier company been around for a while, showing some stability?
- If you have problems with your application, will the supplier be willing and able to provide you with access to experienced consultants, and at what cost?

12.3 Example selections

The previous sections of this chapter have been, out of necessity, somewhat general. This section considers particular example applications, and makes a choice of toolkit for constructing each example system. The analysis of each example is carried out in the following manner:

Description of the application. This will give details about the application domain and about the problems that the application is intended to address.

Outline design. This will analyse the representation and reasoning needs of the application.

Environment requirements. This will specify the other important characteristics that are required of the toolkit. It can be assumed that all developers will want the best development environment available, and that all the toolkits considered have reasonable pricing and support, so the important characteristics requirements will focus on the user interface needs, the outside interface needs and the deliverability needs of the application.

Selection of class, then selection of tool. Having defined the application and the way in which it should be implemented, and identified the environment requirements, all that remains is to perform the two part analysis described in sections 12.1 and 12.2 of this chapter.

12.3.1 "Choice of tool for KBS" application

Description of the application

Imagine that you work for a government agency interested in encouraging the use of KBS technology throughout the country. You decide that one way to achieve this aim would be to develop a system which advises prospective KBS users on what toolkit is best suited for for the application that they wish to build. This toolkit advisory system will be distributed free to a large community of users.

Examples of the type of knowledge that would need to be built into such a system are detailed earlier in this chapter — with any luck the government agency sponsoring the system will buy copies of this book to accompany each copy of the advisory system that is distributed.

Outline design

The system will be built to perform the two-level classification described earlier in this chapter. The system will first classify the type of tool that is needed for the application that the user has in mind. This will be one of:

- Expert system shell
- Integrated toolkit
- Loosely coupled toolkit
- A decision that KBS technology is not suitable

After this initial classification, the system will take into account more detailed issues concerning the chosen class of toolkit in order to select a single tool to employ on the user's application.

Environment requirements

The KBS choosing application will have a simple question and answer interface to the user, in order to ascertain details of the user's proposed application. There will be no need for any interface to code outside of the KBS.

The system will need to be deliverable on a PC, so that it can be distributed on a floppy disc and used by interested parties on hardware to which they are likely to already have access to in their offices.

Selection of class, then selection of tool

This simple classification type of task fits shell technology very well. The task is evidently one of classifying a problem into one of a limited number of possibilities.

Each of the shells examined in chapter 6 would be adequate for implementing this task. Each provides the ability to deliver applications on a PC. LEVEL5 has the tidiest packaging of applications for delivery to people inexperienced in computer usage, but if I didn't already own any of these packages, I would probably choose VP-Expert for this application because it is so cheap.

12.3.2 Car insurance premium evaluation

Description of the application

Many car insurance premiums are very straightforward to calculate — an amount based on age, experience and type of car, a 60% no claims discount, an extra 10% discount for limiting the people allowed to drive the car, etc. A KBS to work in this area would need to calculate premiums for these simple cases, and would also need to detect two sorts of exceptions.

Firstly, there are car insurance proposals that are so risky that the insurance company would not want the business at any price. For example, men aged under 21 that drive sports cars are a notorious risk, so perhaps an insurance company might decide that they are better off without business like that.

Secondly, there are exceptions to the "risky proposal" classifications in the first category. An exception to the young men in sports cars category might be an 18-year-old entrepreneur applying for car insurance — although he is a bad risk, an insurance company might accept his car insurance proposal in the hope that they will also acquire his goodwill and the business insurance custom of his company.

Outline design

This is a decision making system which fits the classification style of system building outlined in chapter 7. The first step towards deciding on the premium to be paid is to make a top-level classification of the application into one of the three areas:

Accept — Calculate the premium for the car insurance, using the standard algorithm for doing so.

Reject — Decide not to accept the insurance proposal. No premium calculation is needed.

High risk — Calculate the standard acceptance premium. Add an extra percentage to the premium to take account of the extra risk being taken.

The top-level classification can be performed using fairly simple rules acting as a checklist of reasons to reject the proposal. There will be further rules considering exceptions to any rejection reasons that are identified.

Environment requirements

Most of the information needed to make a decision in each case will be obtained from a database record which holds the details entered on the original proposal form. The system will need to be able to generate fairly simple reports, including a letter of acceptance or rejection to the applicant, and should prompt the user (an insurance adviser) for any information that is missing from the database record.

The system should run on an IBM mainframe, so that it can be guaranteed that all the insurance advisers use the same insurance premium calculation system, providing uniformity across the insurance company.

Selection of class, then selection of tool

Like the first application, this one can be solved through classification. Each proposal form can be assessed without taking the others into account. The sort of knowledge employed to make a decision about a proposal can be represented as rules. For this reason, an expert system shell again seems perfectly adequate for the application.

As well as the ability to interface to a database, and reasonable reporting facilities, the tool chosen will also need acceptable arithmetic facilities in order to calculate the premium amount (although the calculation might be better done by accessing outside routines if such routines already exist in an earlier computerized system). This may rule out a few of the cheaper shells on the market.

The database facilities supplied in LEVEL5 are ideal for this task. LEVEL5 also meets the other requirements, including availability on an IBM mainframe.

12.3.3 Promotion guidance for employees

Description of the application

A company has discovered through experience that many days of effort are wasted by employees who spend too much time worrying about how best to gain advancement — whether to remain within the company or join a different company. It is decided to help the employees (and indirectly the company) by providing access to a KBS which will give a (fairly) honest expert evaluation of their prospects. This will both save all that idle worrying, and reassure all the employees which the company wishes to keep that their employer recognizes their worth and their work rate.

It should be noted at this point that this application (unlike the other examples in this section) is not based even vaguely on any actual system that has been implemented. I have never heard of any KBS that performs this task, and would think that there are potential problems facing any employer who implemented such a system.

Outline design (1)

A first glance at the problem would certainly place this decision making system in the classification category. It would use details about the employee — age, level of attainment, type of job, results of personality tests, knowledge about personal goals and summaries of internal assessment reports. These details would be combined to reach one of the following decisions:

Stay with company. The employee's best prospects lie in continuing to work for the company. In addition, the system should produce a five-year plan charting the employee's likely progress.

Leave the company. The system would tell the employee the best time to leave, both for the employee and the company.

Stay a while. In the short term, the employee's best interests lie in staying with the company, but in the longer term (specified) the employee should look elsewhere for another job with better prospects.

Outline design (2)

The system outlined above might be useful to many of the employees, but it lacks the ability to take specific circumstances into account. For many employees, their career path will depend on what happens to other people — a boss retires and the second-in-command is promoted; another subordinate does not win promotion because there is someone younger on the same grade who is much more talented.

A more sophisticated system would take these relationships into account when making the classification, using rules like:

```
IF immediate superior is retiring within 3 years
AND there is no other employee on same level as employee
                   with better seniority/conduct profile
AND the company recruits this post internally
AND superiors of immediate superior approve of employee
    THEN employee is in line for promotion
```

This example rule could be implemented as a set of simple propositions, with the user answering questions like "Is there another employee on the same grade with the a better seniority/conduct profile?" and "Does your superior's boss think you are ready for your superior's job?".

Much better would be to build a knowledge base which used information available in the company database to answer such questions automatically using the company's view of the employees. This is too complex to implement using an expert system shell, but could be accomplished using a frame-based representation with knowledge about each employee and about the relationships between all the employees in the company.

Environment requirements

For both designs, much of the information needed to reach a decision will be available in the company database, and so an interface to that data will be necessary. The system needs to be available on the PC on the employee's desk, but all company PCs are networked and have access to the cluster of corporate VAXen where the database of company employee details is held. The best solution (because of the need for company database access) would be for the system to actually run on the company VAXen, although it would be possible for the PCs to run the system and request the data from across the network.

Selection of class, then selection of tool (1)

An expert system shell will be adequate for the simpler version of the system, because the simpler design avoids the complex inter-employee reasoning that is attempted by the second design.

Envisage has some advantages for this type of application. It allows fairly complex reasoning on arrays of records of facts. As well as enabling the simpler system to be constructed, this will give the potential for incorporation of some of the more complex reasoning in the second design. The excellent string handling facilities will facilitate production of a nicely personalized (and so more believable) report.

Selection of class, then selection of tool (2)

The need to represent complex relationships between many different types of item means that a frame representation is necessary for the second design, and so a toolkit is the right choice. The reasoning needing to be done can be performed by using rules which access the frame representation, and so there is no obvious need to use a loosely coupled toolkit to build one's own representation — some sort of integrated toolkit should prove sufficient.

This application is not particularly demanding on the integrated toolkits, and so any of them should be able to perform it adequately. Nexpert is strong on integration with databases, runs on both VAXen and large PCs (allowing us to hedge our bets about where to run the application) and would seem a reasonable choice.

12.3.4 Chemical process plant troubleshooting

Description of the application

A chemical process plant such as the one described in chapter 10 comprises many pipes and tanks, and can undergo physical processes of heating, cooling and pressurization, either in order to produce chemical reactions or as by-products of those reactions. Materials pass through the plant during the reactions, and are changed in chemical nature and in volume during the process.

Such process plants have sensors built in, to detect changes in temperature, pressure, volume, and flow. The task of a complete troubleshooting system on such a plant can be split into three phases:

Detection of anomaly. This is a monitoring activity, and the aim of this phase is to judge whether the sensor readings for the plant can be explained by the processes that are occurring in the plant or whether the most likely explanation for the phenomena observed is a fault rather than the normal operating of the plant.

This phase should operate continuously, and if no suspicious symptoms are encountered, then it will be the only phase of the troubleshooting system to operate.

Identification of cause of the anomaly. Once a fault has been detected, it should be possible to use heuristics to identify the cause of the fault. This will involve further observations about the state of the plant, and possibly some intrusive tests to obtain necessary data. The outcome of this stage should be the identification of the cause of the fault, or the conclusion that there was no fault, or the verdict that the fault is beyond the capability of the system to diagnose.

Remedial action. Where the cause of a fault has been identified, then remedial action should be taken. This may involve repairing part of the plant, or halting the process, or executing plans for emergency action.

It should be noted that this type of system is different from the general process plant running that was described in the RESCU case study. It is harder in that it must concern itself with faulty running of the plant and with the structure of the plant, and yet simpler in that it does not need to know all of the details of how to control the processes.

Outline design (1)

A system to detect most of the important anomalies likely to occur on a chemical process plant would need to have a representation of the relationships between different parts of the plant and a way of reasoning about the effects of different processes across the plant. A frame-based representation, with relations between the different frames would be an adequate way of implementing these requirements.

Where components such as tanks and processes such as flow occurred repeatedly across the process plant, the system should reuse the reasoning linked to those parts or processes. For instance, one useful check that could be repeated across the plant would be to monitor liquid flows through the plant in order to detect leaks of liquid (or of gas), detectable by unaccountable differences between input flow and output flow. More frames giving details about different plant components and processes could be used to express such constraints across the plant, and rules could detect when constraints were violated.

The ability to interpret trends on the plant is also necessary to monitoring — for example, the heating/cooling of parts of the plant over time could be monitored, and inexplicable trends detected before alarms are triggered. Such trends are quite difficult to express symbolically, and it could be that some numerical processing should be interfaced to the KBS to perform trend analysis.

When suspicious symptoms have been detected, the next step is to find the fault(s) that account for the symptoms. This could be done by hypothesizing likely faults for a particular set of symptoms, and performing tests that will confirm or disprove each hypothesis. Both the hypothesis generation and the selection of tests can be implemented using rules (probably rules that will interface to the frame-based representation already constructed). The control of different hypotheses will be made easier by using reasoning facilities for dealing with multiple hypothetical worlds.

When a particular fault has been confirmed, the repair process will depend on the type of fault and the type of repair action needed. It is not likely to be harder to implement than the part of the system already described.

Reasonable guaranteed response will be needed, but what is reasonable will depend on the speed with which events change on the plant. Many process plants change state quite slowly, and the ability to detect trends will mean that the real-time demands of such plants will be quite light (because faults should be detected long before they become critical). However, some types of symptom are likely to be more important than others, and so the system should prioritize the monitoring/diagnosis to ensure that serious faults are monitored more carefully and more frequently.

A final detail that can be important in this sort of system is suitable justifications for any diagnosis reached. These are difficult to construct in any type of tool, but need to be addressed because of the important consequences that may come from the diagnosis. The system should be accountable to the human operators of the plant.

Environment requirements (1)

The user interface should include graphical displays of the plant state, and of the values of important sensors. In order to monitor plant readings on a frequent basis, the monitoring system will need an interface to the plant information — either direct, or via the plant logging system. Very few copies of any particular system will be needed, so there should be no particular problems about delivery systems.

Selection of class, then selection of tool (1)

The system is certainly too complex for an expert system shell — while much of the effect is produced by rules, the interrelationship between components and processes would be difficult to express without a frame-based representation.

Among the integrated toolkits, the description of the system seems to fit ART fairly well. For the most part, the frame-based representation is fairly static, with much of the work being accomplished by powerful rules that gradually move towards a conclusion. The hypothesizing of possible faults also fits ART's Viewpoint facilities very well.

Finally, ART's graphical user interface building facilities are sufficient for implementing the sort of interface discussed above.

Outline design (2)

It is possible to simplify the system described above by leaving out the monitoring phase, and limiting the type of anomaly that can be detected and corrected. Many process plants have certain areas of the plant that are specific causes of concern, and it is possible to build simpler knowledge-based systems that deal only with the problem areas. Concern in these areas might be caused by readings (of temperature or pressure, for example) reaching specific values, or by rapid changes in the value of a reading over time.

Instead of detecting all suspicious conditions, a simpler troubleshooting system would aid the operator by responding when alarms occurred on the plant. This type of help is still valuable. Alarm situations can be difficult for the operator to handle, due to cognitive overload caused by too much information being provided at once. This simpler application could be termed "emergency troubleshooting" or "alarm analysis".

The representation for this simpler system can often be accomplished through the use of rules and simple facts, which brings it within the scope of expert system shells (it is still classification, and the difficult representation of frames and relationships is no longer needed).

However, the demands on the reasoning for this system are fairly rigorous, and so some care needs to be taken in selecting a shell. The simplest representation would be to treat each possible fault as a possible classification, and then to examine each one as a goal. This would have several unwanted effects. Firstly, the KBS constructed in this way would usually ask questions in a fairly unstructured manner, as it pursued and ruled out different goals. Secondly, once a fault had been found, the KBS should stop seeking faults and attempt to repair the identified fault, and that would not happen — all of the other possible faults would be investigated first.

The first problem can be solved by using a shell with good procedural control structure and reasonable modularity — the most significant plant readings can often be used to rule out many of the faults that could happen, and so the ability to modularize the goal structure of the KBS would allow investigation of relevant faults only. This procedural control structure will also be useful for the repair stage of the troubleshooting, as simple repair can often be represented as a set of procedures to follow (perhaps with a few goals to evaluate in order to adapt to the prevailing conditions).

The second problem (stopping searching for faults and starting to perform repair) needs the ability to stop pursuing fault goals, and to invoke repair goals. This probably needs both rudimentary forward chaining and good control structures.

Environment requirements (2)

The graphical interface displaying plant readings might still be useful, and the interface to the relevant process plant sensor readings is vital — the last thing that an operator wants to be doing when there is an emergency on a process plant is to be typing values into a computer program.

Selection of class, then selection of tool (2)

Both LEVEL5 and Envisage have the sort of control structures needed here.

In LEVEL5, the goal/subgoal description would allow the system to focus on likely possibilities, and the other control structures that can be embedded in rules will also be useful. In addition, further modularity can be imposed by splitting the knowledge base into sensible chunks and only chaining to relevant chunks.

In Envisage, the knowledge base can be split into areas, where an area would contain related faults that should logically be investigated at once. When a fault was identified, control could be passed to another area which dealt with relevant repair matters.

12.4 Conclusions

It is conceivable that the previous section of examples might give the wrong impression of the process of selecting tools for particular applications. In each case, a single reasonable tool selection was made for a somewhat hypothetical application. Sadly, there is no single ideal choice for almost any application. A number of tools will be able to handle the application, and there will be compromises to be made in using any of them.

On the other hand, there definitely are choices that are just plain wrong for some applications — either because the application is too complex for the tool, or because the application is so simple that using a complex tool on an expensive piece of hardware would be a complete waste of money.

The intention of this chapter, and the main aim of the book, has been to help knowledge engineers choose the correct tool for the correct application. This is done by identifying the main representation and reasoning needs of the application, and specifying its environmental requirements, and selecting the tool that best fits the application profile.

Appendix A

Next-generation toolkits

Chris Price

I never think of the future,
It comes soon enough.
Albert Einstein.

A.1 Introduction

No-one who has used today's toolkits would doubt that improvements to them are both possible and overdue. One reason for hoping that things will improve is just that building expert systems seems to be harder than it should be. A better reason for this conviction is because we have observed that the application of knowledge can solve users' problems, and so we can expect that it will begin to solve the developers' problems too. The improvements examined in this chapter are all concerned with applying knowledge about how to solve problems and knowledge about the problem domain to the task of simplifying knowledge-based system construction.

The final outcome of improvements to a toolkit should be measurable as better performance in one or more of the following areas:

Development cost. Manpower is the most significant cost in any knowledge-based system development. If it becomes possible to produce the same application with less effort from the expert and/or the knowledge engineer, then the cost of building such applications will fall. This sort of advantage can be expected from more powerful development tools or from better knowledge acquisition tools.

Deliverability. One of the problems with many of the early knowledge engineering tools was that they could not easily be integrated into a deliverable product. You had to buy a copy of the tool for each run-time knowledge-based system that you delivered. This is rather like needing to buy a Pascal compiler for every copy of a Pascal program that you deliver. Most tool suppliers have at least modified this iniquitous practice to one of charging a much reduced fee for each "delivery licence". Other delivery problems are integration with outside programs and lack of a user interface that an ordinary mortal can understand. These problems are also being addressed by the better present-day toolkits.

Robustness. Assuming that the underlying toolkit is robust (not always a valid assumption!), then there is the problem of ensuring that your knowledge-based application covers all problems in its domain, or at least admits its shortcomings rather than giving a wrong answer. This sort of robustness is the responsibility of the knowledge engineer at present, and the sort of validation tools mentioned in section 5.3 can help with this task. Model-based reasoning, explored in section A.4 is a longer term, but very promising, technology for addressing this problem.

Maintainability. Expert knowledge evolves over time, because of changes in understanding of the domain, or because of changes to factors in the domain. Tools are needed to help maintain knowledge-based systems, but the maintainability of such systems will also be improved by better knowledge representation facilities. Higher levels of representation and reasoning will improve the level of description of the expert knowledge, and make it more accessible, more easily understood, and therefore more maintainable.

We will now examine some improvements to knowledge engineering toolkits; improvements which are for the most part still on the research horizon. This exploration will be done in the light of the areas where we have shown that performance needs to be improved, identifying which of these areas are affected by each type of improvement.

A.2 Knowledge reuse

An important way of making KBSs easier to build is by reusing knowledge which is common to a number of different applications. An expert system shell is an example of the simplest level of reuse. It contains a representation and an inference mechanism which has been found to be useful across a range of applications.

If we analyse a typical application, then it is possible to classify the knowledge into five different levels. Take as an example a knowledge-based system to perform project management for the mythical software company of Bambleweeney

Ltd. There are different levels of expert knowledge in such a system. Each level can be reused to some degree, but as the level of generality changes, so does the potential for knowledge reuse.

Underlying representation and reasoning. This is the level that is provided by today's toolkits — basic building blocks with which a wide range of systems can be built.

Task knowledge. It is possible to use the underlying reasoning to perform different tasks, such as *classification*, where tests are used to split up the search space of possibilities.

Generic application knowledge. In the Bambleweeney software project management KBS, this would be knowledge about managing projects, for example knowledge about planning and replanning projects, knowledge about how to resolve problems. Much of this knowledge is not specific to the software industry, but applicable when planning any type of project.

Domain-specific knowledge. This would be knowledge about the characteristics of software projects. Some of this knowledge will be more specific application knowledge (specific details about software projects that make them different from civil engineering projects, for example). Other generic domain knowledge might be relevant for different software applications. For instance, how to work out the cost of having software engineers idle would be relevant to a KBS that decided whether to bid for a piece of work as well as to a software project management KBS.

System-specific details. For a software project management KBS to be of maximum benefit to a company, then it would need to take into account the way in which that company operates, the qualities of its staff, its past record in running projects. All of this knowledge would be very specific to Bambleweeney Ltd, and not much of it could be reused in a software project management KBS for another company.

The pyramid shown in figure A.1 expresses some of the relationship between these types of knowledge. The lower items are general and very reusable, and are applicable to the construction of a wide variety of systems. The items higher in the pyramid are built on the foundations provided by the lower items, and are more specific to particular applications. They have less potential for reuse.

Level One of the pyramid is the only level being regularly reused by most knowledge engineers. Level Two also has a great potential for reuse. It only gives a general distinction between different control strategies, but it is very useful for partitioning a knowledge base. *Generic task abstraction*, considered in subsection A.2.1 is one way of providing this sort of reuse.

Levels Three and Four of the pyramid are the basis for *vertical toolkits*, considered in subsection A.2.2. These could be built on top of a set of generic tasks. They can be regarded as a template for a whole class of applications, where all of the specific details have been stripped out.

Level Five contains the knowledge which is specific to the particular application being built, and so gives the least opportunity for reuse.

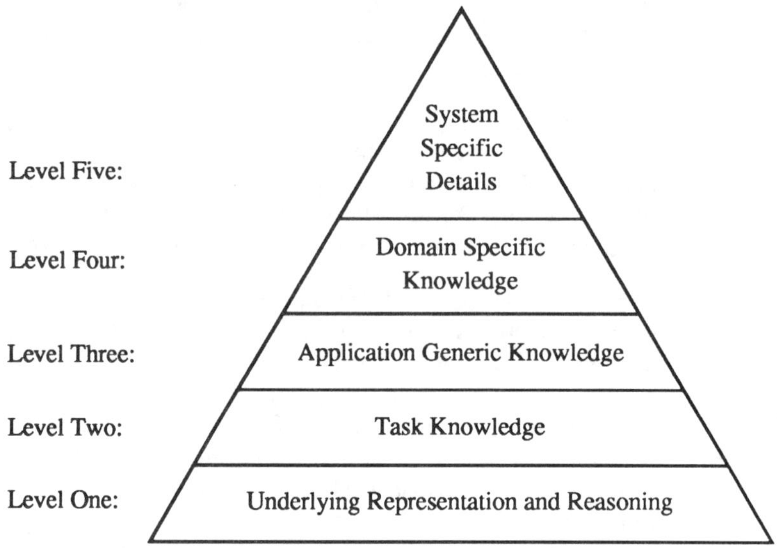

Figure A.1: Different levels of knowledge

A.2.1 Generic task abstraction

Chapter 7 gives an outline of the different types of problem for which KBSs are built. Unfortunately, when a problem-solver is being built for one of these problems, control knowledge about how to solve the problem is often made implicit in the knowledge about the problem itself.

Chandrasekaran, the originator of the generic task concept, argues that the fact that you can write almost any program in a language like OPS5 only confuses the knowledge representation process. Having implemented your system in such a language, it will be unclear which parts of the system represent domain expertise, and which are programming tricks to make the system work.

His solution is to separate out knowledge about how to control the reasoning process from the knowledge about the application domain. He does this by identifying different reusable control strategies (each one is a *generic task*). For each generic task, there is a reusable reasoning module which encapsulates that strategy.

The best way to illustrate this idea is through an example. Consider the chemical process plant example described in section 12.3.4. It breaks the application down into three main phases:

- Detection of anomaly.
- Identification of cause of the anomaly.
- Remedial action.

It was observed in chapter 12 that a simpler version of this application would assume that detection had occurred (through a sensor on the plant reaching a critical value) and would just concentrate on the problems of diagnosis and repair. This simpler application could be built in a modular manner using the following generic tasks:

Hierarchical classification. This can operate at several levels. For example, it could first attempt to localise the area of the plant where the problem must be. This would be followed by a more detailed examination of the sorts of fault that might have caused the alarm. In each case, the classification is attempting to move down a tree of possibilities like the one pictured in figure A.2. It is aided by the next generic task to be examined.

Hypothesis matching. Given a hypothesis (a possible classification in this case) and a set of data describing the problem state (the state of the plant), this task returns a likelihood that the hypothesis matches the situation. In this case, the classification task would use this information to decide between different possible faults.

Assembly of compound hypotheses. In some cases, the problem will be caused by a number of faults, rather than a single fault. That will mean that no single hypothesis will account for the symptoms. In that case, this task will attempt to identify a combination of faults that will account for the symptoms.

Plan selection and refinement. Repairing faults on the process plant is a matter of executing a plan. In some cases, those plans are very simple (turn on the cooling water), but in other cases it may be necessary to have a skeletal plan which needs to be filled in with particular details in order to address a complex situation.

Knowledge-directed information retrieval. This task enables information to be both accessed and interpreted (an intelligent database task). It could be used to help fill in particular details in the repair plans.

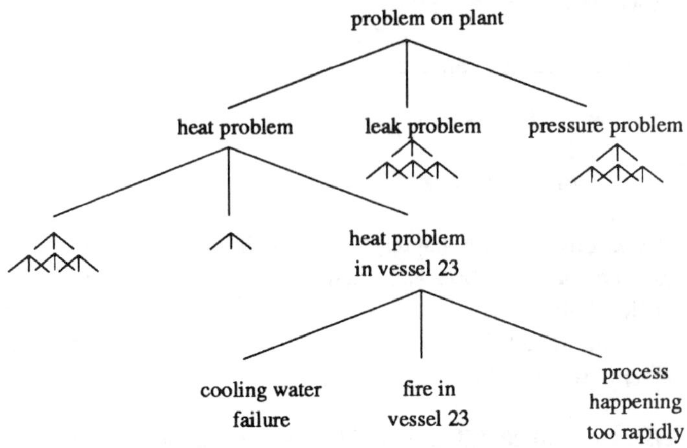

Figure A.2: Chemical plant diagnostic hierarchy

Figure A.3 shows the relationship between the generic tasks, the way in which the tasks are employed in the application, and the sorts of information in each task.

Consider the situation where a high-temperature alarm occurs on the plant. The classification task focusses on the plant vessel where the sensor was attached. It generates hypotheses for why the contents of the vessel might be too hot. These hypotheses are passed to the hypothesis matcher. It may have to examine other symptoms that might support or refute the hypotheses (pressure in the same vessel, temperature in attached pipes, readings of liquid flow meters etc.). The hypothesis matcher will return a measure of likelihood for each hypothesis.

In this case, the only hypothesis with strong support is that there is a fire in the vessel, and it accounts for all of the symptoms, so no assembly of hypotheses is needed.

The repair action for when a fire breaks out on the plant calls for execution of a general plan dictating what must be done. The plan includes considering the shutdown of nearby processes (in order to minimize the risk of explosion), calling the fire brigade, and immediate action to tackle the fire. The best strategy for tackling the fire will depend on the type of fire that has occurred. In this case, it has been identified as an oil-based fire. A knowledge base about types of fire, their particular dangers, and how to deal with each type can be interfaced to the

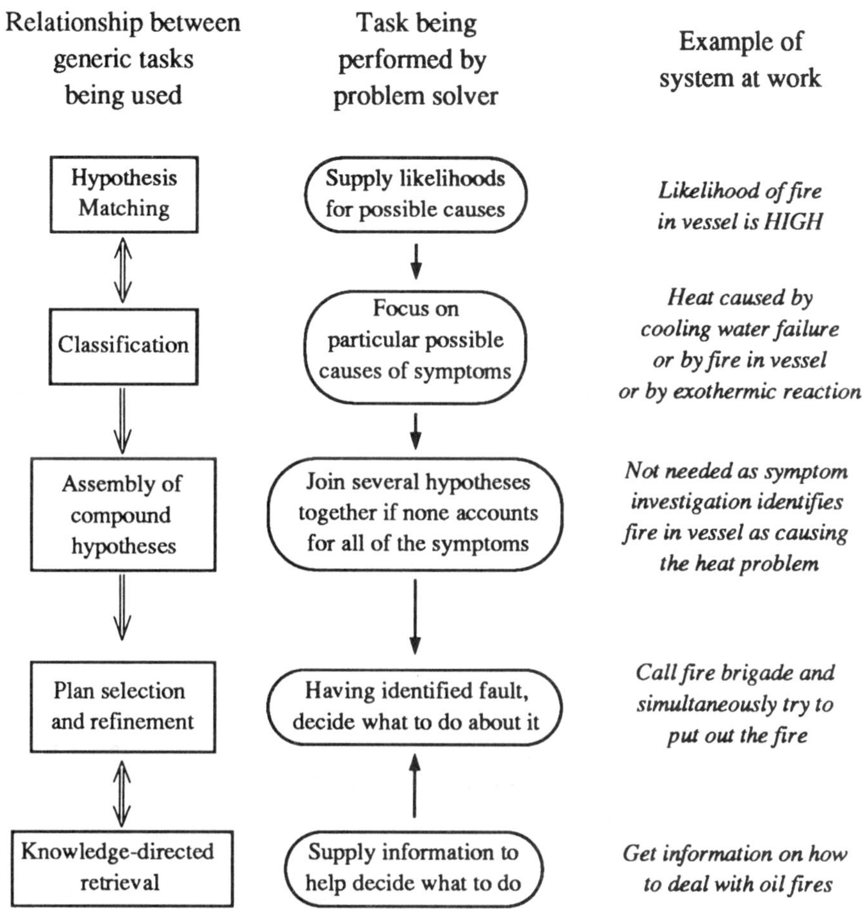

Figure A.3: Chemical process plant diagnostic system

plan refinement system in order to provide the knowledge needed to refine the plan.

This example has illustrated the use of several of the generic tasks identified by Chandrasekaran's group. However, it does not exhaust the types of generic task that they have identified, nor the ways in which each task can be used. Each task is applicable in many different types of application.

Benefits of generic task abstraction:

Generic abstraction of tasks can make it easier to build knowledge-based systems for the following reasons:

Control of reasoning is appropriate. Because the form of reasoning varies for each type of generic task, the type of reasoning can be chosen to suit the problem in hand, rather than forced on a problem where it is inappropriate.

System construction is much less haphazard. Knowledge about how to control the reasoning has been separated from the declarative type knowledge in the system, and so it is easy to differentiate between the two. This facilitates the maintenance of the declarative knowledge in the system.

The development cost should be reduced. It should become easier (and therefore cheaper) to build knowledge-based systems in this manner.

Drawbacks of generic task abstraction:

The representation is no longer uniform. Different types of concept are represented in different ways (unlike OPS5, for instance, where all expressions look the same). However, one could argue that uniformity has already been abandoned as a goal once knowledge engineers start using a hybrid mixture of rules and frames for representation and reasoning.

Cleverer knowledge acquisition tools are needed. Because each task represents knowledge in a different way, different knowledge elicitation tools will be needed to obtain knowledge for each generic task. On the positive side, there already exists a problem with acquiring different types of knowledge. Building knowledge elicitation tools that match the generic tasks may give us a chance to partially solve that problem.

Linking tasks is difficult. Not enough work has been done on the problems of building the sort of system that has been outlined in figure A.3, where a wide range of generic tasks are joined together to make a single problem-solving system. General methods need to be developed which will give guidance concerning how to couple generic tasks together.

To some extent, generic abstraction applies *software engineering* principles at the knowledge-based system design level. It encourages you to break your system down into recognized types of control unit that are already implemented, providing standard structures into which domain knowledge can be fitted. This brings the same benefits to knowledge-based system design as it does to other software engineering applications.

A.2.2 Vertical toolkits

A vertical toolkit is a blueprint for a specific class of applications. It has much of the knowledge about how to perform that type of application, but little of the knowledge that is specific to any particular application.

Attempts at vertical toolkits have been made for several of the different types of application outlined in chapter 7. Some of these toolkit attempts have been more successful than others. The most advanced area in this respect is simple diagnosis, where a number of toolkits have been built and are commercially available. This section will outline two different diagnostic toolkits available today — KLUE and TestBench, and then briefly describe other attempts at vertical toolkits.

KLUE

The KLUE development system runs on top of KEE, and produces "C" code that can run on an IBM PC. The intention of KLUE is to substantially reduce the amount of knowledge engineering involved in building a diagnostic expert system, by presenting the knowledge in the system in such a way that the experts themselves can both understand the system and maintain it.

This is done by representing the knowledge as a decision tree. Adding extra tests or new diagnoses means adding *question nodes* or *potential problem nodes* to the tree and linking them together with *answer links*. Simple instructions for action can be attached to problem nodes.

This decision tree representation is one with which many diagnostic experts will be familiar, and it makes the investigation strategy pictorially understandable to non-programmers. The accessibility of the fault tree representation allows the experts to build simple diagnostic expert systems of the level that could be managed in one of the expert system shells described in chapter 6. This can be achieved with very little input from trained knowledge engineers.

TestBench

TestBench relies on the same basic idea as KLUE — diagnostic knowledge can be represented as a classification tree, and once that tree has been built, it can be used as a basis for diagnosis. However, TestBench allows a greater variety of knowledge to be specified in the tree. This means that it is probably applicable to a wider range of diagnostic applications. On the other hand, it is harder to use — it is necessary to understand the significance of a larger number of "programming constructs", and the way in which they interact.

TestBench allows embellishment of the simple fault tree with, among other details:

- multiple causes for particular faults;
- lists of possible tests to confirm the classification
- the cost of performing each test (allowing the prioritization of testing);
- information about whether the repair must be confirmed to have worked before the diagnosis can be pronounced "correct".

Like KLUE, TestBench applications are developed on a workstation, and can be targetted to a PC.

Other areas

There has been research into building specialized toolkits to help the construction of knowledge-based systems in several other areas:

Project planning. An Alvey project, called "PLANIT", in the UK has developed a research project planning assistant. The system uses a Petri Net representation to encode the causal relationships between project resources, activities and the activity outputs of project plans. The Petri Net plan is then used as a fact-base by three expert systems, each concerned with a different generic area of project planning, to project the repercussions of updates to the plan, and to find solutions to plan failures.

Process control. Esprit project P820 has been researching the construction of a toolkit especially for building KBS applications for process control systems. The toolkit built on this project is a much looser association of tools relevant to that area than is the case with most vertical toolkits. It also aims to be useful for different types of application in that domain.

Configuration. Coherent Thought Inc. have announced a "Configuration Template", which understands configuration management, and can be configured for different types of configuration. In fact, this company is developing a range of vertical tools and may well emerge as a leader in the development of this type of toolkit.

Benefits of vertical toolkits

Reduced development cost. If an application matches the structure of one of these tools, then the time necessary to build the application can be significantly reduced. The reduction is most significant at the design stage. In effect, an "off the peg" design for the whole system has been chosen.

The system builder need be less sophisticated. The process of building applications has been simplified (because many design decisions are made automatically), which means that applications can be successfully built by developers with less experience.

Maintenance is easier. Where a group of developers have developed several similar systems with one of these tools, then the different applications should have a great deal in common. This should make it much easier for the applications to be supported by other members of the group instead of just by the original developer.

Drawbacks of vertical toolkits

There are very few drawbacks to this sort of toolkit. They really are a good idea. The main reasons why they are not in widespread use as yet are:

Motivation. The market for each such vertical tool needs to be large enough and rich enough to encourage toolkit builders to build such a tool.

Identification of commonality. It must be possible to identify both the types of representation and reasoning that are needed in the particular application area, and the common knowledge used in building that type of application. This usually implies that the tool builders need to have already implemented several applications of that type.

Overblown claims. Some toolkits of this type claim a greater degree of generality than they can actually deliver. It is still necessary for developers to examine the features provided by such tools and consider whether the toolkit can encompass all of the characteristics of the proposed application.

A.3 Advanced knowledge acquisition

Approaches to automation of knowledge acquisition can be identified and classified in three main categories.

Knowledge elicitation for simple representations. Many of today's knowledge acquisition tools (for example, the automated repertory-grid technology described in chapter 5) are really only useful in the elicitation of knowledge for performing simple classification tasks. Usually, the knowledge acquired in this way can be represented in a form suitable for rule-based expert systems. Where the problem to be solved does not fit well with this sort of reasoning, this type of knowledge acquisition is not very useful. Most complex problem-solving systems will need different types of knowledge.

Knowledge elicitation for application areas. A second strand of knowledge acquisition research has concentrated on developing tools to elicit knowledge for problem solving systems in particular domains, e.g. KNACK [Klinker et al.] elicits knowledge for the construction of report writing expert systems. The theoretical standpoint of these systems is that domain-specific tools are necessary for the development of KBSs with specialized problem solving characteristics.

However, this can only be justified for frequently occurring applications or in high-value situations, because each new type of problem or new domain involves building or modifying tools and significant implementation effort.

Knowledge acquisition methodologies. Several much more general knowledge acquisition methodologies have emerged, e.g. KADS[Hayward 87], KEATS [Motta et al.]. These methodologies are applicable to knowledge acquisition in a wide range of domains. KADS will be considered in some detail as an example of where advanced knowledge acquisition might be leading.

KADS is both a methodology for knowledge acquisition, and a set of tools to support that methodology. The methodology involves investigating the domain, and identifying the type of application needed before developing the system.

During domain investigation in KADS, the basic aim is to build a *Conceptual Model*. This is a description of the knowledge which will need to be built into the future KBS, but at a higher level of abstraction than would normally be used when actually building the knowledge-based system.

The main tools which KADS provides for knowledge acquisition are general tools which focus on the conceptual model building phase.

Protocol Editor (PED). The knowledge engineer can use PED to edit transcripts of interviews. PED enables the annotation of related concepts in the edited transcripts with hypertext-like links. It is possible to use these links to group related information together (e.g. in a process plant application, all plant readings that are significant in a particular alarm situation, or all combinations of alarms that are important enough to check for).

PED assists the knowledge engineer in forming an impression of what concepts and structures, and what relations between those concepts and structures are relevant in the domain.

Concept Editor (CE). This allows the flexible construction of hierarchies of concepts, displaying them both graphically and textually. A simple example of this might be an is-a hierarchy — giving inheritance between related concepts.

Knowledge engineers can also define their own relations and build hierarchies which show those relations between different domain objects.

KADS also provides tools to assist with identifying the type of application that is intended, and in providing a framework description for different types of application. The **Interpretation Model Librarian (IML)** contains a number of *interpretation models*. These are template descriptions of different sorts of application. The knowledge engineer can study these library descriptions and attempt to map the intended application on to one of them (using the information supplied by the PED and the CE). Alternatively, if the correct type of interpretation model is identified at the start of knowledge acquisition, that interpretation model can be used to focus the conceptual model building effort.

If none of the existing interpretation models fits the application, it is possible to use the **Conceptual Model Editor** to alter an existing interpretation model into one which does match the application.

The interpretation models describe the functions which the KBS will perform, leaving gaps for the concepts on which those functions are performed.

The third and final stage of KBS development will involve the bringing together of these two descriptions to make a complete system. KADS has no tools to automate this process, although there are suggestions that this is a fruitful future area of research.

Advantages of KADS

KADS provides an usable methodology for KBS development. The KADS methodology attempts to bring KBS development closer to normal software engineering practices, with domain exploration being done during the requirements analysis stage of system development. KADS is independent of any particular type of toolkit, and has been used to describe systems which have then be implemented on a wide range of toolkits.

There are tools to support the KADS methodology, and signs that more specific tools will be developed as KADS progresses.

Drawbacks of KADS

While the KADS methodology is not limited to one application area (unlike a system such as KNACK), its general applicability means that the level of automation provided in the KADS knowledge elicitation tools is lower than is the case with KNACK. Tools such as the KADS Protocol Editor and the KADS Concept Editor are basically knowledge editing tools — allowing the knowledge engineer to create links between different concepts in transcripts, or to build simple semantic networks.

The solution to this problem probably lies in developing tools which can be associated with the interpretation tasks in the interpretation model library. However, such tools would need to be tied to particular types of representation, and possibly even to particular toolkits, detracting somewhat from the number of situations in which KADS can presently be applied.

A.4 Model-based diagnosis

Consider a human expert performing the sort of diagnosis on a chemical process plant that is outlined in figure A.3 earlier in this appendix. In frequently encountered diagnostic situations, the expert may use simple classificatory heuristics. However, when faced with an unfamiliar situation, (s)he has theoretical knowledge about the chemical processes happening in the plant, and about the structure of the plant. This knowledge can be used to mentally model different scenarios that might account for the behaviour being observed. For example:

> *If there was a fire in vessel A, then that would account for the rise in temperature at point X, and an increase in temperature at that point would cause evaporation from vessel J. That would account for the fumes observed around vessel J.*

Computer systems able to utilize such knowledge can be termed *model-based* diagnosticians. Model-based diagnosis uses knowledge about the entities, structures and interactions in a particular domain as a basis for diagnosis.

The key feature of model-based diagnosis is that the model-based diagnostician maintains a model which *mirrors* the important structure and features of the domain, so that analyses and predictions may be carried out with a high degree of authenticity. This is in contrast to heuristic-based diagnosis where the knowledge used to perform the diagnosis bears little relation to the physical structures in the domain.

Process plant experts often bring to bear on plant problems their knowledge of chemistry, of chemical engineering, and of the design of the plant, as well as the theory and practical experience of running the plant.

Performing model-based diagnosis

When there is a problem on a process plant, it could have been caused by any of the following occurrences:

- The structure of the plant is faulty (e.g. a pump not joined to a pipe).
- The function of a part of the plant is faulty (e.g. a pump not working).
- One of the chemical processes is happening faster than expected.
- One of the chemical processes is happening slower than expected.
- An ingredient of one of the processes is missing or in too little quantity or in too great quantity, thereby altering the process.
- There is an extra ingredient, altering the process.
- A sensor has failed, and so a process is not started or not stopped.
- There is an extra process occurring for some reason.
- A sensor is producing the wrong reading.

Some of these descriptions are inter-related — for instance, too much of an ingredient could make a process occur too quickly.

It is possible to identify possible explanations for faults on a piece of process plant by hypothesizing changes to the model of the device, and deriving the behaviour of the changed process plant through simulation. The behaviour of the changed model can be compared to the behaviour of the actual faulty plant. If the behaviours match, then the hypothesized alteration(s) to the model is a plausible explanation for the observed symptoms. That is, the proposed alteration(s) could represent the actual alteration(s) which have affected the process plant. If this type of simulation is done for all possible alterations to the model, than all possible explanations which can account for the observed symptoms will be found.

This is a very simple description of the principle of generating explanations of faulty behaviour using a model of the system being diagnosed. In practice, generating a simulation of process plant behaviour for every possible combination of alterations, and then comparing with the behaviour of the real process plant is usually impossible on computational grounds. Knowledge about performing diagnosis and about the domain can be used to decide which models to generate and compare. The use of such knowledge is vital for realistic diagnosis.

The next few sections will consider the type of domain model that is needed in order to perform model-based diagnosis.

Why not numerical models?

It needs to be possible to map the results of running the model on to the real world fairly easily. In practice, this means reasoning symbolically in such a way that it is straightforward to interpret the analysis of the model. This requirement will usually rule out the use of a numerical simulation to perform model-based diagnosis, but sometimes an abstraction from a numerical model can be employed.

One solution to the problems with employing numerical models for this type of diagnosis is to build models based on qualitative reasoning instead. In areas where exact values are either not significant for the outcome of the simulation (for example, failure mode effects analysis) or not available, this type of simulation has been used. It involves identifying critical (landmark) values for observed variables and then basing the reasoning on those landmarks instead of on continuous expressions. Many qualitative reasoning systems use just the three values (+, 0, -) for variables. The advantages of this approach over a numerical simulation are:

- A qualitative simulation can be performed in cases where a numerical simulation would be impossible because of incomplete or only qualitative information being available in the domain.
- A qualitative simulation can be performed much more rapidly than a comparable numerical one, and needs much less computing power. This is because of the comparative simplicity of the model.
- The symbolic representation of a qualitative model matches closely the structure of the device being modelled, making it easier for qualitative systems to produce explanations and justifications at an appropriate level for human comprehension than is the case with numerical models of a domain.

What should be modelled in a given domain?

In order to build a model-based diagnostic system, it is necessary to identify suitable modelling primitives in the particular domain — there are several reasonable alternatives to be considered:

Models of physical structure and behaviour This type of model is used for diagnosis of systems that can be described in terms of their components and the way in which the components are joined together (often the case with man-made systems).

The structure of the whole device is described — the components that comprise the device, and the ways in which those components are linked together — but not the behaviour of the whole device. The device behaviour is synthesized from the device structure and the behaviour of the components. The behaviour of the component is described independent of any particular device. In practice, this means describing its behaviour over a wide range of circumstances.

For diagnosis, it is possible to specify failure modes for each type of component, or to just treat behaviour of a component as unknown in the case where it is incorrect. Either way, possible incorrect behaviours of the whole device can be obtained by simulating a device with a component or components with incorrect behaviour.

There are several advantages to modelling the structure and behaviour of a device:

- High degree of modularity.
  The behavioural description of each component can be encapsulated in a module. These modules are reusable in a variety of devices. Failure modes can also be related to these modules. In the case of mechanical devices, connections between components are so important to the behaviour of the whole device that they are also best treated as modules of behaviour.
- Strong mapping to real device.
  If the simulation is carefully based on device structure and component behaviour, then it is possible to alter the structure or alter a component's behaviour, and the device simulation will alter automatically to reflect those changes.

The suitability of models of structure and behaviour depends on the domain. It is not suitable for domains where behaviour of the whole cannot easily be synthesized from behaviour of components (for example, many medical domains). Another restriction is that it is only applicable for devices with fairly small numbers of components — reasoning about the behaviour of gases, liquids or polystyrene beads in this way is not sensible. Reasoning about chemical processes using structural models is unlikely to be fruitful.

Logical models of structure and behaviour This is similar to reasoning from structure and behaviour, described above, but the structure used is the logical structure of the device, not the physical structure. It has been used successfully in electronic domains. The simulation employed ignores the physical aspects of the circuits for the most part, and concentrates on the logical relationships between components implied by the connections. There can be additional problems, even for electronic applications in cases where the physical structure is significant to the diagnostic problem (for example, in the detection of bridging faults).

The advantages and drawbacks of the logical models are similar to those listed for physical models, except that the model maps onto the logical structure of the device not the physical structure. Logical models are much more appropriate for electronic devices than for devices where the physical structure is significant.

Process models Forbus [Forbus 88] has developed a language for describing the processes that occur in physical phenomena. It is able to describe such processes as liquid flow, boiling, evaporation, and cooling. These processes are modular, and can be used to describe the behaviour of a whole system. The working of a refrigerator, for example, could be described in terms of the processes mentioned plus a few others.

This type of modelling is useful for reasoning about systems (like the process plant example) where the processes happening in the system are its most important features. There are some difficulties in using this type of model for performing diagnosis, because the relationship between the components of the system and the processes happening in the system are not always clear.

Causal models This type of model is often the simplest to build for a single application. The behaviour of the whole device is explicitly embedded in the representation. A causal model of a flush toilet would contain details of relationships like *when the toilet is flushed, the water flows from the cistern to the toilet bowl* and *the flow of water from the cistern to the toilet bowl causes an increase in the height of water in the bowl.* In that particular example, the causal model is similar to the *result* of running a process model for the toilet — an explicit declaration of all of the states that the toilet can be in, plus details of how to move from state to state.

Such models can be very useful for diagnostic purposes. The reasoning of the model can be reversed to explain what might have gone wrong. In this particular case, if the height of the water in the bowl is not increasing (when the toilet has been flushed), it could be because the water is not able to flow from the cistern to the bowl.

However, causal models suffer from the same problems as heuristic systems. The model builder must explicitly enumerate all possible faults that can occur to the whole device (and all possible states that it can be in). If the device is redesigned with a slightly different structure, then the whole model must be reappraised, and a new analysis performed by the diagnostic system builder to obtain all possible faults on the device.

Therefore, while causal models are easy to build, they have much in common with the heuristic expert systems on which model-based systems are hoping to improve.

This discussion of different modelling styles implies that the style chosen will depend on what is being modelled. In fact, what is often needed for an application is a mixture of these styles — human experts seem to be able to adapt their reasoning about a system depending on the type of information needed, linking their models of process to the components which cause those processes to happen. This is beyond the ability of model-based systems that can be built today.

Advantages of model-based diagnosis

Reuse. It is possible to modularise the knowledge base around components and processes that can be used in many different devices or systems. Once the effort has been made to build these descriptions in the first place, further systems in the same area are much easier to build.

Robustness. Experts often miss out details of "obvious" system faults when listing possible faults. Reusing descriptions of components or processes, including the faults that can happen to them, helps to ensure that such obvious faults are included automatically.

Heuristic expert systems for process plant diagnosis often have difficulty dealing with the possibility that sensors might be faulty. For the model based diagnostic system, sensors can be included as part of the model, and sensor faults can then be treated in the same way as any other faults on the plant.

Maintainability. Man-made systems are often redesigned during their lifetime. If a heuristic diagnostic system is built to diagnose a particular product or plant, then it is hard to decide where to change the diagnostic system when the structure of the thing being diagnosed changes. A model-based diagnostic system would need its structural model changed.

Building a diagnostic system based on a model of the system being diagnosed has significant potential advantages in terms of system robustness, reuse and maintainability. The key word here is "potential" — while there has been a significant degree of success building heuristic-based diagnostic systems [Feigenbaum et al.], model-based diagnostic systems are mostly still at the research stage.

Drawbacks of model-based diagnosis

Deciding what to model in a domain A methodology is needed which describes what should be modelled in a domain in order to produce a diagnostic system with a certain level of ability.

Modelling limitations. Human experts are very adaptable in their modelling abilities. They can switch the level of their modelling and the content of their models to match a changing investigation very easily. Model-based diagnosis is unable at present to match this flexibility.

Integration of heuristic work and model-based work. It was observed at the start that human experts can switch between the generation of hypotheses from their experience, and the generation of hypotheses from their internal model of the thing being diagnosed. Again, model-based diagnosis cannot match that flexibility.

A.5 Further reading

Generic tasks. Chandrasekaran and his group at Ohio have published numerous reports on the benefits and properties of generic tasks over conventional ways of building expert systems. [Chandrasekaran 87] is a good introductory paper on generic tasks given by invitation at the IJCAI-87 conference. Other papers ([Chandrasekaran 86], [Bylander and Chandrasekaran] and [Chandrasekaran 88]) provide more details of the research. There is also a book which goes into much more detail about using generic tasks for simple design [Brown and Chandrasekaran].

Vertical toolkits. [Stefanini et al.] describes the early work on Esprit project P820 looking into toolkits for process control applications.

[PLANIT 86] details the described work on project planning systems.

Advanced knowledge acquisition. [Hayward 87] is a good review of the basic KADS idea, and there is a book with more details of the methodology [Hickman et al.]. The KADS project has produced many documents with more specific details, available directly from the Department of Social Science Informatics, University of Amsterdam, 196 Herengracht, 1016 BS Amsterdam, The Netherlands.

Model-based diagnosis. [Forbus 88] looks at the use of model-based reasoning in a range of engineering applications. [Davis and Hamscher] explains the mechanics of performing model-based diagnosis very well. A survey article by Cohn [Cohn 89] gives an excellent introduction to qualitative reasoning, and [Weld and de Kleer] contains many of the important research papers in the field over the last ten years.

Appendix B

Details of toolkits mentioned

ART

In the United States: Inference Corporation, 5300 West Century Boulevard, Los Angeles, CA 90045. Telephone: (213) 417-7997.

Configuration Template

In the United States: Coherent Thought Inc., 3350 West Bayshore Road, Suite 205, Palo Alto, CA 94303. Telephone: (415) 493-1555.

Envisage

Envisage is now sold by Systems Designers as SD-Adviser:

In the United Kingdom: Systems Designers Scientific, Pembroke House, Pembroke Broadway, Camberley, Surrey. Telephone: 0276-686200.

G2

In the United States: Gensym, 125 Cambridge Park Drive, Cambridge, MA 02140. Telephone: (617) 547-9606.

Goldworks

In the United States: Gold Hill Computers, Inc., 26 Landsdowne Street, Cambridge, MA 02139. Telephone: (617) 621-3300.

In the United Kingdom: Artificial Intelligence Limited, Greycaine Road, Watford, Hertfordshire, WD2 4JP. Telephone: 0923-247707.

KEE (and **KLUE**)

In the United States: Intellicorp, 1975 El Camino Real West, Mountain View, CA 94040. Telephone: (415) 965-5500.

In the United Kingdom: Intellicorp Ltd, 10 Jewry Street, Winchester, Hampshire, SO23 8RZ. Telephone: 0962-735348.

KES

In the United States: Software A&E, 1600 Wilson Boulevard, Suite 500, Arlington, VA 22209. Telephone: (703) 276-7910.

KLUE See *KEE*.

Knowledge Craft (and **TestBench**)

In the United States: Carnegie Group Inc., Five PPG Place, Pittsburgh, PA 15222. Telephone: (412) 642-6900.

In the United Kingdom: Carnegie (U.K.) Limited, Coworth Park House, Coworth Park, Ascot, Berkshire, SL5 7SF. Telephone: 0990-872904.

Leonardo

In the United Kingdom: Creative Logic, Brunel Science Park, Kingston Lane, Uxbridge, Middlesex, UB8 3PQ. Telephone: 0895-74468.

LEVEL5

In the United States: Information Builders, Inc., 1250 Broadway, New York, NY 10001. Telephone: (212) 736-4433.

In the United Kingdom: Information Builders, Station House, Harrow Road, Wembley, Middlesex, HA9 6DE. Telephone: 081-903-6111.

MUSE

In the United Kingdom: Cambridge Consultants Limited, Science Park, Milton Road, Cambridge, CB4 4DW. Telephone: 0223-358855.

Nexpert-Object (and **Nextra**).

In the United States: Neuron Data, Inc., 444 High Street, Palo Alto, CA 94301. Telephone: (415) 321-4488.

In the United Kingdom: Software Sciences Limited, Meudon Avenue, Farnborough, Hampshire, GU14 7NB. Telephone: 0252-544321.

NEXUS

In the United States: Human Intellect Systems, 1670 South Amphlett Boulevard, San Mateo, CA 94402. Telephone: (415) 571-5939.

In France: MindSoft, 3 Rue de l'Arrivée, BP63, 75749 PARIS Cédex. Telephone: (1) 45 38 70 12.

POPLOG (and **KERIS**, **RULES**, and **FLEX**)

In the United States: Computable Functions Inc, 35 South Orchard Drive, Amherst, MA 01002. Telephone: (413) 253-7637.

In the United Kingdom: Integral Solutions Ltd, Unit 3, Campbell Court, Bramley, Basingstoke, Hampshire, RG26 5EG. Telephone: 0256 882028.

TestBench See *Knowledge Craft*.

VP-Expert

In the United States: Paperback Software International, 2830 Ninth Street, Berkeley, CA 94710. Telephone: (415) 644-2116.

In the United Kingdom: Paperback Software UK Limited, The Widford Old Rectory, London Road, Widford, Chelmsford, Essex, CM2 8TE. Telephone: 0245-265017.

Appendix C

Affiliations of authors

Michael Z. Bell,
Spar Aerospace Ltd,
1700 Ormont Drive,
Weston,
Ontario,
CANADA,
M9L 2W7.

John Hunt,
Department of Computer Science,
University College of Wales,
Aberystwyth,
Dyfed,
SY23 3BZ,
United Kingdom.

Ryllan Kraft,
Systems Designers Scientific,
Pembroke House,
Pembroke Broadway,
Camberley,
Surrey,
United Kingdom.

Bob Moore,
Software Sciences Limited,
Meudon Avenue,
Farnborough,
Hampshire,
GU14 7NB,
United Kingdom.

Chris Orgill,
Department of Computer Science,
University College of Wales,
Aberystwyth,
Dyfed,
SY23 3BZ,
United Kingdom.

Chris Price,
Department of Computer Science,
University College of Wales,
Aberystwyth,
Dyfed,
SY23 3BZ,
United Kingdom.

Baggy Shah,
Coopers and Lybrand Deloitte,
Plum Tree Court,
London,
EC4A 4HT,
United Kingdom.

Dave Wilson,
Information Builders,
Station House,
Harrow Road,
Wembley,
Middlesex,
HA9 6DE,
United Kingdom.

Appendix D

Trademarks

ART is a trademark of Inference Corporation.

Envisage is a trademark of Systems Designers plc.

Goldworks is a registered trademark of Gold Hill Computers, Inc.

IBM is a registered trademark of International Business Machines Corporation.

KEE is a registered trademark of Intellicorp.

KERIS is a trademark of GEC-Marconi Limited.

KES is a trademark of Software A&E.

Knowledge Craft is a trademark of Carnegie Group, Inc.

LEVEL5 is a trademark of Information Builders, Inc.

Macintosh is a registered trademark of Apple Computer, Inc.

Microsoft Windows is a registered trademark of Microsoft Corporation.

Nexpert-Object and **Nextra** are trademarks of Neuron Data, Inc.

POPLOG is a trademark of the University of Sussex.

Smalltalk-80 is a registered trademark of ParcPlace Systems, Inc.

Symbolics and **Genera** are trademarks of Symbolics, Inc.

Sun is a trademark of Sun Microsystems, Inc.

UNIX is a registered trademark of AT & T.

VAX and **VMS** are trademarks of Digital Equipment Corporation.

VP-Expert is a trademark of Paperback Software International.

All other trademarks and registered trademarks are the property of their respective trademark holders.

Bibliography

[Anderson 89] J. Anderson. *POP-11 COMES OF AGE: the advancement of an AI programming language*, Ellis Horwood, 1989.

[Bailey, Kraft and Leitch 87] M. G. Bailey, R. Kraft, R. R. Leitch. *RESCU — A Real-Time Expert System*, in Proc. Int. Conf. on Control of Industrial Processes, Milan, Italy, pp485–502, 1987.

[Barrett and Beerel] M. L. Barrett and A. C. Beerel, *Expert Systems in Business: A Practical Approach*, Ellis Horwood, 1988.

[Boehm] B. Boehm. *A Spiral Model of Software Development and Enhancement*, Software Engineering Notes, August 1985.

[Boose and Gaines] J. Boose and B. Gaines (eds). *Knowledge Acquisition Tools for Expert Systems*, Academic Press, 1988.

[Boose 88] J. H. Boose. *Uses of repertory grid centred knowledge acquisition tools for knowledge-based systems*, International Journal of Man–Machine Studies volume 29, pp287–310, 1988.

[Born 88] G. Born. *Quality in Expert Systems Development*, Proceedings 4th International Expert Systems Conference, London, pub. Learned Information, 1988.

[Bratko] I. Bratko. *Prolog programming for Artificial Intelligence*, Addison-Wesley. 1986.

[Brown and Chandrasekaran] D. C. Brown and B. Chandrasekaran. *Design Problem Solving: knowledge structures and control strategies*, Morgan Kaufmann, 1989.

[Bylander and Chandrasekaran] T. Bylander and B. Chandrasekaran. *Generic tasks for knowledge-based reasoning: the "right" level of abstraction for knowledge acquisition*, International Journal of Man–Machine Studies, vol 26, pp231–243, 1987.

[Brownston 85] L. Brownston, R. Farrell, E. Kant, N. Martin. *Programming Expert Systems in OPS5*, 1985.

[Buchanan and Shortliffe] B. G. Buchanan and E. H. Shortliffe. *Rule-based Expert Systems: The MYCIN Experiments of the Stanford Heuristic Programming Project*, Addison-Wesley, 1984

[Chandrasekaran 86] B. Chandrasekaran. *Generic Tasks in Knowledge-based Reasoning: High-level Building Blocks for Expert System Design*, IEEE Expert, pp23–30, Fall 1986.

[Chandrasekaran 87] B. Chandrasekaran. *Towards a functional architecture for intelligence based on generic information processing tasks*, in Proceedings IJCAI'87, pp1183–1191, 1987.

[Chandrasekaran 88] B. Chandrasekaran. *Generic tasks as building blocks for knowledge-based systems: the diagnosis and routine design examples*, in The Knowledge Engineering Review, vol 3(3), pp183–210, 1988.

[Charniak & McDermott] E. Charniak and D. McDermott. *Introduction to Artificial Intelligence*, Addison-Wesley, 1985.

[Charniak et al.] E. Charniak, C. Riesbeck, D. McDermott and J. Meehan. *Artificial Intelligence Programming*, second edition, Lawrence Erlbaum Associates, 1987.

[Clancey 85] W. J. Clancey. *Heuristic classification*, in Artificial Intelligence, vol.27, pp289–350, 1985.

[Cohn 89] A. G. Cohn. *Approaches to qualitative reasoning*, in Artificial Intelligence Review vol.3 no.2&3, pp177–232, 1989.

[Conklin] J. Conklin. *Hypertext: An Introduction and Survey*, IEEE Computer, pp17–41, 1987.

[Cox] B. J. Cox. *Object-Oriented Programming: An Evolutionary Approach*, Addison-Wesley, 1986.

[Davis and Hamscher] R. Davis and W. Hamscher. *Model based reasoning: troubleshooting*, in "Exploring artificial intelligence: survey talks from the national conference on artificial intelligence", publ. Morgan Kaufmann, 1988.

[Davison and Kraft 90] S. J. Davison and R. Kraft. *COGSYS: Real-time Decision Support for Process Control*, Proceedings 10th Intl. Workshop on Expert Systems and their Applications, Avignon, 1990.

[Dowsing et al.] R. D. Dowsing, V. J. Rayward-Smith, C. D. Walter. *A First Course in Formal Logic and its Application in Computer Science*, Blackwell Scientific Publications, 1986.

[Dyer et al.] M. Dyer, M. Flowers, J. Hedges, *Edison: An Engineering Design Invention System Operating Naively*, Proceedings 1st Conference on Applications of AI in Engineering Problems, (ed) Sriram & Adey, pp327–341, Springer-Verlag, 1986.

[Engelmore and Morgan 88] R. Englemore and A. Morgan. *Blackboard Systems*. Addison-Wesley, 1988.

[Feigenbaum et al.] E. Feigenbaum, P. McCorduck, H. P. Nii. *The Rise of the Expert Company*, Times Books, 1988.

[Forbus 88] K. Forbus. *Intelligent Computer-Aided Engineering*, in AI Magazine, Fall 1988.

[Forgy] C. L. Forgy *Rete: a fast algorithm for the many pattern/many object pattern match problem*, Artificial Intelligence, vol.19, pp17–37, 1982.

[Gaines and Boose] B. Gaines and J. Boose (eds). *Knowledge Acquisition for Knowledge-based Systems*, Academic Press, 1988.

[Gilb] T. Gilb. *Principles of Software Engineering Management*, Addison-Wesley, 1988.

[Goldberg and Robson] A. Goldberg and D. Robson. *Smalltalk-80: The Language and its Implementation*, pub. Addison-Wesley, Reading, MA, 1983.

[Green et al.] C. Green, D. Luckham, R. Balzer, T. Cheatham, C. Rich. *Report on a knowledge-based software assistant*, in Readings in Artificial Intelligence and Software Engineering, ed. C. Rich and R. Waters, Morgan Kaufmann, 1986.

[Greenwell] M. Greenwell. *Knowledge Engineering for Expert Systems*, Ellis Horwood, 1988.

[Harston and Hix] H. R. Hartson and D. Hix. *Human-Computer Interface Development: Concepts and Systems*, ACM Computing Surveys, pp5–92, Vol 21 (1), 1989.

[Hart] A. Hart. *Knowledge Acquisition for Expert Systems*, Kogan Page, 1986.

[Hawley] R. Hawley (ed). *Artificial Intelligence Programming Environments*, Ellis Horwood, 1987 (especially chapter 2 on POPLOG, chapter 10 on KEE).

[Hayes-Roth et al.] F. Hayes-Roth, D. Waterman, D. Lenat. (eds) *Building Expert Systems*, Addison-Wesley, 1983.

[Hayward 87] S. Hayward. *How to build knowledge-based systems: techniques tools and case studies*, in Esprit '87, Achievements and Impact, pp665–680, 1987.

[Hickman et al.] F. Hickman, J. Killin, L. Land, T. Mulhall, D. Porter and R. Taylor. *Analysis for Knowledge-Based Systems: A Practical Guide to the KADS Methodology*, Ellis Horwood, 1989.

[Hunt and Price] J. E. Hunt and C. J. Price. *POPLOG for WIMPS*, in POP-11 Comes of Age: The Advancement of an AI Programming Language, ed. J. Anderson, pub. Ellis Horwood, 1989.

[Hutchins et al.] E. L. Hutchins, J. D. Holland and D. A. Norman. *Direct manipulation interfaces*, in User Centered System Design, ed. D. A. Norman and S. W. Draper, pub. Lawrence Erlbaum Assoc., Hillsdale, N.J., 1986.

[Kahn 85] G. Kahn, S. Newlan, J. McDermott. MORE: An intelligent knowledge acquisition tool, Proceedings IJCAI-85, pp581–584.

[Kidd 87] A. L. Kidd. *Knowledge Acquisition for Expert Systems: A Practical Handbook*. Plenum, 1987.

[Klinker et al.] G. Klinker, D. Boyd, S. Genetet, J. McDermott. *A KNACK for knowledge acquisition*, Proceedings AAAI-86, 1986.

[Laurent 86] J. P. Laurent, J. Ayel, F. Thome, D. Ziebelin. *Comparative Evaluation of Three Expert System Development Tools: KEE, Knowledge Craft, ART*, in Knowledge Engineering Review 1(4), pp18-29, December 1986.

[Lee] M. H. Lee. *Intelligent Robotics*, Halsted Press, 1989.

[Leitch and Dulieu 88] R. R. Leitch and M. R. W. Dulieu. *RESCU Revisited: A Review of a Practical Real-Time Expert System*, in Research and Development in Expert Systems IV, Proc. of Expert Systems '87, Cambridge University Press, pp267–275, 1988.

[Leitch and Kraft 88] R. R. Leitch and R. Kraft. *A Real-Time Knowledge-Based System for Product Quality Control*, in Proc. of Int. Conf. Control 88, IEE Publ. No. 285, pp281–286, 1988.

[Luger and Stubblefield] G. F. Luger and W. A. Stubblefield. *Artificial Intelligence and the Design of Expert Systems*, Benjamin/Cummings 1989.

[Marcosian et al.] L. Marcosian, L. Abraído-Fandiño, S. Katzman. *Knowledge-Based Software Engineering using REFINE*, to appear in "Handbook of Computer-Aided Software Engineering", ed P. Ng, Van Nostrand Reinhold.

[Meyer] B. Meyer. *Object-Oriented Software Construction*, Prentice-Hall, 1988.

[Morgan 88] A. Morgan. *Real-Time Expert Systems for Industrial Applications*, in Proc. of Fourth Int. Expert Systems Conf., pp 149–157, 1988.

[Motta et al.] E. Motta, T. Rajan, M. Eisenstadt. *Knowledge acquisition as a process of model refinement*, Open University HCRL Technical Report 40, to appear in Int J Man–Machine Studies, 1989.

[Myers] B. A. Myers. *Creating User Interfaces by Demonstration*, pub. Academic Press, Inc., 1988.

[Nguyen et al.] T. A. Nguyen, W. A. Perkins, T. J. Laffrey, D. Pecora. *Checking an Expert Systems Knowledge-Base for Consistency and Completeness*, Proceedings IJCAI'85, pp375–378.

[Odette and Dress] L. Odette and W. Dress. *Engineering intelligence into real-time applications*, in Expert Systems vol. 4(4), November 1987.

[O'Keefe] R. M. O'Keefe, O. Balci, E. P. Smith. *Validating Expert System Performance* IEEE Expert, Winter 1987.

[Orgill] C. H. Orgill *An online mobility model for robotic assemblages using orthogonal physical constraints*, in IEEE Workshop on Artificial Intelligence for Industrial Applications, pp401-410, Hitachi City, Japan, May 1988.

[Pepper 86] J. Pepper and G. Kahn. *Knowledge Craft: An Environment for Rapid Prototyping of Expert Systems*, in Proceedings SME Conference on Artificial Intelligence for the Automotive Industry, Detroit, March 1986.

[PLANIT 86] Alvey IKBS Special Interest Group on Planning, Proceedings Alvey IKBS Planning Workshop 5, March 1986.

[Pountain 88] D. Pountain. *Pop goes the Macintosh*, BYTE Magazine, August 1988.

[Preece 89] A. Preece. *Verification of rule-based expert systems in wide domains*, in Research and Development in Expert Systems VI, ed. N. Shadbolt, pp66–77, Cambridge University Press, 1989.

[Price and Hunt 89a] C. J. Price and J. E. Hunt. *Simulating Mechanical Devices*, chapter 11 of "POP-11 COMES OF AGE: the advancement of an AI programming language", edited by James Anderson, published Ellis Horwood, 1989.

[Price and Hunt 89b] C. J. Price and J. E. Hunt, *Using Qualitative Reasoning for Diagnostic Expert Systems*, in Research and Development in Expert Systems VI, ed. N. Shadbolt, pp12–23, Cambridge University Press, 1989.

[Quinlan] J. R. Quinlan. *Induction of Decision Trees*, in Machine Learning 1(1), pp81-106.

[Ramsay, Barrett and Sloman] A. Ramsay, R. Barrett and A. Sloman. *POP-11: A Practical Language for Artificial Intelligence*, Ellis Horwood, 1985.

[Reichgelt and van Harmelen] H. Reichgelt and F van Harmelen. *Relevant Criteria for Choosing an Inference Engine in Expert Systems*, in Expert Systems 85, (ed) M. Merry, Cambridge University Press, 1985.

[Shaw 88] R. Shaw. *Reasoning in Real Time*, Control and Instrumentation, Vol 20, No. 9, pp 81–83, 1988.

[Shneiderman] B. Shneiderman. *Designing the User Interface, Strategies for Effective Human-Computer Interface*, pub. Addison-Wesley, 1987.

[Smith et al.] D. C. Smith, C. Irby, R. Kimball, B. Verplank and E. Harslem. *Designing the Star user interface*, BYTE Vol 7 (4), pp 242–282, April, 1982.

[Sommerville] I. Sommerville *Software Engineering*, 3rd edition, Addison-Wesley, 1989.

[Stallman and Sussman] R. M. Stallman and G. J. Sussman *Forward reasoning and dependency directed backtracking in a system for computer aided circuit analysis*, Artificial Intelligence vol. 9, pp 135–196, 1977.

[Stefanini et al.] A. Stefanini, F. Arlabosse, A. Cavanna, P. Courtin, M. Levin, R. Leitch, P. Martin. *A toolkit for building KBS applications for process control*, in Esprit '87, Achievements and Impact, pp985–1003, 1987.

[Stefik and Bobrow] M. Stefik and D. G. Bobrow. *Object-oriented Programming: Themes and Variations*, AI Magazine, 1986.

[Tesler] L. Tesler. *The Smalltalk Environment*, BYTE vol 6 (8), pp90–147, August 1981.

[Thompson and Thompson] Thompson and Thompson, *Finding Rules in Data*, BYTE Magazine, pp149–158, November 1986.

[Vaughn] R. Vaughn. *Expert systems come out of their shells*, Systems International, March 1988, pp35–41.

[Wasserman and Shewmake] A. I. Wasserman and D. T. Shewmake. *The role of prototypes in the user software engineer methodology*, in Advances in Human-Computer Interaction, vol 1, ed. H. R. Harston, pub. Ablex, Norwood, N. J., pp191–210, 1985.

[Waters 86] R. Waters. *The Programmer's Apprentice: A Session with KBEmacs*, in Readings in Artificial Intelligence and Software Engineering, ed. C. Rich and R. Waters, Morgan Kaufmann, 1986.

[Welbank] M. A. Welbank. *A Review of Knowledge Acquisition Techniques for Expert Systems*, BT Research Labs, Martlesham Heath, Ipswich, UK.

[Weld and de Kleer] D. S. Weld and J de Kleer. *Readings in qualitative reasoning about physical systems*, Morgan Kaufmann, 1989.

[Wheldon 87] A. G. Wheldon. *An overview of the Alvey Community Club projects in industry*, in Proc. of 4th European Conf. Automated Manufacturing, pp 453–458, 1987.

[Wilensky] R. Wilensky. *Common LISPcraft*, Norton, 1986.

[Williams and Kraft 89] T. P. Williams and R. Kraft. *COGSYS: An Expert System for Process Control*, in Proc. of Fifth Int. Expert Systems Conf., London, June 1989.

[Winston 84] P. H. Winston. *Artificial Intelligence*, second edition, Addison-Wesley, 1984.

[Winston and Horn] P. H. Winston and B. K. P. Horn. *LISP*, third edition, Addison-Wesley, 1989.

Index